I0828581

Heroines
of
Popular Culture

Heroines
of
Popular Culture

809.
9355
2
H 559

edited by

Pat Browne

Bowling Green State University Popular Press
Bowling Green, Ohio 43403

BIND COVER IN

R0123545825
HUMCA

HOUSTON PUBLIC LIBRARY

INDEXED IN _MLA, ENE IV_

Copyright © 1987 by Bowling Green State University Popular Press

Library of Congress Catalogue Card No.: 87-72240

ISBN: 0-87972-408-0 Clothbound
       0-87972-409-9 Paperback

Cover design by Gary Dumm

For Alicia

Contents

Introduction
Pat Browne

Heroines of Popular Culture examines literature and history to reveal women heroes. Heroes have traditionally been male but this study reveals that females as well as males can fit the definition of hero as defined by Joseph Campbell. The hero must journey forth from the world into a region of supernatural wonder, he must meet with supernatural forces and win, he then returns with the "power to bestow boons on his fellow man." Often, however, the hero's quest or journey is a metaphor for the personal quest for self-awareness. As such, women as well as men can be heroic.

But through the centuries men have treated women heroes as invisible. They have kept women stored away, like explosives in a warehouse, priding themselves on the treasures they possess, yet afraid to unleash that power lest it tend to overpower its possessor. But education of women, which began in the nineteenth century, helped to bring about an awareness to women of their heroic capabilities.

Education, industrialization, and democracy have changed the social world. The hero's preeminence has been diminished. Many of the areas once conquered by men are now conquered by machines. In an age when the differences between the heroic and the unheroic are not as obvious and great as they were in the past, the hero's role—although perhaps as desired and envied as it was in the past—is not so evident in the everyday world.

The democratization of the hero from the heroic to the unheroic has, in fact, allowed for the rise of women. Again, the reasons are fairly clear. As the role of the hero, the need for the heroic, has diminished, there has been less defensiveness on the part of men to defend their exclusive role as hero because prizes have been reduced. So, now that the prize of heroism is less coveted, men are more willing to recognize the heroic in women.

It is ironic that democracy has at the same time tended to diminish the stature of the hero at the same time it has allowed for the hero's growth. Perhaps it is more accurate to say that democracy has changed the nature of the hero's role, the society she serves, the means by which individuals become heroes, and therefore, has unleased women's potential heroic stature. Democracy is allowing women to demonstrate what they

and men have known all along, that if they were given the opportunity
they could be equals with men in all ways. Now, given the opportunity,
they are demonstrating their rise to equal power with men.

The essays in this volume chart some of this rise. No single volume,
of course, could possibly cover the rise of one half of the human race.
The geography of that trip requires a library of maps. But this volume
points the compass and sets the motion.

Joanna Mink discusses the emergence of woman as hero in the nineteenth
century. Two interesting movements, social and literary, contributed to the
rise of the female hero. The "woman question" was a prominent topic among
social theorists and intellectuals from the 1830's onward but little was done
about it until later in the century when the push for female education was
begun. As woman became literate they could read and write of women's
heroism. Gail Walker's essay on Victorian sexuality suggests that *East Lynne*
was radical for its time in that it gives a sympathetic picture of the adulterous
wife's transgressions, repentance, and sufferings. The heroine was allowed
to act out her feelings—her adulterous liasion—but perhaps because of the
author's ambivalence, she was also made to suffer. Another kind of heroine
is May Welland of *The Age of Innocence*. Gwendolyn Kennedy describes
May as "a character of much potential. Intelligent, intuitive, loving, and
a survivor.... May is one of the last representatives of the true honor and
nobility when it [society] was at its zenith." Unfortunately, this cost May
the love due to her from her husband whose honor, position, and integrity
were preserved by her. Valerie Broege looks at Adela Quested in the novel
and film versions of *A Passage to India* from the perspective of Jungian
psychology. She discusses how Adela Quested, whose last name suggests
heroism as defined by Campbell, achieves heightened self-awareness and
integration as she travels to India. Broege compares and contrasts the ways
in which E.M. Foster, the novelist, and David Lean, the filmmaker, portrayed
Adela. Elizabeth Bell turns to history for her discussion of heroines. Bell
addresses the role of women in aviation. In *The Oxford History of the
American People*, the mention of women in aviation takes up four lines
in a volume of 1153 pages. Bell discusses this negligence and gives us an
overview of women in aviation from Amelia Earhart to Sally Ride. T.J.
Ross discusses the role of Margaret Sullavan in the film *Only Yesterday*
and how her style comes across as heroic for its representation of "grace
under pressure." Anne Kaler tells us about Marion Zimmer Bradley's
inspiration for her heroines in the fiction she writes. By binding together
traits from medieval convents, from the Amazon Warriors, and from medieval
women's societies, Bradley is able to put together an ideal figure for her
heroines to follow. This idealized figure or muse is known as a sisterhood
and includes traits of the heroic character. Unlike Marion Bradley, Stephen
King, an enormously popular writer, features ordinary human characters

in his fiction. They become heroic because they confront unspeakable horrors with courage and conviction. Carol Senf writes about one of King's strongest heroines, Donna Trenton of *Cujo*. To save herself and her son Tad, Donna must abandon the notion that she is a heroine to be rescued, an idea popular in fiction. Only after doing that can she become heroic and a suitable representative of a modern American woman. Professor Donaldson's essay on Margaret Atwood's *Surfacing* and Maxine Hong Kingston's *The Woman Warrior* begins with a discussion of Joseph Campbell's definition of a hero. She then discusses how these two books treat the pattern and nature of heroic quests. In the final section, Donaldson considers the contributions made by female heroes. Diane Calhoun-French turns to romance literature—that of "Silhouette's Intimate Moments" series—to study heroines. Though the careers followed by the main characters (jockey, charter yacht captain, land developer) are outside of the traditional careers heroines in literature normally engage in, these heroines' lives are never shaped by their experiences on the job. In fact, their jobs seem to be affected primarily because of the heroes' animal magnetism which makes it impossible for the heroines to do their work. The heroines of "Intimate Moments" though purportedly presenting the *new* woman are in fact recounting *old* lies. Scarlett O'Hara, heroine of Margaret Mitchell's *Gone With The Wind*, is the opposite of the Intimate Moments' heroines. As Ann Egenriether demonstrates, Scarlett is a heroine because she survives, triumphs, and flourishes in the world of men. Heroes abound in popular thought but as Charles Piehl writes, "the predominant heroes of American history have been male and white." This was certainly true in the mythology of the Old South. Robert Gwathmey, an artist who is the subject of Piehl's essay, gives us paintings with anonymous black women as heroines who are worthy of recognition by blacks and whites. In the thirteen pictures which illustrate his essay we are brought fact-to-face with forgotten heroines who should be given their due. Suzanne Frentz, a writer of soap operas as well as a university professor, brings us new insights into the role of soap opera heroines. Our soap opera heroines have left the simple life of Helen Trent and other radio soap opera stars and have moved into the electronic age, meeting and conquering with courage the problems they face. Just as the late nineteenth century brought more heroines in drama, the twentieth century, particularly the 1970's and 1980's, brought us heroines in popular music. Women have increasingly taken over roles previously held by that of male heroes of popular culture—they write their own music, play "masculine" instruments (drums and electric guitar), and/or lead male bands. They are becoming leaders instead of followers. Frank Oglesbee discusses a number of heroic female rock musicians.

These essays make obvious that the heroic world of literature and life is becoming a world filled with heroines as well as heroes. Women have ventured forth from their everyday worlds, encountered troubles and emerged triumphant.

The Emergence of Woman as Hero in the Nineteenth Century

JoAnna Stephens Mink

In her discussion of classical tragedy, Mary Lefkowitz claims that "women are so often the central figures of tragedy because they are by nature victims of the traditional values of society" (4). It is not my purpose here to develop the thesis of the woman as victim; there are a multitude of excellent critical and scholarly works which more than adequately support that point.[1] Instead, I shall focus on the positive, on the strong British women writers in the nineteenth century and on the strong portrait of woman that emerges in the course of the century, a portrait to which both men and women writers contributed the brushstrokes.

"The birth of the woman as Hero occurred, insofar as one may date such an event, in 1880, when almost at the same moment Ibsen and James invented her," asserts Carolyn Heilbrun in *Toward a Recognition of Androgyny.* "Within a year of each other, each had conceived her [the woman hero's] first major, tragic work, and each had determined that in this new work a woman would bear the burden of the tragic action" (49). Heilbrun is referring, of course, to Ibsen's *A Doll's House* and James' *The Portrait of a Lady.* If we accept Heilbrun's "birth date," we also must realize that this almost simultaneous birth did not just happen; no natural accident produced this twin birth. Rather, both Ibsen and James were responding to "something in the air," to a new perception of womanhood, to what had come before Nora Helmut and Isabelle Archer ever made their appearances.

As is true with so many contemporary concerns, we need to understand past events and trends in order to put current events and trends into perspective. Similarly, an understanding of the nineteenth century in Britain is necessary for an understanding of the twentieth century in America because of the many factors which helped shape our cultural heritage. As Granville Hicks points out in *Figures in Transition,* "The social phenomena of the nineteenth century still are part of our lives." The new mercantile and professional class which arose amidst the flowering of capitalism and industrialism eventually became a powerful force within Great Britain. In the course of its rise, this new middle class gave birth to or accepted sets of ideas adapted to the process of its growth, ideas which Hicks says were loosely organized by utilitarianism and evangelicalism. "Those ideas became part of the intellectual world of the Victorian authors, and how they approached the ideas, whether they accepted or rejected or modified them, is a matter of some importance"—not only in understanding more clearly what occurred in the nineteenth century but also in understanding more clearly what is occurring today, in our own culture (Hicks 65). In other words, study of the nineteenth century is important to us in the twentieth because of the parallels in cultures.

In the latter part of the eighteenth century, the increased concern with the individual influenced the concerns articulated in the literature of the times. W. Austin Flanders says in *Structures of Experience* that the struggle "to achieve a sense of the essential self" is of "primary importance" in eighteenth-century poetry and the emerging novel. But "The struggle is always doomed to failure," contends Flanders, because "the very awareness of the problem precludes its solution in a psychologically stable sense, because the process of self-discovery presupposes an alienated consciousness" (31). The emerging novel in the eighteenth century has come to be seen by contemporary critics as "an expression of a new concern with individual, immediate quotidian experience and the subordination of group or communal values to personal life" (Flanders 6). This subordination of the community—and the accompanying emphasis on the individual—is important, not only in the historical development of the novel, but also in the evolution of the literary hero (or heroine) in the nineteenth century.[2] Victorian novelists and poets were concerned with social changes: writing became an increasingly social act rather than a private one, and the main concern of many writers was with the relationship between the individual and his or her society.

Two broad, intertwining movements, social and literary, contributed to the rise of the female hero. On the social front, from as early as 1830 onward, the "woman question" was a prominent topic among social theorists and intellectuals.[3] By the 1870s, general interest was so great that the *Examiner* collected and reprinted articles that had appeared in this popular weekly in a separate volume titled *The Woman Question*. The reason is given in "Words of Weight" in this special volume: "The rapid growth of literature on the 'woman question' indicates a prevailing impression that hitherto society has failed to draw from women all the good they are capable of doing, that it leaves their powers insufficiently developed" (qtd. in Graver 168).[4] But in spite of the efforts of John

Stuart Mill and others, women remained second-class citizens. In fact, "Woman's serfdom was sanctified by the Victorian conception of the female as a priestess dedicated to preserving the home as a refuge from the abrasive outside world" (Altick 53). Woman was fragile, non-intellectual, Patmore's Angel in the House.

Underneath this fragile facade, however, things other than the pot on the stove were beginning to boil. A push for female education began in the nineteenth century, an education that encompassed more than needlepoint and waterpainting. Many people no longer supported the relationship between men and women which Tennyson's king describes in *The Princess*:

> Man for the field and woman for the hearth:
> Man for the sword and for the needle she:
> Man with the head and woman with the heart:
> Man to command and woman to obey.

Lower-class women remained chained to their machines, but middle-class women began to take some steps toward improving their lot. Cheltenham Ladies' College, established in 1853, signified the first move toward providing for girls a secondary education comparable to that received by boys. In 1848, Queen's College in London was established, and in 1869 and 1879 respectively, women's colleges were established at Cambridge and Oxford, although women could not take degrees at either institution until 1920-21 (Altick 55). In *The Subjection of Women* (1869) Mill puts forth the idea that women should have "the power of learning," and that equality of partnership in marriage requires "that women be fully capable of surviving independently outside the family, for only if they are free to preserve their autonomy are they free to marry on equal terms" (qtd. in Graver 173). In addition to concerns over female education, the push for legal rights for women began in the middle of the century. In 1882 the Married Women's Property Act, consolidating several acts of the previous decade, gave women considerably more power over their own property than they had been allowed by the common law. This act had a significant effect on the public image of women as individuals (McMurtry 222).[5] Life, of course, was not rosy for women, but the future was more hopeful than it had been at the beginning of the century. Slowly, women gained in political and economic power.

On the literary front, the novel had become established as a reputable genre. The form of the novel, less restrictive than that of poetry or drama, lent itself to exploration of the minds and motivations of characters. Many authors used the novel to put forth ideals of morality. In fact, in 1851 one writer in *Fraser's* complained that the English novel was too moralistic: "We are too didactic, thinking too much of the moral, and too little of the story through which it is enforced" (qtd. in Stang 69). Writers often used the novel as a means of social reform. Elizabeth Gaskell sought to expose the plight of the working class in *Mary Barton* and *North and South*. Charles Dickens is probably one of the most noteworthy examples of a writer who sought to right the wrongs of the times by exposing them in his popular novels, *Hard Times, Bleak House*, and *Oliver Twist*, for example. And near the end of the century, publication of Thomas Hardy's *Jude the Obscure* was one of the factors leading to the establishment of Ruskin College for the working class. The novel's purpose was to teach, to be moralistic. After *Esther Waters* was banned by Smith's Library because of its content, for instance, Smith's accepted it back onto their list when Gladstone approved the book's morality (Cruse, *After the Victorians* 49).

In the novel, nineteenth-century writers merged their social concerns with their tragic view of the world; consequently, in the nineteenth century "the novel becomes the medium of tragedy." George Eliot, for example, deliberately set out to write tragedy, says Barbara Hardy, "and her novels are tragedies in a strictly technical sense, not because they show pain and evil, crime and punishment, but because they impose a moral pattern which shows the pain as productive" (32). Charlotte Brontë, an author as well as a woman who needed to support herself and her family, was concerned with the role of work in a woman's life: "The insistence that women as well as men need fulfilment in work is one of the new elements of reality in Charlotte Brontë's novels, and must have found an echo in many hearts," claims Geoffrey Tillotson. "In *The Professor* even marriage does not rule it out," and the need for worthwhile occupation for single women is one of the leading themes of *Shirley* (198-99). In the novel women writers responded to the changing role of work in women's lives, the integration of work and marriage. In this new relationship, the figure of woman finally is elevated to the heroic. In other words, there appears to be a relationship between a woman's work and her status as a hero.

Throughout history,   the idea of the hero or heroine has changed, but some common attributes remain. The hero, claims Bill Butler, "is an archetypal figure, a paradigm who bears the possibilities of life, courage, love—the indefinables which themselves define our human lives" (6). In his seminal work *The Hero with a Thousand Faces*, Joseph Campbell says that the hero, "a personage of exceptional gifts" (37), is "the man or woman who has been able to battle past his personal and local historical limitations to the generally valid, normally human forms" (19-20). Clearly, heroism is "a vital aspect of human behavior and human endeavor"; consequently, the idea of the hero is at the center of our cultural thinking. While we should not worship the hero, Jenni Calder asserts that because the hero "represents the best that is in ourselves," we should be open in our response to the hero (ix, xi). Three Victorian novels—*Jane Eyre, The Tenant of Wildfell Hall,* and *Middlemarch*—by offering portraits of the Woman as Hero, serve as a touchstone for tracing the evolution of the literary hero. *The Odd Women,* written near the end of the century, shows another aspect of this evolution, placed in an urban, as opposed to a rural, setting.

Jane Eyre's demand for a measure of individual freedom echoes the cries of all powerless individuals who are the victims of industrialization and political disenfranchisement (Heilbrun 59). Jane represents one of the first women to achieve her goals on her terms and, thus, her story marks a change in the evolution of the literary hero. Charlotte Brontë was fighting for the recognition of the governess' "equality in spirit, mind and soul" (Thomson 48). Jane saw herself as a woman first and a dependent second: "Purely literary considerations apart, *Jane Eyre* was of the two [*Jane Eyre* and *Vanity Fair*] the more revolutionary document, the Magna Charta of governesses" (Thomson 46). But the implications of *Jane Eyre* go further than one class of women, for Jane represents not just governesses but all women of the common, ordinary, middle class. Dennis Porter claims that Jane Eyre is not the heroine of a fairy tale; hers is the "triumph of a plain, middle-class woman over the obstacles of wealth and class and beauty, as well as over the antithetical demons of aggressive male sexuality (Rochester) and inhuman religious fervor (St. John Rivers)" (549).

Critical response to *Jane Eyre* has come a long way from its immediate reception. Jane received harsher treatment than her contemporary Becky Sharp: her love-affair with Rochester shocked "all those good Victorians who held that no modest young lady should feel for her betrothed anything stronger than a coy and decorous affection." In fact, many years were to pass before "any young lady could admit that she had read and enjoyed the book without bringing shame on her own head and on the heads of her parents" (Cruse, *The Victorians* 264-65). Jane's "crime," asserts Patricia Thomson, was that she indulged herself in the passions and emotions that only the upper classes were privileged to experience, feelings that submissive governesses were not allowed to possess (47). Present-day critics, especially feminist critics, now view Jane Eyre as the champion of women's rights in the middle of the nineteenth century, when women were not allowed to wish for such rights, much less demand them. Adrienne Rich, for example, finds that "Jane's sense of herself as a woman—as equal to and with the same needs as a man—is next-door to insanity in England in the 1840s" (98). Perhaps in *Jane Eyre* Brontë has, in effect, shown the two sides of the Byronic hero. Rochester is a male Byronic hero while Bertha and Jane, taken together, represent the female Byronic hero, since both of their characters seem to be based on sexuality, either in terms of excess in Bertha's case, or in terms of restraint in Jane's. Only at the novel's end do we see this bifurcated nature subdued, when Jane's rationality dominates.

There are some obvious parallels in discussion of the Jane/Bertha portrait and Jane's potential for heroism. The novel is built on many contrasts, of character as Eric Solomon points out (216), and of symbolism as M. A. Blom demonstrates (359). Moreover, Peter Grudin notes Jane's potential for violence as a child in the Red Room, a potential which we later see acted out in the adult Bertha: "As the figurative representation of something unspeakable and as a projection of Jane's own dark potentials, Bertha is used to show why Jane must act as she does" (145). Their relationship is similar to that of Dorian Gray and his portrait: Bertha is a grossly exaggerated symbol of what Jane could become if her violent tendencies were not sublimated (Grudin 153-54). As Rich says, "Jane never feels herself to be going mad, but there is a madwoman in the house who exists as her opposite, her image horribly distorted in a warped mirror" (98). Similarly, Sandra M. Gilbert and Susan Gubar point out that Thornfield's attic, imprisoning the mad Bertha, "soon becomes a complex focal point where Jane's own rationality...and her irrationality...intersect" (348). There is a clear relationship between the mysteries which Grace Poole hints at and Jane's search for the mystery of her own life (Gilbert and Gubar 351).

In his discussion of the nineteenth-century heroine, H. M. Daleski shows that she is often torn in two; one way of representing that division is her strong attraction to two lovers "who are presented as thoroughgoing opposites and embody opposed tendencies within herself." He gives as examples Tess, Catherine in *Wuthering Heights*, and, to some extent, Lizzie Hexam in *Our Mutual Friend* (4). A similar situation shows the conflict within Jane's nature; her dilemma of having to choose between Rochester and St. John reflects "her own central conflict between abandon and control." Jane, however, is different from some other heroines because she is able to make a decisive choice (Daleski 6). Her two significant choices are refusing to become Rochester's mistress and refusing to marry St. John. She bases her decisions on the dictates of her conscience and on Christian morality, but these are not the real reasons: her decision is "the product not of a belief in these tenets but of a resurgence of selfhood" (Blom 361). The secret of Jane's triumph, then, and the primary element that marks her as a step in the evolution of the hero, is her insistence on self, that she will be what she wants to be and what she can be.

This insistence, I think, mirrors the cultural changes taking place in Victorian society, the growing push for female education and female equality which I discussed at the beginning of this essay. In this light, the ending of *Jane Eyre* causes some concern. "Reader, I married him," states Jane in Chapter 38. But, we may wonder, at what cost. Jane becomes increasingly passive at the end of the novel and, finally, buries herself at Ferndean with the half-blinded and maimed Rochester. She announces her marriage in triumphant tones, hardly in the voice of the "new woman," hardly as Rhoda Nunn would have done. By returning to the Bertha/Jane character, we may perhaps discover the reason. Lee R. Edwards claims that the demonic side of Jane's heroism, the Bertha side, "is bleached away by the conclusion of her tale" (*Psyche as Hero* 88). Her dark side, the id, has been suppressed. Moreover, there is no place for Jane's type of heroism in Brontë's view of contemporary life. Jane is diminished by marriage and "Happiness is ransomed by heroism" (Edwards 91). Jane's capacity for heroism has no outlet; she is subjected to the same kind of stifling environment as were other women of her time. While her announcement of her marriage appears triumphant, we, the readers, are left to decide her true happiness. Granted, her end is disappointing to twentieth-century readers. But heroism is not limited simply to specific acts but defined in terms of capacity or attributes as well. Within the constraints of her environment, Jane Eyre exhibits the capacity for heroism and, up until the end of the novel, generally fulfills that capacity. Consequently, even though her heroism may be limited because her final choice is conventionality, she is a necessary link in the development of the woman as hero in the nineteenth century.

Almost simultaneous with Jane Eyre's birth was the birth of a woman whose end was also conventional, even though her life was not. In *The Tenant of Wildfell Hall*, Anne Brontë paints the portrait of one of the first women in fiction to support herself in a non-traditional, that is, "non-feminine" way. In the following lines taken from her poem "To Cowper," Anne Brontë attempts to point out the similarities and differences in their religious beliefs. These lines are, I think, more important in that they show her identification (as well as, I suppose, the identification that many Victorian women in similar circumstances would have felt) with Helen Graham's plight:

> The language of my inmost heart
> I traced in every line;
> *My* sins, *my* sorrows, hopes and fears,
> Were there—and only mine.

These lines also serve as a kind of epitaph to the struggles which only a woman could feel, the struggle to maintain her independence, both as an individual and as a woman in a social structure that defines her as dependent. In *The Tenant of Wildfell Hall*, Brontë paints a verbal portrait of a woman who struggles with social conventions as well as philosophical arguments, all of which serve to keep her "in her place" as a woman as well as an artist. By the end of the novel, Helen achieves heroic stature, at least when compared to the women of her time.

Thomson's comments about Jane Eyre, when reworded slightly, apply to Helen Graham as well: "One of a tribe of [Victorian wives] whose especial heritage was submission, she yet indulged herself in passions, emotions and resentments that were the privileges of the [male sex]" (47). Just as Charlotte Brontë was fighting for the recognition of the governess' "equality in spirit, mind, and soul," so does Anne Brontë fight for the rights of all women, particularly those imprisoned in unhappy marriages, to remain individuals in their own right. Moreover, she goes one step further: Helen is not only independent in much the same way as Jane Eyre retains her selfhood, but she accomplishes this feat in a manner traditionally reserved for men—through painting. For these reasons, we may assign the title of *hero* to Helen for her accomplishments because, after all, she is successful: she supports herself and her son and servant through her own artistic efforts, and, perhaps more important, she refuses to relinquish her own selfhood, her God-given right to remain an individual even in the repressive social climate in which she was mired.

The word *artist* conveys many images, but the essence of their meaning is that the individual creates through a variety of media—painting, music, writing—a picture of herself as well as of her subject. This Helen (as well as Brontë) achieves. One of Helen's art forms, in addition to her painting, is her diary. It serves as a means of communication, documentation, and consolation and, in fact, fulfills three functions of discourse: communication with others (she gives it to Gilbert Markham to read), documentation of facts (of her marriage and her plight), and self-expression. By looking at Helen's two forms of art, her painting and her diary-writing, we can trace her development as a character and as a hero.

Helen's artistic efforts and the function of art in her life are the means by which Brontë shows Helen's development. To make this development clearer, I have divided the chronology of the novel into six stages, each of which marks Helen's maturation as an individual and as a woman:

Stage One: Chapters 16 through 22

In stage one, as a young girl approaching womanhood, Helen uses painting solely for self-expression. The chapters in stage two cover the time immediately before and after her marriage to Arthur Huntingdon. At this time, her vehicle is her writing; her diary is a means of self-expression, documentation, and consolation. Painting is not mentioned in stage two, except as a means of socializing; at social events art, specifically music, serves as a convenient topic of conversation which is non-threatening and non-revealing. Stage three depicts Helen's life after five years of marriage. She now thinks of her painting as a means of escape; she wonders how much money she can make from her talent, and begins to think of her art as a means of support when she shall have left her now completely besotted husband. In stage four, the opening of the novel at Wildfell Hall, painting serves as a topic of conversation and helps promote the developing romantic feelings between Helen and Markham. Although not actually mentioned, an undertone of this stage is the idea that painting is Helen's means of survival; we realize later that Helen has been supporting herself by secretly selling her paintings. Helen returns to Arthur in stage five, and here her diary becomes her means of consolation and self-expression. There is no mention of her painting, and there are no references to art or writing after Arthur's death. Instead, in stage six the final maturation of the characters and resolution of the plot take place.

At the beginning of her chronicle, Helen's art is a form of self-expression, but she hides these manifestations of her feelings. Her pictures of Arthur, for example, are partially rubbed out, and she is embarrassed when he finds one and her feelings are exposed. She then uses her art in order to survive, which in a way is a means of self-expression because her painting enables her to leave Arthur, to raise her son the way she chooses, and to make a happier life for herself. In other words, because she paints as a means to an end, the novel gives few details of her satisfaction with the paintings themselves, only suggestions of what she is able to obtain through them. The variety of roles which Helen's art plays in her life can be compared to the role which Jane Eyre's paintings fulfill. The most detailed description of Helen's paintings comes when Markham has surreptitiously caught a glimpse of them: "It was a view of Wildfell Hall, as seen at early morning from the field below, rising in dark relief against a sky of clear silvery blue, with a few red streaks on the horizon" (67) and

There was one in an obscure corner that I had not before observed. It was a little child, seated on the grass with its lap full of flowers. The tiny features and large, blue eyes, smiling through a shock of light brown curls, shaken over the forehead as it bent above its treasure, bore sufficient resemblance to those of the young gentleman before me, to proclaim it a portrait of Arthur Graham in his early infancy. (70)

Jane's paintings, on the other hand, are described in vivid detail:

These pictures were in water-colours. The first represented clouds low and livid, rolling over a swollen sea: all the distance was in eclipse; so, too, was the foreground; or, rather, the nearest billows, for there was no land. One gleam of light lifted into relief a half-submerged mast, on which sat a cormorant, dark and large, with wings flecked with foam: its beak held a gold bracelet, set with gems, that I had touched with as brilliant tints as my palette could yield, and as glittering distinctness as my pencil could impart. Sinking below the bird and mast, a drowned corpse glanced through the green water; a fair arm was the only limb clearly visible, whence the bracelet had been washed or torn. (110).

The comparison is obvious. Helen paints primarily in order to support herself, while Jane's art is primarily a means of self-expression. Rochester is interested in seeing them in order to learn about her, which is why the paintings are described in such detail. Through discussion of them Rochester becomes a sympathetic listener to Jane's views of the world. Helen's feelings that she cannot disclose any secrets about herself are reinforced by the limited descriptions of her paintings.

In *The Tenant of Wildfell Hall*, Anne Brontë has achieved a major change in the role of art and of work in a woman's life. In her Introduction to this novel, Winifred Gerin notes that in 1848 "wives—and still more the children of a marriage—were wholly subject to the husband's control" (1). In 1913, May Sinclair "said that the slamming of Helen Huntingdon's bedroom-door against her husband reverberated throughout Victorian England" (Brontë 1). If it were not for her artistic talents, Helen would not have been able to take this stance. Helen's slamming of the bedroom door marks a major step in the evolution of the female hero, a step which Nora Helmut would take even further when she slams the door of their home against both her husband and her children.

In summarizing the importance of *The Tenant of Wildfell Hall*, Gerin claims that Helen is "one of the very first married women in fiction who is both competent and resolved to keep herself not by any of the accepted means as housekeeper, companion, governess, but as a painter selling her canvasses to dealers" (*Anne Brontë* 251). Only after her success in supporting herself and her son does she enter into a happy marriage with Markham. Inga-Stina Ewbank believes that this is not a feminist novel in the obvious sense. Helen does not complain of her legal position, even though she is virtually a prisoner in her own home and even though she cannot divorce Huntingdon, no matter what he does. These points, says Ewbank, do not seem to have occurred to Brontë: "And yet, through the very nature of its central concern, this novel is feminist in the deepest sense of the word" (84). Brontë has given us "a wonderfully useful paradigm of the female artist" in Helen Graham (Gilbert and Gubar 81). She has also given us one of the first female heroes in the nineteenth century. The contest between Helen and Huntingdon is presented on both the physical and spiritual levels; "In the former, inevitably, the man triumphs; in the latter, the woman"(Gerin, *Anne Brontë* 248). "The psychological insight and moral imagination displayed in the character of Helen" enlarge the moral theme of the novel (Ewbank 81). Because Helen Graham triumphs on the more important spiritual level, and because she achieves this triumph through her intellect and her talents, she finally achieves heroic stature, signifying an important change in the evolution of the literary hero.

If, as twentieth-century readers, we are dismayed by the conventional endings of *Jane Eyre* and *The Tenant of Wildfell Hall* because both Jane and Helen decide at the end of their stories to marry men who many people feel are not really worthy of them, Dorothea Brooke's marriage to Will Ladislaw is probably even more difficult to accept. The ending of *Middlemarch* has long been a subject of critical controversy. More pertinent to this discussion, Dorothea's heroic stature is problematical.

"The possibility of the woman hero," claims Edwards, "is contingent only on recognizing the aspirations of consciousness as human attributes; it is the absence of this understanding that has kept Psyche and her heroic daughters so long in shadow." Furthermore, "if heroism is defined in terms of external action alone and heroic actions are confined to displays of unusual physical strength...or social or political power, then physiology or a culture that limits women's capacities in these areas thereby exclude women from heroic roles" (*Psyche as Hero* 11). In order to resolve whether or not she achieves heroic stature, we must put Dorothea and *Middlemarch* into the context of Eliot's views of heroism. Eliot's scientific thought was influenced by her friendships with Herbert Spencer and, of course, George Henry Lewes. She and Lewes read the books and articles of Darwin, Tyndall, and Huxley, and the latter two were frequent visitors (Cosslett 74). Since she was part of the mainstream of philosophical thought in the Victorian Period, she was aware of the efforts being made by the women's movement. Eliot was even more concerned with the plight of the person, male or female, in society. Largely in response to the influence of the scientific writers of the Victorian Period, Eliot "moves from a vision of the restrictive, reductive external limitations to human aspiration, to a vision of effective human participation within an organic structure" (Cosslett 99). Her novels are concerned with the tragic and, consequently, with the heroic. Furthermore, there is running through her work the idea that tragedy is a common experience, and we find that Eliot's heroes, male and female, are representative of the human experience.

After *Adam Bede* all of Eliot's novels, with the exception of *Silas Marner*, concern the figure of the female hero. This choice, points out Hardy, has several consequences: Maggie, Romola, and Dorothea all share the "ex officio disability of being women." Eliot seems to have needed a disability for the compassionate appeal of her tragedies. It is not a question of class but of gender: "The woman's disability, like the inferior chances of the Poor Man or the Younger Son of folk-tale, provides the handicap." This handicap plays a large part in "determining the quality of the tragic suffering and redemption" (Hardy 47). Although some of Eliot's female characters become governesses, none is a Jane Eyre. Esther Lyon is a governess, but we do not see her at work, and Mary Garth is a reluctant teacher. Dorothea, on the other hand, is an heiress without an occupation. Since I have framed this discussion within the context of woman's work, the pertinent question here is: Is Dorothea a hero?

"There are few prophets in the world; few sublimely beautiful women; few heroes," writes Eliot in *Adam Bede* (Chapter 17). "Any 'low subject' may be elevated: all that is needed is to consider it a parable in order to enoble it," Mario Praz says in summarizing Eliot's observations in Chapter 35 of *Middlemarch*. Praz continues, "But absolute greatness, hundred per cent. heroism—do they really exist? [Eliot] asks; and in this question, and in the inferences she derives from her own doubtful answer, she finds herself in agreement with Thackeray and Trollope" that there are no heroes, only heroic acts (335). In the Finale, Eliot explains why Dorothea does not achieve the heroic stature of St. Theresa or Antigone:

there is no creature whose inward being is so strong that it is not greatly determined by what lies outside it. A new Theresa will hardly have the opportunity of reforming a conventual life, any more than a new Antigone will spend her heroic piety in daring all for the sake of a brother's burial: the medium in which their ardent deeds took shape is forever gone. (811)

As Tess Cosslett explains, "So instead of a Promethean victory of force against external obstacles we are given an image of human power restricted and broken by external conditions" (99). Edwards points out in "Women,

Energy, and *Middlemarch*" that neither Dorothea nor Eliot "can see a way to realize" the desire to lead "a grand life here—now—in England" (688). In other words, Eliot seems to say that no woman can attain the heroic stature of a St. Theresa because Victorian society is different and does not allow for such instances of heroism.

Apparently, society qualifies heroism. Frank Kermode believes that Dorothea fails to attain heroic stature because "the kind of activity open to her is not much different from Miss Noble's when she steals sugar from a well-stocked table to give to poor children" (Afterword *Middlemarch* 817). The metamorphosis of Dorothea Brooke into Dorothea Casaubon Ladislaw, says Edwards, marks the surrender "of heroic claims and appetites in favor of the more limited and contingent existence" (*Psyche as Hero* 65). Like Jane Eyre, Dorothea seems to be prevented by society and by convention from realizing her heroic capabilities. Yet she possesses many of the characteristics of the hero. Dorothea's chief virtue is her sympathetic nature. Even at the beginning of the novel, when she has not yet become aware of her own capacity for suffering and before she undergoes her palingenesis, she sympathizes with the plight of others. Her means of achieving some relief for the poor is to build cottages. Sir James sees these plans only as a bit of whimsy, and Celia thinks that Dorothea just wants to keep herself busy. They are partly correct in that Dorothea is idealistic, but her main objective, like St. Theresa's, is to help others. Her sympathetic nature is fully developed after her palingenesis. When she is talking with Rosamond, for example, Dorothea tries to comfort her: "The waves of her own sorrow, from out of which she was struggling to save another, rushed over Dorothea with conquering force" (773). She moves to total unawareness of herself, total unselfishness: "Her immediate consciousness was one of immense sympathy without check; she cared for Rosamond without struggle now" (774). Dorothea has, by this point, relinquished her egoism and, I believe, by moving out of herself, beyond herself, as it were, moved into the sphere of heroism.

Unlike St. Theresa, however, Dorothea is bound by the constraints of Victorian society which said that a woman should subordinate her aspirations to those of her husband. After her marriage to Ladislaw, "Many who knew her thought it a pity that so substantive and rare a creature should have been absorbed into the life of another and be only known in a certain circle as a wife and mother." But, Eliot points out, "no one stated exactly what else that was in her power she ought rather to have done" (809). Edwards wonders about and regrets Eliot's ending of the novel with this limited vision of Dorothea—and womankind: "Had George Eliot been able to find some system of values by which such a woman could live, she might have succeeded in breathing life again into Saint Theresa's dessicated image" ("Women" 692). What Edwards does not take into account is that Eliot herself qualifies the sphere of Dorothea's influence because Dorothea desires to lead "a grand life" in *England*. Eliot is even more explicit that "Certainly those determining acts of her life were not ideally beautiful. They were the mixed result of young and noble impulse struggling amidst the conditions of an imperfect social state" (811). A twentieth-century Dorothea would probably not have behaved as did Dorothea Ladislaw. She would have had more opportunities to express her heroic capacities—and Eliot would have been able to allow her to express them instead of ensnaring her in the bondage of societal dictates. Such hypothetical qualifiers aside, however, I believe that the character of Dorothea contributes to the evolution of the literary hero in the nineteenth century because she represents woman's ability to transcend then-popular stereotypes of the Angel in the House, of woman as the "weaker vessel." Certainly, Dorothea has the capacity to become heroic; the forces of a conservative, repressive society are what keep her from achieving her potential.

The society which George Gissing depicts in *The Odd Women* is different from the provincial life Eliot describes in *Middlemarch*. All of his life Gissing was concerned with the problem of the social status of women. He urged his sisters "to take their studies more seriously than girls generally did, and he wrote to them that he preferred the kind of knowledgeable and self-reliant woman who could travel alone" (Korg 185). Gissing's opinions on women were more consistent and uncompromising than were his opinions about other matters. His favorite novelists were George Eliot, Charlotte Brontë (*Villette* was one of his three favorite novels [Halperin 1941]), and George Sand. "An enemy of the Victorian myth of the inferiority of women," says Jacob Korg, "he believed firmly that women were the intellectual and spiritual equals of men" (185). *The Odd Women* is in many ways Gissing's response to the educational and legal reforms of the Victorian Period (Korg 187), reforms such as the Married Women's Property Act of 1882 which I discussed earlier in this essay. The novel is about women, untrained and with no formal education, trying to live in a changing society of the late 1880s. Two of its major themes are the contrasts between youth and age and the relationship between work and marriage in a woman's life. In light of what we know of Gissing's own life and his unhappy marriages, it is not surprising that the themes of poverty and marriage appear in many of his novels, in *New Grub Street*, for example. In *The Odd Women* Gissing explores the importance of work and marriage in women's lives and, thus, his novel ties together the ideas which I have mentioned in my discussion of *Jane Eyre*, *The Tenant of Wildfell*

Hall, and *Middlemarch* and serves as a concluding statement on the evolution of the Woman as Hero in the nineteenth century.

Throughout the course of the novel, the Madden sisters and their friend Rhoda Nunn, all "spinsters" in their thirties (only Monica is younger, twenty-one, and only she marries) battle for economic and emotional survival in the Victorian "male world." Rhoda's means of independence is to set up a school, the purpose of which is to teach women to be independent by training them as typists. This choice reflects Gissing's own ideas about female education as a means toward achieving equality. In a letter to his friend Eduard Bertz, he explains:

> The average woman pretty closely resembles, in all intellectual considerations, the average male *idiot*—I speak medically. The state of things is traceable to the lack of education, in all senses of the word.... That type must disappear, or at all events become altogether subordinate. (qtd. in Cunningham 132; see also, Korg 185-86).

While Rhoda struggles to maintain her feminist philosophy and her independence through work, Monica tries the traditional route for women—marriage. But the marriage is doomed. One of the reasons (aside from Widdowson's generally despicable character) is that Monica "is not an emancipated woman, but merely a girl who has responded to some of the new ideas about equality and has grown accustomed to a freer life than old-fashioned marriage allowed" (Korg 188-89). In other words, she is not committed to the "new woman" image, and in her lack of commitment and understanding (a reflection, perhaps, of her youth) she fails.

Although she bears very little resemblance to the dilettantish "professional" violinist Alma Rolfe in *The Whirlpool*, Rhoda in a sense also fails because she is unable to follow through with her feminist ideals and enter into a free-love relationship with Everard Barfoot. That Gissing would even allow Rhoda this choice is, as Marcia R. Fox points out in her Introduction to the novel, rare: the scene is "an extraordinary passage for a Victorian male to have written. It suggests how deeply Gissing was able to envision the allure of a satisfying career to a professional woman, in an era when few authors could conceive of women as anything but wives and mothers" (viii). Many critics consider *The Odd Women* a significant feminist novel. Indeed, Gail Godwin's *The Odd Woman* is a modern-day response to its themes. However, I question whether Gissing's view was so optimistic. At the end of the novel, as Rhoda holds Monica's child (she has died in childbirth), she gazes at the infant: "The dark, bright eye was Monica's. And as the baby sank into sleep, Rhoda's vision grew dim; a sigh made her lips quiver, and once more she murmured, 'Poor little child!' " (Gissing 336). Poor little child, indeed, for this little girl, Gissing seems to be saying, will grow up, only to have to make the same decisions, endure the same struggles as her aunts endured. In writing this novel, Gissing "paid tribute to the women [and, I would add, the men] of his era who were attempting to change the social order" (Fox viii). But I do not believe that Gissing was as optimistic as many would have him be.

The Odd Women does, however, mark a fitting end to this discussion of the emergence of the Woman as Hero in the nineteenth century. Its themes reinforce those of Charlotte Brontë, Anne Brontë, and George Eliot, as well as of other nineteenth-century authors and thinkers (John Stuart Mill, Henrik Ibsen, and Thomas Hardy, for instance)—all of whom believed that, if heroism is possible, then it belongs to women as well as to men. James W. McFarlane's comments about Nora Helmut apply to many women who contributed to the evolutionary progress of the Woman as Hero: "She is, to adapt an idea of Schiller's, a 'sublime criminal,' a person whose transgression is against the unfeeling and unsympathetic laws created by male-dominated society, but whose deeper motives are honorable and admirable" (4). It is for those honorable motives, exemplified in Jane Eyre, Helen Graham, Dorothea Brooke, and Rhoda Nunn, that we admire the portrait of woman that emerges at the end of the century. Surely, heroism "is a human necessity, capable of being represented equally by either sex" (Edwards, *Psyche as Hero* 11). By the end of the nineteenth century, the evolutionary path of the woman as hero merges more closely with that of the man.

Notes

[1]This list, which is supplementary to my works cited, is by no means exhaustive: Nina Auerbach, *Woman and the Demon: The Life of a Victorian Myth* (Cambridge: Harvard UP, 1982); Olive Banks, *Faces of Feminism: A Study of Feminism as a Social Movement* (New York: St. Martin's, 1981); Elizabeth Janeway, *Man's World, Woman's Place: A Study in Social Mythology* (New York: Morrow, 1971); Ellen Moers, *Literary Women: The Great Writers* (New York: Doubleday, 1976); Martha Vicinus, ed. *Suffer and Be Still: Women in the Victorian Age* (Bloomington: Indiana UP, 1972) and *A Widening Sphere: Changing Roles of Victorian Women* (Bloomington: Indiana UP, 1977).

[2]In this essay, I use the term *hero* to stand for what many critics have termed the *heroine* so that no pejorative associations will be connected with this figure.

[3]For further discussion, see Sally Mitchell, *The Fallen Angel: Chastity, Class and Women's Reading, 1835-1880* (Bowling Green: Bowling Green U Popular P., 1981): 100ff.

[4]For further discussion of the role of women in middle-class Victorian England, see Viola Klein, "The Historical Background," *Women: A Feminist Perspective*, ed. Jo Freeman, 3rd ed. (Palo Alto: Mayfield, 1984): 519-32.

[5]For discussion of events leading up to the Passage of this act, see Lee Holcombe, "Victorian Wives and Property: Reform of the Married Women's Property Law, 1857-1882," *A Widening Sphere: Changing Roles of Victorian Women*, ed. Martha Vicinus (Bloomington: Indiana UP, 1977): 3-28.

[6]Rochester is throughout most of the novel a rather typical Byronic hero; only at Ferndean are we presented with a more Victorian interpretation, that his maiming and partial blindness suggest that "the cause of the suffering in the past and its avoidance in the future are related to the character of Rochester's sexuality" (Porter 547). Consistent with mid-nineteenth-century views, Rochester's alienation is a rationally chosen, voluntary exile, whereas Bertha's is involuntary and based on passion.

Works Cited

Altick, Richard D. *Victorian People and Ideas*. New York: Norton, 1973.

Blom, M. A. *"Jane Eyre*: Mind as Law unto Itself." *Criticism* 15 (1973): 350-64.

Brontë, Anne. *The Tenant of Wildfell Hall*. 1848. Intro. Winifred Gerin. New York: Penguin, 1979.

Brontë, Charlotte. *Jane Eyre*. 1847. Ed. Richard J. Dunn. New York: Norton, 1971.

Butler, Bill. *The Myth of the Hero*. London: Rider & Co., 1979.

Calder, Jenni. *Heroes: From Byron to Guevara*. London: Hamish Hamilton, 1977.

Campbell, Joseph. *The Hero with a Thousand Faces*. 2nd ed. Princeton: Princeton UP, 1968.

Cosslett, Tess. *The "Scientific Movement" and Victorian Literature*. New York: St. Martin's, 1982.

Cruse, Amy. *After the Victorians*. London: Allen, 1938.

_____. *The Victorians and Their Books*. London: Allen & Unwin, 1935.

Cunningham, Gail. *The New Woman and the Victorian Novel*. New York: Macmillan, 1978.

Daleski, H. M. *The Divided Heroine: A Recurrent Pattern in Six English Novels*. New York: Holmes & Meier, 1984.

Edwards, Lee R. *Psyche as Hero: Female Heroism and Fictional Form*. Middletown: Wesleyan UP, 1984.

_____. "Women, Energy, and *Middlemarch*." 1972. Rpt. *Middlemarch*. George Eliot. Ed. Bert G. Hornback. New York: Norton, 1977. 683-93.

Eliot, George. *Middlemarch*. 1872. Afterword. Frank Kermode. New York: NAL, 1964.

Ewbank, Inga-Stina. *Their Proper Sphere: A Study of the Brontë Sisters as Early-Victorian Female Novelists*. Cambridge: Harvard UP, 1966.

Flanders, W. Austin. *Structures of Experience: History, Society and Personal Life in the Eighteenth-Century British Novel*. Columbia: U of South Carolina P, 1984.

Gerin, Winifred. *Anne Brontë*. 2nd ed. London: Lane, 1976.

Gilbert, Sandra M. and Susan Gubar. *The Madwoman in the Attic: The Woman Writer and the Nineteenth-Century Literary Imagination*. New Haven: Yale UP, 1979.

Gissing, George. *The Odd Women*. 1893. Intro. Marcia R. Fox. New York: Norton, 1977.

Graver, Suzanne. *George Eliot and Community: A Study in Social Theory and Fictional Form*. Berkeley: U of California P, 1984.

Grudin, Peter. "Jane and the Other Mrs. Rochester: Excess and Restraint in *Jane Eyre*." *Novel* 10 (1977): 145-157.

Halperin, John. *Gissing: A Life in Books*. New York: Oxford UP, 1982.

Hardy, Barbara. *The Novels of George Eliot: A Study in Form*. London: Athlone, 1959.

Heilbrun, Carolyn G. *Toward a Recognition of Androgyny*. New York: Norton, 1964.

Hicks, Granville. *Figures in Transition: A Study of British Literature at the End of the Nineteenth Century*. New York: Macmillan, 1939.

Korg, Jacob. *George Gissing: A Critical Biography*. Seattle: U of Washington P, 1963.

Lefkowitz, Mary. *Heroines and Hysterics*. New York: St. Martin's: 1981.

McFarlane, James Walter. Introduction. *The Oxford Ibsen*. Vol. V. Henrik Ibsen. Trans. James Walter McFarlane. London: Oxford UP, 1961.

McMurtry, Jo. *Victorian Life and Victorian Fiction: A Companion for the American Reader*. Hamden: Archon, 1979.

Porter, Dennis. "Of Heroines and Victims." *Massachusetts Review* 17 (1976): 540-52.

Praz, Mario. *The Hero in Eclipse in Victorian Literature*. London: Oxford UP, 1956.

Rich, Adrienne. "Jane Eyre: The Temptations of a Motherless Woman." 1973. Rpt. *On Lies, Secrets and Silence: Selected Prose, 1966-1978*. New York: Norton, 1979.

Solomon, Eric. "*Jane Eyre:* Fire and Water." *College English* 25 (1963): 215-17.

Stang, Richard. *The Theory of the Novel in England, 1850-1870*. New York: Columbia UP, 1959.

Thomson, Patricia. *The Victorian Heroine: A Changing Ideal 1837-1873*. London: Oxford UP, 1956.

Tillotson, Geoffrey. *A View of Victorian Literature*. Oxford: Clarendon, 1978.

The "Sin" of Isabel Vane: *East Lynne* and Victorian Sexuality

Gail Walker

Mrs. Henry Wood's sensational—and sensationally popular—novel, *East Lynne*, was first published serially in the *New Monthly Magazine* beginning in January of 1861. By 1895 over 400,000 copies had been sold in England, the novel had been published in America in at least two dozen pirated versions, and innumerable adaptations had been done for the stage (Mitchell vii). Thus phenomenally popular in its own day, the novel obviously fulfilled a need for its Victorian audience, reflecting that audience's belief in the centrality of woman's position in the social fabric and the seriousness of the consequences for society and the individual of a failure to fulfill the demands which culture placed on women as guardians of the public morality.

For the modern reader, however, *East Lynne* is perhaps remarkable chiefly for the light it sheds on the ambiguities and ambivalences of the Victorian attitude toward female sexuality; as Jeanne B. Elliott suggests, Mrs. Wood "presents the conventional response to questions which her great contemporaries considered in a far more profound and searching manner" (330).[1] Whether the novel's implied norms of acceptable sexual conduct reflect actual behavioral patterns and social judgments or mere stereotypes, the fact that the norms are expressed at all through the vehicle of the popular novel indicates a widespread need on the part of the Victorian middle-class reading audience for the kind of sexual "safety" that the enunciation of rigid sexual standards might supply.

Sally Mitchell suggests that *East Lynne* was in many ways a radical work for its time, creating as it does a very sympathetic portrait of the adulterous wife's guilt, repentance, and consequent suffering; Mitchell cites the comment of a contemporary of Mrs. Wood, Adeline Sergeant, that much of the novel's popularity lay in public reaction against "inane and impossible goodness" in fictional heroines (vii). In the same vein, Elaine Showalter includes *East Lynne* among her list of subversive novels which, she maintains, gave expression to a "wide range of suppressed female emotions . . . tapping and satisfying fantasies of protest and escape" (159). Undeniably, the portrayal of the heroine, Lady Isabel Vane, is in many ways sympathetic, yet equally undeniably the fate of Lady Isabel exemplifies the Victorian obsession with female sexual purity through the extreme severity with which her misconduct is punished. Not only does she lose status and name (quite literally—she first ceases to be "Lady" Isabel and then becomes Mrs. Vine), home, security, and reputation after her fall from virtue, but she is also led by her creator to return in disguise to the home of her wronged husband as governess to her own children, forced to become a witness of his marital happiness with his second wife, and placed at the deathbed of her younger son, whose death is presented as the result of her own failures as a mother.

The heroine of *East Lynne* thus exemplifies, for us as for its original audience, the consequences of violating the restrictions placed on female sexuality. As Winifred Hughes points out, "What holds [Wood's fiction] all together is the rule of propriety, in its most rigid and conventional sense. The fact that this rule is continually broken only serves to strengthen it; the offenders are fully aware of the terms of their offenses . . ." (112). However, the "sin" of Isabel Vane involves a greater transgression than mere illicit sexual activity; the novel reinforces the popular moral stereotype that female sexuality is in itself illicit, for its rather complicated plot suggests that the seduction of the heroine is in fact a punishment visited upon her for her earlier failure to abide fully by the sentimental ideal of true womanhood with which mainstream Victorian culture sought to neutralize the threat of female sexuality.[2]

Before turning to an examination of the novel itself, however, one must first examine the popular stereotypes of female sexuality embodied in the public ideal of woman as wife and mother. As Duncan Crow points out (22-26), much of middle-class Victorian morality stems from the reaction of the emerging, largely fundamentalist industrial middle-class against what it perceived as the extravagance and promiscuity of the "Georgian" age, a period of sexual license for men and women alike in which it was commonly said that few men could be certain of the paternity of their sons. The middle-class custodians of Victorian morality sought to contain this potential for social chaos by creating a public mythos of the female, dichotomized as woman and demon (see Auerbach, *Woman and the Demon*), by means of which women's sexual behavior could be controlled in the interest of familial and social order. Peter Gay demonstrates the likelihood that, in reality, Victorian sexual attitudes were not as simple, sexual behavior and sexual pleasure not as sharply separated in practice as the public moral stance of the time once led us to believe, yet the pervasiveness of stereotypical images of virtue and vice in both fictional and non-fictional material about and for women[3] suggests the strength of Victorian culture's need to control female sexuality.

According to the rather contradictory interpretation of female sexuality proclaimed by the moral and medical establishment, normal young women experienced little or no sexual feeling before their physical initiation. W. R. Greg, an influential writer on popular issues of the day, commented in a July 1850 article entitled "Prostitution" in the *Westminster Review* that "In men, in general, the sexual desire is inherent and spontaneous, and belongs to the condition of puberty. In the other sex, the desire is dormant, if not non-existant, till excited; always till excited by undue familiarities; almost always till excited by sexual intercourse" (Murray 410). A few years later Dr. William Acton, the most prominent of Victorian specialists in sexual and reproductive theory, and a practicing physician, reassured his contemporaries that "the majority of women (happily for them) are not much troubled with sexual feeling of any kind"—in fact, by Dr. Acton's definition, a woman who experiences sexual pleasure is abnormal: "As a general rule, a modest woman seldom desires any sexual gratification for herself. She submits to her husband, but only to please him; and, but for the desire of maternity, would far rather be relieved of his attentions." Indeed, according to Acton, "The best mothers, wives, and managers of households, know little or nothing of sexual indulgences. Love of home, children, and domestic duties, are the only passions they feel" (Marcus 31).[4] Daughters of the middle and upper classes (the sentimental ideal of womanhood was essentially a class phenomenon which had little application to the laboring classes, as Fraser Harrison points out) were taught to regard this absence of sexuality as both their natural condition and their greatest virtue, at the same time as they were socialized to regard marriage and reproduction as the sole appropriate goal and purpose of their lives. Thus on her wedding night the bride "lost" that which before marriage was held to be the principal source of her value.

The resulting psychological and sexual dilemma was resolved, on the public level, through the pious sentimentalities with which love, marriage, and especially motherhood were surrounded. As Harrison comments, "The role of the wife was transfigured, for upon her was bestowed the mystical identity of a priestess through whose selfless ministrations the altar of domesticity was supposed to be kept spotless; at the same time, the virtue of self-sacrifice was venerated as the quintessence of femininity" (42).[5] The myth of the "angel in the house" enabled Victorian culture to minimize women's sexual nature while at the same time authorizing them to perform the sexual function of reproduction. Because a truly feminine woman should shrink from the sexual requirements of marriage (and no woman who did *not* shrink was "feminine" in the deepest sense), the only excuse for a genuinely modest young woman's entering into marriage was a sentimental ideal of affection, devotion, and emotional dependency—untinged of course by any hint of sexual impulse; having married, the modest woman was supposed to look to motherhood for consolation for the ensuing shock to her natural delicacy. Physical awareness and sexual yearnings, however vague and unfocused they might be, were no part of the publicly acknowledged pattern of female behavior. A young woman who possesses such impulses and passions, *whether she acts on them or not,* has sinned already, without need of overt action. Inculcated through the precepts of Church and Chapel, reinforced through volumes of advice for the guidance of young ladies, and made emotionally persuasive through the medium of the popular novel, which presented both models of impossible virtue for young female readers to emulate, and also examples of virtue fallen to terrify them into conformity with received standards of public sexual behavior, the myth implies that there is no such thing as innocent (female) sexuality. This is the lesson of *East Lynne.* The seduction of Isabel Vane, midway through the novel, is both consequence of and retribution for her earlier "crimes" against Victorian sexual mores.

The ambivalence of the author toward her character (an ambivalence surely reflective of Mrs. Wood's audience as well, to the extent that the popular novelist is an indicator of prevailing cultural norms), is apparent first of all in the tension between guilt and justification with which Mrs. Wood surrounds the heroine in the first section of the novel, focusing on Lady Isabel's marriage to Archibald Carlyle. The first "sin" of Isabel Vane is that she marries without that sentimentalized fiction of love which supposedly authorized a delicately nurtured female to submit to her husband—a fact which she stammeringly acknowledges to Carlyle: "I ought to tell you, I must tell you...though I have said yes to your proposal, I do not—yet—It has come upon me by surprise...I like you very much; I esteem and respect you: but I do not yet love you" (102). The novelist creates for her heroine a dilemma which has no tenable solution, for Isabel's circumstances are such that marriage is her only honorable means of self-preservation, but the only marriage offered to her is one that leads her to violate the mythos of the ideal woman. Orphaned by the death of her dissolute father the Earl of Mount Severn and left penniless to the charity of distant relatives, Isabel is deprived even of the shelter of her home at East Lynne, which the Earl had sold almost on his deathbed to Carlyle, an industrious middle-class solicitor. Carlyle's reaction to Isabel at their first meeting establishes her initial conformity to the ethereal ideal of innocent maidenhood, for he is "not quite sure whether it was a human being: he almost thought it more like an angel" (8)—the "angel" of course being free from any taint of sexuality. Isabel's appeal for Carlyle lies in her beauty, unworldliness, and helplessness, qualities which the author obviously expected her audience to accept as the appropriate attributes of a young girl of good breeding; these qualities in themselves constitute some justification for Isabel's actions, thus enabling the author to create sympathy for her while simultaneously and covertly condemning the action which Isabel takes in accepting Carlyle as a means of escape. The image of purity evoked by the simile would allow the audience to ascribe her display of wayward sexual impulse to her unprotected situation following the death of her father.

The ambiguity of the novel's attitude toward Isabel (are we as readers meant to condemn the social order which creates Isabel's dilemma, the mythos of the ideal woman, or Isabel herself for failing to preserve her sexual "integrity"?) is underscored by the fact that Isabel's eventual seducer is introduced into the novel at this early point, as a complicating factor in the decision which Isabel is required to make about a marriage of convenience to Carlyle. Although she responds with passivity to her newly accepted fiance's first attempt at lovemaking, she is not, the novel implies, innocent in the truest sense; her second "sin" is that prior to her acceptance of Carlyle she experiences an attachment, clearly based on sexual attraction, to Captain Francis Levison. Even as she considers Carlyle's proposal of marriage, Isabel's thoughts dwell on the "other man": "It is not only that I do not love Mr. Carlyle, but I fear I do love, or very nearly love, Francis Levison. I wish *he* would ask me to be his wife!—or that I had never seen him" (101). When Francis unexpectedly enters the room where she waits for Carlyle, "her heart beat wildly," and the sternly moral voice of the narrator comments that "said beating might have convinced her that she ought not to marry another" (101). Only when Levison makes clear that he has no intention of marrying her does she accept Carlyle. She has, in fact, violated the Victorian ideal of true womanliness long before her conventional "fall" into the trap of seduction.

Subsequent events of the novel make clear that Isabel's misconduct as wife is the outgrowth of her earlier sexual "transgressions." As wife she misunderstands and distrusts the husband whom she has never been able to love properly because another man had touched her emotions first; aware of her own failure to love, she falls into the delusion that Archibald is in love with another woman and regrets having married her, so that the way is open for a chance meeting with Francis Levison to re-arouse the earlier passions which she ought never to have experienced.[6] The narrative description of their encounter coyly indicates Isabel's intense excitation, in a passage that recalls the wildly beating heart of the episode above: "What was it that caused every nerve in her frame to vibrate, every pulse to quicken? *Whose* form was it that was thus advancing, and changing the monotony of her mind into a tumult?" (171). When Levison follows her to East Lynne, her earlier attraction to him, combined with her distrust of her husband, makes her an easy victim of his practiced seduction. Her previous lapses from "virtue" have prepared the way, psychologically, for her final "fall."[7]

Interestingly, however, having established the existence of this physical attraction, doubly illicit because Isabel is both female and wife, the novel makes jealousy of Carlyle's supposed involvement with another woman to be the primary motivation for Isabel's elopement with Levison, suggesting Mrs. Wood's awareness that her audience's continued sympathy for Isabel was dependent upon denying or obscuring her sexuality.[8] Even *the* sexual transgression above all others could not be permitted to have a genuinely sexual motivation, on the woman's part,[9] nor could she be permitted to experience even brief pleasure: "Even in the first days of her departure, in the fleeting moments of abandonment, when it may be supposed she might momentarily forget conscience, repentance was sharply wounding her with adder stings" (237). In keeping with the novel's need to reinforce received cultural norms of female behavior even as it evokes sympathy for the erring heroine, Isabel is made to feel immediate remorse: "Never had she experienced a moment's calm, or peace, or happiness, since the fatal night of quitting her home" (237). The lesson of Isabel's experience is that surrender to illicit sexuality destroys the capacity for sexual pleasure.

A further component of Isabel's suffering is the anguished longing she experiences for the children she has abandoned but has not ceased to love: "Oh! that she could see her children but for a day, an hour? that she might press one kiss upon their lips!" (327). Motherhood, the social reward of the virtuous wife, becomes the source of the fallen Isabel's greatest suffering, for not only does she lose the children of her marriage, but she must also undergo the humiliation of bearing out of wedlock a child who is the visible evidence of her shame: when that child dies, her response is relief and remorse rather than grief.

The novel's implied norms of female sexual behavior are emphasized through the related plot involving the secondary heroine, Barbara Hare— the object of Isabel's jealousy whom Isabel wrongly imagines that her husband loves. Like Isabel, Barbara is guilty of the "sin" of an unmaidenly attachment unsolicited by its object. She loves Archibald Carlyle passionately, continues to love him even after he marries Lady Isabel, and suffers all the predictable anguish—moral and emotional— appropriate to her immodest behavior. One of the key scenes of the novel involves her pursuing Carlyle and making an avowal of her passion to him, an action which leaves her overcome with shame and humiliation (137-39). However, Barbara does *not* commit the further sin of giving herself to a husband whom she does not love, despite considerable pressure from her father to do so. Her passionate feelings are a violation of true womanliness and purity, for she should not have experienced them, but having given her heart she remains faithful (i.e., she does *not* give her body to another man, even within marriage, as Isabel had done), so her punishment is less severe than Lady Isabel's. Following Carlyle's divorce from Isabel, Barbara becomes his wife (and of course a mother— a virtuous woman's sexual initiation must be "redeemed" by motherhood, just as a fallen woman's sexual misconduct must be punished by illegitimate childbirth, usually occurring after her seducer has tired of her and cast her off, as Levison abandons Isabel).

Not at all incidentally, the marriage of Carlyle to Barbara becomes the novel's primary means of punishing the guilty Isabel. Disguised, disfigured and maimed by the railway accident which kills her illegitimate child, Isabel returns to East Lynne to serve as governess to her own children, to witness Barbara's triumphant wifehood, and to discover too late that she does indeed love the husband she had wronged: "Terribly, indeed, were their positions reversed; most terribly.... Barbara was now the honoured and cherished wife, East Lynne's mistress. And what was she?...an interloper, a criminal woman..." (362). Wild with remorse and anguish, she watches her son die of consumption, his death clearly the result of having lacked his mother's care in the early stages of his illness—a terrible warning of the way in which the sins of the mother might fall upon her child. Then at last Lady Isabel is allowed to die, a sacrificial offering to the Victorian mythos of love, motherhood, and female sexuality.

The complex of tensions which the novel generates of sympathy and condemnation for its central character, the careful framework of cause and justification with which the author surrounds Isabel's actions juxtaposed against the extreme severity with which her transgression is punished, point both to the ambivalence of the Victorian middle-class audience itself toward its own public ideal, and to an implicit recognition that the continuance of the ideal requires the most stringent kinds of social and moral sanctions on women's erotic freedom. Thus *East Lynne*'s heroine suffers not only for her violation of the letter of the ideal, but for her failure to adhere to its spirit, her seduction itself being the consequence of her earlier "sins."

Notes

[1]Elliott asserts that Isabel Vane is "caught between the demands of her own nature and the rigid standards imposed upon her by her sex and class. In brief, her tragic fate...arises from her inability to live up to the ideal of the Lady" (330-331). For Elliott, however, the sexual element of the ideal is less significant than its social and educational components, leading her to slight the novel's sexual concerns. She argues that "Isabel's frustration with her social environment and the demands of her domestic situation create the central conflict" (334) and lead her to utilize a relationship with Levison as the only available means of escape from an intolerable dilemma. Elliott comments only briefly about Isabel's sexual/erotic frustrations, basically in order to discount them as a motivating force in the novel, whereas, I believe, mingled fascination with and fear of the potential for social disorder implicit in women's sexuality is for its creator the novel's deepest motivating force.

[2]Hughes unfortunately simplifies the moral complexity of Wood's world by suggesting only the adultery itself as Isabel's transgression (112-113).

[3]Sally Mitchell, *The Fallen Angel: Chastity, Class and Women's Reading 1835-1880* has an interesting discussion of the relationship between contemporary fiction and the norms of female sexual behavior.

[4]Although the book from which this passage is taken, *The Functions and Disorders of the Reproductive Organs* (1857), is as Steven Marcus points out "part fantasy, part nightmare, part hallucination, and part madhouse" (13), it was favorably reviewed on publication and went through numerous editions in both England and America; its popularity suggests, at the least, that Acton's contemporaries regarded his opinions as functional, that is, contributing to the security of the social framework, regardless of whether they corresponded to anyone's particular, individual experience. In other words, Acton's popularity implies that he was saying something which his readers wanted to believe. Indirect confirmation of Acton's views is suggested by the complaint of an early feminist writer that the married woman "is not permitted to feel, or desire.... The obedient instrument of man's sensual gratification, she is not permitted even to wish for gratification for herself" (1825; William Thompson, *Appeal of One-Half the Human Race, Women, Against the Pretensions of the Other Half, Men, to Restrain Them in Political and Thence in Civil and Domestic Slavery*, quoted in Murray 11).

[5]Sarah Lewis' *Woman's Mission* (1839), which went through thirteen editions by 1849, is typical in proclaiming that women "have fewer worldly interests, and are by nature and education less selfish.... Naturally disposed to reverence, to worship, to self-sacrifice, for the sake of a beloved object...the regenerators of society" (quoted in Murray 24). The feminist Ann Richelieu Lamb attests equally to the pervasiveness of this exalted concept of woman's moral responsibility: "As far as manners and morals are concerned, a book can scarcely be opened without meeting therein the assertion, that woman is the secret and silent spring which keeps us all right; that in her hands is placed that mighty engine 'the morals of society'; that she is the keeper of the soul of the social system" (Murray 28).

[6]Hughes notes that "Apparently Wood cannot bring herself to let her heroine knowingly violate a perfect home and a perfect marriage" (113), so Isabel must be made to experience delusion as a prelude to seduction.

[7]The author of a popular mid-century book of advice for young ladies, W. Nicholson, in *How To Be a Lady* (Wakefield; Wm. Nicholson and Sons, c. 1850),

comments that "Many a girl has been ruined in consequence of a very slight deviation from propriety, which has led to others of a more serious nature" (cited in Gorham 71). Mrs. Wood's audience would have found entirely credible the idea that Isabel's earlier, relatively justifiable and understandable deviations from the ideal of virtue would have weakened her ability to reject the final transgression.

[8]Showalter maintains that although "Wood adopts a moral and prudential tone...she clearly sympathizes with the feelings of the wife who is neither deceived not mistreated, but sexually frustrated and simply bored to death" (172). What Showalter calls the "urgency of Mrs. Wood's message" (173), however, is less a mark of covert sympathy for women's sexual frustration than of covert fear of women's capacity for sexual fulfillment. The ambivalent but proper Mrs. Wood, like many in her audience, could sympathize with Isabel's plight but was terrified by the prospective consequences for society of actions like hers.

[9]W. R. Greg in the *Westminster Review* article on "Prostitution" (July 1850) comments that "a vast proportion of those who...come upon the town, fall in the first instance from a mere exaggeration and perversion of one of the best qualities of a woman's heart. They yield to desires in which they do not share, from a weak generosity which cannot refuse anything to the passionate entreaties of the man they love" (quoted in Murray 410).

Works Cited

Auerbach, Nina. *Woman and the Demon: The life of a Victorian Myth.* Cambridge: Harvard UP, 1984.

Crow, Duncan. *The Victorian Woman.* N.Y.: Stein & Day, 1982.

Elliott, Jeanne B. "A Lady to the End: The Case of Isabel Vane." *VS*, 19/3 (March 1976), 329-44.

Harrison, Fraser. *The Dark Angel: Aspects of Victorian Sexuality.* N.Y.: Universe, 1977.

Hughes, Winifred. *The Maniac in the Cellar: Sensation Novels of the 1860s.* Princeton: Princeton UP, 1980.

Gay, Peter. *The Bourgeois Experience: Victoria to Freud.* Vol I. *Education of the Senses.* N.Y.: Oxford UP, 1984.

Gorham, Deborah. *The Victorian Girl and the Feminine Ideal.* Bloomington: Indiana UP, 1982.

Marcus, Steven. *The Other Victorians: A Study of Sexuality and Pornography in Mid-Nineteenth-Century England.* Norton Paperback. N.Y.: Norton, 1985.

Mitchell, Sally. *The Fallen Angel: Chastity, Class and Women's Reading 1835-1880.* Bowling Green: Bowling Green U Popular Press, 1981.

Murray, Janet Horowitz. *Strong-Minded Women and Other Lost Voices from Nineteenth-Century England.* N.Y.: Pantheon, 1982.

Showalter, Elaine. *A Literature of Their Own: British Women Novelists From Bronte To Lessing.* Princeton: Princeton UP, 1977.

Wood, Mrs. Henry. *East Lynne.* Ed. Sally Mitchell. New Brunswick: Rutgers UP, 1984.

The Unsung Heroine—
A Study of May Welland in
The Age of Innocence

Gwendolyn Morgan

The criticism which surrounds Edith Wharton's *The Age of Innocence* includes extensive analyses of the characters of Newland Archer and Ellen Olenska. However, surprisingly little attention is devoted to that of May Welland who, as the third point of Archer's triangle, surely must be of significance. Most scholars[1] are content to accept Newland's view of his wife and dismiss her as "physically magnificent but mentally equipped with no more than the clan negations" (Parrington, 152). As such, she becomes merely a symbol of the stifling society which "traps" Archer in a meaningless life or at most, as Widmer (35) claims, the mechanical agent of that society in bringing about his undoing. Louis Coxe provides a notable exception to this general opinion when he suggests that May is the only noble or tragic character in Wharton's story:

I believe that if any character in this novel partakes of the heroic nature it is indeed May Welland, she of the pink and white surface and the candid glance, whose capacity for passion and sacrifice her husband never knew. (159)

Yet even Coxe is content to define May as a simple young woman whose only distinction lies in her intuitive knowledge of her husband's illicit love and in her determination to suffer silently and nobly. This devoted wife does not understand the why or how of the situation and is unable to effect any change in her own or Newland's understanding of their human conditions.

While Coxe's perception that May Welland is not merely a "marble statue" in Newland Archer's parlor is significant, I do not believe even this critic has given May her due. May is a much more complex character, both in her personality and in her function in the novel, than the martyred wife depicted in his conclusions. The following discussion provides an alternative interpretation.

The generally accepted view of May Welland probably stems from the narrative voice employed in *The Age of Innocence*. Although the story is told in the third person, the narrator is not omniscient; almost everything, including the depiction of other characters, is filtered through the consciousness of Newland Archer. The reader is thus tempted to accept the hero's misconceptions and prejudices as "fact." Newland's view of May—and that of the majority of Wharton's critics—is succinctly put in his reflection that

he would always know the thoughts behind [May's brow], that never, in all the years to come, would she surprise him by an unexpected mood, by a new idea, a weakness, a cruelty or an emotion. (295)

Yet there is ample evidence in the novel that his perception is not to be trusted. First, Newland frequently finds himself erring in his interpretation of May and her behavior: he is startled when she intuits his affection for another woman (147); he senses something "superhuman" in her suggestion that he marry his former mistress (150); he cannot deceive her regarding his "business" trip to Washington (282); and he is shocked to find she believes him to be having an affair with Ellen (339). When, in the epilogue, Dallas reveals that May had always known of his "sacrifice," Newland begins to realize that he never understood the depth of her perception or feeling (356). Newland's frequent discoveries that he has misunderstood his wife indicate that she is not to be accepted as the person he thinks she is. The second, and more important, reason for rejecting Newland's view of his wife is that it is in conflict with her actions. Each of the major characteristics attributed to her can be refuted or, at least, extenuated.

The major features of Newland's May are ones of negation. She is perceived as lacking in intelligence and individuality, the product of social forces and conventions which she is unable to transcend. She is, for Newland, filled with a "false innocence" which has destroyed her "instinctive guile." Finally, May is viewed as being incapable of sincere emotional response and deep passion. Taking each of these in turn, one discovers that Newland's charges against her character are unjustified.

While May is certainly not portrayed as possessing genius neither is she stupid. Ellen recognizes her intelligence immediately (64) and, given the Countess Olenska's frankness in stating her opinions (e.g. the Duke is "the dullest man I ever met" (64) and the van der Luyden's stately drawing room is "gloomy" (73)), it is unlikely that she is merely trying to ingratiate herself with Archer. Furthermore, she restates her opinion of May after she has come to know Newland well enough to drop any such pretense (167). Archer himself initially believes May to be an intelligent young woman (45, 120, 167, etc.) and apparently only begins to question the fact after he becomes dissatisfied with his marriage. Indeed, any indication on May's part that she wishes to develop her mind soon becomes a source of irritation to her husband:

> In the days of their engagement she had simply (as he now perceived) echoed what he told her; but since he had ceased to provide her with opinions she had begun to hazard her own, with results destructive to his enjoyment of the works commented on. (294)

It is little wonder, then, that May does not attempt to demonstrate her mental capacities to her husband. Her actions, however, indicate a sharpness of perception and a keen analytical ability. Her evaluation of Newland's impulsive flight to St. Augustine is a case in point. She senses that there is more to his persistent, agitated plea for an early marriage than the passion of a lover, and suggests that he may have ceased to care for her (147). She successfully traces the beginning of the "difference" in him to the announcement of the engagement (i.e. when he met Ellen), and refuses to be cajoled into dropping the subject (148). May then identifies the real reason for his wish, of which he himself appears to be unaware:

> "Yes," she said at length. "You might want—once and for all—to settle the question: it's [the early marriage] one way." (148)

May is, in fact, superior in intellect to most of the other New York women. Although Newland expects his wife, like his mother and sister, to have no understanding of his professional life (140, 269), he is unable to deceive her when he cancels his "business" trip to Washington because Ellen is coming to New York. She carefully analyzes and destroys his alibi on the basis of the very understanding he expects her to lack:

> "Oh, I'm not going," Archer answered.
> "Not going? Why, what's happened?" Her voice was as clear as a bell, and full of wifely solicitude.
> "The case is off—postponed."
> "Postponed? How odd! I saw a note from Mr. Letterblair to Mama saying he was going to Washington tomorrow for the big patent case... You said it was a patent case, didn't you?"
> "Well—that's it: the whole office can't go, Letterblair decided to go this morning."
> "Then it's *not* postponed?"...

May's intelligence is closely connected with "instinctive guile," the basis of human nature which Newland believes has been replaced in her by "false innocence" (46). Contrary to Newland's perception it is instinct and intuition which give May much of her strength, and examples of these abound in the novel. She "senses" his love for another woman when he comes to St. Augustine, though at the time she does not know it is Ellen. She intuitively finds "the one disarming answer to his plea for haste" which can reconcile Newland to a long engagement (95) and divines his true motive for wanting to visit Washington (266). Perhaps the best examples of May's intuition are to be found in her instant understanding of Newland's unspoken motives and feelings, such as when he enters the Mingott box at the opera with the intention of "backing up" the Wellands and Countess Olenska:

As he entered the box his eyes met Miss Welland's, and he saw that she had instantly understood his motive, though the family dignity which both considered so high a virtue would not permit her to tell him so. (17)

In the post-Darwinian age, the drive for self preservation is commonly recognized to be the strongest of instincts, and there is no purer example of this in *The Age of Innocence* than May's use of pregnancy to save her marriage. May not only tells Ellen she is expecting before she is sure of her condition, knowing this is the one way to drive her cousin from New York, but lies to Newland about the subject of their conversation (326). Only after the farewell dinner, when she tells Newland of her now confirmed pregnancy, does May admit her earlier lies (343). Surely this determination to fight for her home and husband using any means available (and, notably, the most "natural" ones) is an example of "instinctive guile" at its best.

May's possession of a high degree of intuition and instinct does not preclude the possession of an equally strong sense of social convention and correctness. On the contrary, throughout the novel she is shown to be a master of the social graces, always, as Newland notes, able to do and say the "right thing" (24). Yet her respect for convention and tradition does not mean that she is their slave, merely that she believes in the "old order" which Newland, until the end of the novel, attempts to reject. May, in fact, often transcends the behavioral formulas of her New York society when they are insufficient for her purposes or interfere with her emotional expression. Early in the story, when May tells Newland that he should marry the woman he loves (whom she mistakenly believes to be his former mistress) even if it involves a divorce, she states her understanding of the need to rise above convention:

"I've wanted to say this for a long time," she went on. "I've wanted to tell you that, when two people really love each other, I understand that there may be situations which make it right that they should—should go against public opinion." (149)

The very suggestion that he involve himself in such a scandal for the sake of love is, to Newland, so "recklessly unorthodox" as to be "superhuman" (150). It is certainly not the gesture of an unthinking slave of society.

May shows her ability to ignore protocol and convention on numerous other occasions. She insists that Newland "be kind" to Ellen because he is "the only person in New York who can talk to her about what she really cares for" (120), despite the fact that, as Archer knows, "a man who's just engaged doesn't spend his time calling on married women" (32). She prefers the romance of honeymooning in a country hide-away over the "usual bridal suite in a Philadelphia or Baltimore hotel" (187), flaunts convention and surprises Newland by kissing him passionately "in full Fifth Avenue" on their wedding day (187) and actually suggests some years later he go to Paris, offering him the opportunity to see Ellen:

She had indeed proposed that her husband should go to Paris for a fortnight, and join them on the Italian lakes after they had "done" Switzerland; but Archer had declined. (351)

May loves her New York society and is usually happy to live within its bounds. However, she recognizes the times when one can and should act contrary to its conventions and traditions and does so herself when she feels it to be justified. May's qualification for the acceptability of breaking social codes is deep and enduring love, and this leads us to the last charge against her character—an incapacity for passion and deep emotion.

May's New York, with its gracious society, "nuances of feeling" and dignified behavior, is very dear to her. Some of her greatest moments of happiness come from her triumphs within its conventions, such as her victory at the archery contest, the perfect pageantry of her wedding, and the successful social "vindication" of Ellen and confirmation of her marital situation which result from the farewell dinner. Yet May is capable of willingly breaking behavioral codes when she feels the need to express her love for Newland Archer. Her passionate embrace on the wedding day, her agreement to an early engagement announcement, her concession to his desire to "move up" the wedding against her parent's wishes, and her agreement to a country honeymoon are all unorthodox actions joyfully performed out of love for Newland. Less joyful but greater proofs of her love and understanding are her offer to free Newland from their engagement so that he might marry another woman, and her suggestion that he go to Paris alone (with the implication that he see Ellen), both discussed earlier. The violation of the taboos of the society so dear to her illustrate the depth of May's love for Newland.

May's everyday behavior also demonstrates a love and dedication to Newland which contrast sharply with the latter's inconsideration for his wife. She delights in such simple pleasures as driving home together, yet offers no reproach when her husband forgets his promise to pick her up at her grandmother's house and leaves her to find her own way home (293). At the van der Luyden's dinner May makes an attempt to defend Ellen's visit to Mrs. Beaufort out of what appears to be consideration of her husband's feelings:

A flush rose to May's forehead. She looked across the table at her husband, and said precipitately: "I'm sure Ellen meant it kindly." (319-20)

Defending the women she believes to be her husband's mistress could not have been an easy gesture.

May's fight to keep her husband despite his apparently greater love for Ellen is often viewed as an example of May's automatic and unyielding social behavior. The use of an unconfirmed pregnancy to drive Ellen away from Newland, and of a confirmed one to prevent him from following the Countess to Europe, might be viewed as selfish or dishonest. In addition, May's determination to host a farewell party for Ellen, so painful to the frustrated lovers, might even be considered cruel and certainly her husband views it as such. To Newland, it was "the old New York way of taking life without effusion of blood," and a warning to him that unless he abided by society's rules it would destroy him (335). Yet it may well be that these actions are the greatest proofs of May's love. Before their marriage, May urges Newland to consider carefully his obligations to and feeling for another woman, stating that she "couldn't have [her] happiness made out of a wrong—an unfairness— to somebody else" (149). In rejecting the freedom thus offered him and in marrying May, Newland has made a commitment to her that would be "a wrong" and "an unfairness" to break. Divorce is not possible for her, and without it living with Ellen would be morally wrong. Furthermore, not only is the desertion of a possibly pregnant wife for another woman the action of a cad, but the implication[2] of being sexually involved with both wife and mistress at the same time would debase both relationships. In preventing his desertion, May stops Newland from doing what she perceives as an injury not only to her but to himself. Given his basic sense of decency, Newland's desertion of May would ultimately destroy his self-respect, and any life he might have with Ellen would be ruined by the knowledge that it was built on a dishonorable, hurtful and immoral act. May has, therefore, no choice but to fight for the husband she loves so much, for to allow him to leave would destroy both their lives.

Just as May's fight to keep her husband can be viewed as an act of great love, so can her insistence on going through with Ellen's farewell party. The dinner is not merely a means of preserving New York society's decorum: it returns to both Ellen and Newland public dignity and honor. The overt denial of the perceived love affair and avowal of respect for the lovers preserve their social position and acceptability. Rigid New York society, it seems, has been coerced into publicly supporting Newland and Ellen, a stand which it cannot later (at least without further cause) repudiate. This vindication of Newland and avowal of his worthiness is what makes it possible for society to later accept his authority in community affairs and to respect him as a "good citizen." Painful though it may be, May knows the dinner party is necessary to preserve her husband's standing in their New York world and to assure him a future in it.

May Welland, then, is a character of much potential. Intelligent, intuitive, loving and a survivor, she could have been the heroine of *The Age of Innocence*. Yet she is not. Instead, she spends her life married to a man who never comes to know or love her until years after her death. In a society which, as Irving Howe notes, "had entered its decline" (10), May is one of the last representatives of the true honor and nobility which characterized it at its zenith. To May belong the "nuances of feeling," the highly developed sense of decorum and decency, the nobility of character and the honorable spirit. Her capacity for generosity and self-sacrifice is matched only by that of Ellen, who is from another world. There is evidence that the young May is indeed seeking for a kindred spirit, a man who, like her, is capable of appreciating and preserving "what is good in the old order," while being able to transcend its narrowness and hypocrisy. Initially, May and Newland are so attuned to each other's thoughts that they can commune in thought and action without speaking:

Her eyes said: "You see why Mama brought me," and his answered: "I would not for the world have had you stay away." (17)

. . .

His joy was so deep that this blurring of the surface left its essence untouched; but he would have liked to keep the surface pure too. It was something of a satisfaction to find that May Welland shared this feeling. Her eyes fled to his beseechingly, and their look said: "Remember, we're doing this because it's right." (23-4)

And so May finds Newland, who did not want merely a hollow shell of New York convention, but a "miracle of fire and ice" which combined the best of their society's tradition with vitality, worldliness and spiritual richness (7). Unfortunately, Newland is convinced that, though May has this potential, she must be "created," that she has not the innate ability to fulfill that role. After meeting the vital and individualistic Ellen Olenska, he loses interest in "creating" his ideal May and dismisses her as a mechanical product of society, a "blind Kentucky cavefish" who needs someone to mould her and breathe a soul into her in order to become a real individual. Thus, Newland keeps May in a doll house similar to Nora Helmer's. Never allowing her to express opinions freely, never accepting her as an individual, he discards her in all her potential when he discards her society. Only after Dallas tells him that she had appreciated all along the "sacrifice" he made for her does Newland begin to glimpse a May he never knew. It is this knowledge—that May was indeed heroic, noble and passionate—that gives his life meaning in retrospect. With this new understanding, Newland cannot bring himself to face Ellen again, though there is now nothing to keep them apart, for to do so would be to reject all the values of his New York life and the significance of *May's* sacrifice for him. Newland has indeed missed the "flower of life," but the flower was not necessarily his Countess. As Louis Coxe notes,

what Newland has lost is not Ellen, but May, whom he never took pains to know or to love, May, who knew all along the extent and fullness of her husband's "sacrifice." (157)

The tragedy of *The Age of Innocence* is not the thwarted love affair of Newland and Ellen but that of Newland and May; it is not the destruction of Newland's spirit by a rigid and unforgiving society but the denial of May's great potential by her rigid and unforgiving husband. Newland's "epiphany" is only made possible by May's preservation of his honor, position and integrity. Unfortunately, it has also cost May her own epiphany and the love due her by her husband.

Notes

[1] E.g., see Tuttleton, Walton and Nevius.
[2] Everyone except Newland and Ellen themselves believes their love affair has been consummated.

Works Cited

Auchincloss, Louis. *Pioneers and Caretakers*. Minneapolis, U of Minnesota P, 1961.

——— "Edith Wharton and Her New Yorks." *Reflections of a Jacobite*. Boston: Houghton Mifflin, 1962. Rpt. in *Edith Wharton: A Collection of Critical Essays*. Ed. Irving Howe. Englewood Cliffs: Prentice-Hall, 1962.

Brown, E. K. "Edith Wharton." *Etudes Anglais*, 1938. Rpt. in *Edith Wharton: A Collection of Critical Essays*. Ed. Irving Howe. Englewood Cliffs: Prentice-Hall, 1962.

Coxe, Louis O. "What Edith Wharton Saw in Innocence." *New Republic* June 27, 1955. Rpt. in *Edith Wharton: A Collection of Critical Essays*. Ed. Irving Howe. Englewood Cliffs: Prentice-Hall, 1962.

Howe, Irving. "Introduction: The Achievement of Edith Wharton." *Edith Wharton: A Collection of Critical Essays*. Ed. Irving Howe. Englewood Cliffs: Prentice-Hall, 1962.

Nevius, Blake. "On *The Age of Innocence*." *Edith Wharton*. Los Angeles: U of California P, 1953. Rpt in *Edith Wharton: A Collection of Critical Essays*. Ed. Irving Howe. Englewood Cliffs: Prentice-Hall, 1962.

Parrington, Vernon L. "Our Literary Aristocrat." *Edith Wharton: A Collection of Critical Essays*. Ed. Irving Howe. Englewood Cliffs: Prentice-Hall, 1962.

Tuttleton, James W. *The Novel of Manners in America*. Chapel Hill: U of North Carolina Press, 1972.

Walton, Geoffrey. *Edith Wharton: A Critical Interpretation*. Rutherford: Fairleigh Dickinson UP, 1970.

Wharton, Edith. *The Age of Innocence*. 1920. Rpt. New York: Charles Scribner's Sons, 1970.

——— *A Backward Glance*. New York: D. Appleton Century, 1934.

Widmer, Eleanor. "Edith Wharton: The Nostalgia for Innocence." *The Twenties*. Ed. Warren French. Deland, Fl: Everett/Edwards, 1975.

Wilson, Edmund. "Justice to Edith Wharton." *The Wound and the Bow*. New York: Oxford UP, 1974. Rpt. in *Edith Wharton: A Collection of Critical Essays*. Ed. Irving Howe. Englewood Cliffs: Prentice-Hall, 1962.

The Journey Toward Individuation of Adela Quested in E. M. Forster's and David Lean's *A Passage to India*

Valerie Broege

At first glance Adela Quested in E.M. Forster's *A Passage to India* seems unprepossessing as a potential heroine. Described as a "queer, cautious girl,"[1] who is not blessed with great charm or physical attractiveness, she also suffers from a deficiency in the heart's affections. Nonetheless, as her last name implies,[2] she is a questing person and in going to India and in the course of her experiences there enacts in broad terms the archetypal journey of the hero, as outlined by Joseph Campbell.[3] Although Forster has said that he couldn't read Freud or Jung himself, their work was filtered to him through Proust's ways of looking at character.[4] The purpose of this essay, then, is to discuss from the perspective of Jungian psychology the path by which Adela achieves greater self-awareness and integration, culminating in what Carolyn Heilbrun has called her act of public heroism, in which "she performs the one act most difficult for all of us: she makes a fool of herself in the cause of justice."[5] In my paper I will be comparing and contrasting the ways in which Forster the novelist and David Lean the filmmaker have developed their portraits of Adela, commenting where applicable on the relative effectiveness of their treatments of her when these differ.

Adela has come to India with her prospective mother-in-law, Mrs. Moore, in order to help her to decide whether to marry Ronny Heaslop, a young Englishman who is the City Magistrate in Chandrapore. Early on Adela expresses the desire to see the real India (p. 24), and for both Forster[6] and Lean,[7] who are highly adept at capturing the feel of a place, India takes on a prominent symbolic function. Jungian analyst and writer

41

Marie-Louise von Franz has remarked on the importance of landscape in constellating inner psychic moods, the nature of which correspond to different spirits of place.[8] Through the eyes of various of his British and Indian characters, Forster presents images of India as a mystery and a muddle, a place where nothing "is identifiable; the mere asking of a question causes it to disappear or to merge in something else" (p. 86). The country's vastness, dense population, multiplicity of cultures, fields, hills, jungles, fierce sunlight, and monsoon rains make it a difficult place to comprehend as a totality: there are a "hundred Indias" (pp. 136, 210, 263). In attempting to assess the inner meaning of all these aforementioned views of India, I think that at bottom they reflect the archetype of the uroboros, as delineated by Jungian Erich Neumann.[9] The uroboros is a symbol of a state of undifferentiated unconsciousness, which can be equated with chaos. Thus, by coming to India, Adela has entered a zone of accentuated unconsciousness, in which things out of the ordinary might be expected to happen to her. Adela says she hates mysteries, while the more mystically inclined Mrs. Moore says she likes them, but hates muddles (p. 69). Mrs. Moore also thinks that the odd surroundings of India confuse one's sense of what is really important (p. 98). Particularly in Lean's version of the story one gets the impression that Mrs. Moore has a true appreciation of the uroboric presence of India in her remark to Adela that India forces one to come face to face with oneself, and that can be very disturbing. She also comments after Adela's frightening experience in the Marabar Caves that India is a dangerous place for new arrivals.

C. G. Jung has posited that the human psyche contains four functions—thinking, feeling, intuition, and sensation. Most people develop one or two of these functions to a greater extent than the other two, which would in consequence tend to be more primitive and unconscious in their operation. E. M. Forster makes it very clear throughout his novel that thinking is Adela's superior function, while her functions of sensation and especially feeling are at a low level.[10] In the eyes of Fielding, the British Principal of the Government College in Chandrapore, Adela is a prig, "one of the more pathetic products of Western education" (p. 119). Fielding further characterizes her as going "on and on as if she's at a lecture—trying ever so hard to understand India and life, and occasionally taking a note" (p. 119). She has a "hard schoolmistressy manner" and was examining life (pp. 244-245). Forster tells the reader that for Adela plans had been a passion from girlhood; that she is dry, honest, reliable; has a well-equipped mind (pp. 134-136); and has been accustomed to years of intellectualism (p. 211). Adela's usual approach to problem-solving is to think things out rather than to trust her feelings (pp. 193-194). But Forster suggests that mere thinking is not enough in India: "How can the mind take hold of such a country?" (p. 136).

It is precisely because of the inferior feeling function of Adela in particular and the English in general that Anglo-Indian relations have proven to be difficult. British people have been taught that feeling is bad form and hence are afraid of and bottle up their emotions,[11] while the Indians are described as being a very emotional people (p. 65). Dr. Aziz, the main Indian character in Forster's novel, emphasizes that Indians need "kindness, more kindness, and even after that more kindness" (p. 117). In Aziz's opinion, kindness is the only hope for India; he believes that "we can't build up India except on what we feel" (p. 117). Fielding thinks that Indians cannot be fooled in knowing whether they are liked or not (p. 260). Therefore, it becomes easier to understand Aziz' viewpoint that the English "could not help being so cold and odd and circulating like an ice stream through his land" (p. 71).

Adela's failure to perceive and value her feelings in relation to her personal dilemma vis-à-vis her intended husband Ronny ultimately leads to the tragedy of the Marabar Caves episode. Prior to this incident both Forster and Lean offer ample evidence of Adela's uncertainty and vacillation in matters of the heart, in which she is at a loss. Because of Ronny's bigotry and rigidity in his attitudes toward the Indians, Adela has her doubts about marrying him and becoming part of the snobbish local Anglo enclave. Much to her surprise and distress, Adela first realizes after half an hour had gone by that in a conversation initiated by Aziz in the presence of Fielding and Professor Godbole about gorging on mangoes in the rain she had said that she was not going to settle in India (pp. 73, 82-83).[12] Later in a conversation with Mrs. Moore, Adela still cannot figure out why she said this when she didn't mean it (p. 98).

Both the novelist and the filmmaker later depict Adela as calmly and rationally telling Ronny at a polo match that she will not marry him. They do not quarrel, and Adela remarks that " 'We've been awfully British over it, but I suppose that's all right' " (p. 85). Yet she feels inwardly that "a profound and passionate speech ought to have been delivered by one or both of them" (p. 85). But such an outburst does not occur since Ronny is equally endowed with the quintessentially English stiff upper lip.

Adela's continuing confusion about what her true feelings toward Ronny are is illustrated in an episode that occurs shortly thereafter. An old Indian, the Nawab Bahadur, arrives on the scene and offers to take the young couple for a spin in his car. While riding after darkness falls, Adela's hand touches Ronny's, because of a jolt, and they each become sexually aroused and silently interpret this to mean that all their difficulties are only a lovers' quarrel (p. 88). Nevertheless, Forster gives the reader the impression that all is not well in his statement that "a spurious unity descended on them, as local and temporary as the gleam that inhabits a firefly" (p. 88). Then a collision occurs with something that Adela takes to be a buffalo or a hyena. This is a type of synchronous event in which the animal that hits the car mirrors the animal instinct of sexuality that has affected the couple.

In his movie version of *A Passage to India* Lean has elected to interpolate an original incident of his own in place of what has just been described. In my opinion, Lean has acted wisely in that his scene is more visually exciting and dramatic, while still evoking a similar spirit of place in regard to the nature of India and Adela's response to it. In this scene Adela goes bicycling in the countryside. As she cycles on a narrow dirt path amid high weeds, I was reminded of a labyrinth, and indeed Adela meets her own personal Minotaur. First she encounters remnants of stone statuary in the grass, then comes upon plants and flowers of phallic appearance and the overgrown ruins of an old temple. She gazes at the stone carvings of three couples in sexual embrace. Suddenly a horde of angry monkeys descends and chases her away from the site. Again one gets shots of an erotic statue and the phallic plants and flowers.

In constructing this scene Lean has said that he wished to depict the sexual stirrings and awakening of desire within Adela. Lean's impression of Adela in Forster's novel was that she is "an absolute stick," and he thought she is quite uninteresting. Therefore, Lean wanted to fill out her character a little more than Forster did and make her a more believable person, on the whole, as far as her sexuality is concerned. Lean feels that India can have a catalytic sexual effect on some people, such as Adela. Lean meant the scene to be somewhat sexually frightening, which he achieves through a roaring noise and the monkeys pursuing Adela.[13]

Adela's terrified reaction to the monkeys demonstrates just how alienated she is from her animal instincts and body.[14] James Hillman states that the repressions of our human shadow have been projected upon the monkey as an image of natural wisdom.[15] Furthermore, monkeys can stand for the polymorphous perversity of the pleasure principle.[16] Yet the monkey is also a liminal creature who can point to higher realms of being as seen in the fact that the esteemed Hindu monkey god, Hanuman, has supernatural powers, can change his shape and size at will, can make himself invisible, has incredible strength and speed, and can fly through the air as well as leap over oceans.[17] Thus, the presence of monkeys in Lean's temple scene can point to the fact that Adela is nearing a threshold of awareness concerning parts of her psyche that have been formerly repressed.

However, her immediate reaction is regressive in that after fleeing the ancient shrine, she goes to Ronny's house crying, but not communicating what she has seen, and avers that she wants to marry him. Thus, her hysterical reaction shows that she is still possessed by her inferior feeling function and wants to find a safe, sane, and logical haven with a fellow British partner to avoid facing her anarchic eroticism lying below the surface of her normally bland exterior.

But later that night it becomes clear that her problem has not thereby been resolved. Unable to sleep, Adela looks out the window "into which wafts the sweetly sensuous aroma of blooming frangipani."[18] In a kind of foreshadowing of the Marabar Caves episode, fantasy images of erotic statuary appear in conjunction with the flowers. Also there is the sound of thunder and rain. Rain can symbolize fertility, the emotions, and the liquefying of rigid consciousness. As shall be seen, throughout his film Lean makes effective use of rain falling in important scenes, highlighting various stages in Adela's journey toward wholeness.

For Adela, the visit to the Marabar Caves marks her deepest descent into the unconscious; in Joseph Campbell's terms, she is in the belly of the whale. Interestingly enough, even when Forster was writing *A Passage to India* he knew that something important happened in the Marabar Caves, "and that it would have a central place in the novel"— but he did not know what it would be. Forster saw the Caves as representing an area in which concentration can take place, a cavity. "They were something to focus everything up: they were to engender an event like an egg."[19]

Forster sets the stage for the climactic episode by several earlier references to the Marabar Caves, so that they are definitely on the reader's mind. Even in the very first line of his novel, the Caves are mentioned as being twenty miles away from Chandrapore. The Caves are seen as a potential source of danger when Dr. Aziz warns Mrs. Moore that leopards from the Marabar Hills might be roaming during the night in Chandrapore (p. 21). Significantly, Adela is drawn to the Marabar Hills upon her arrival, looking at them through a nick in the cactus hedge at the stuffy English club and thinking them lovely but untouchable (pp. 45-47). While gazing at the hills, she contemplates what her future married life with Ronny will be like and sees it as rather sterile and divorced from the spirit of India (p. 47). Already the reader can sense a conflict in Adela between her conservative, thoughtful approach to life and the emotional vitality that India represents and which is repressed in her.

Later Adela and Mrs. Moore are invited by Aziz to tour the Marabar Caves. Before this expedition takes place, Ronny and Adela have their misadventure during their car ride with the Nawab Bahadur. Note that their accident occurs on the *Marabar* Road.

In "Part II: Caves" Forster devotes quite a lengthy section to a description of the Marabar Hills and their Caves. Chaman Sahni points out that Forster modeled his Marabar Caves on the Barabar Caves, which actually exist near the town of Gaya.[20] Forster emphasizes the incredible antiquity of these hills, that they are older than anything in the world (p. 123), "older than all spirit," and that "there is something unspeakable" in them (p. 124). This description suggests that the Caves symbolize the primordial realm of the archetypes and as such are likened to infinity and eternity (p. 150). Sahni thinks they represent matter, the primeval matrix of nature.[21] One is again reminded of the uroboros, the unconscious as conceived as the chaos of undifferentiated elements, particularly since the uroboros is often represented by a snake eating its own tail, and snakes and worms are mentioned by Forster in conjunction with the Caves (pp. 147-148, 150, 208). Sahni sees the expedition to the Marabar Hills as analagous to a journey back into the timeless past, "an effort to fathom the mystery of the Primal Cause, a quest for Ultimate Reality, for a Timeless Absolute in relation to which our time-bound existence acquires meaning and significance."[22] Wilfred Stone equates the Caves to the "primal womb from which we all came and the primal tomb to which we all return; they are the darkness before existence itself."[23]

It seems as if on one level Adela is compelled by her own inner promptings to undergo her shattering experience to come in these Caves. Forster describes the Marabar Hills as looking romantic in certain lights and at suitable distances, as they do for Adela, once again from the vantage point of the club, that bastion of English respectability. (p. 126).

As in the case of Forster, Lean also gives the filmgoer a number of clues to foreshadow the centrality of the Marabar Caves in the story. The movie opens on a rainy day with Adela buying her ticket to India at a steamship office. Her eye is caught by a poster of the Marabar Caves on the wall. James Hillman has mentioned that for some individuals with an inferior feeling function their love fantasies are stirred only through travel posters of distant places.[24] Upon the arrival of Mrs. Moore and Adela in India, Adela looks at the Marabar Hills from the back of the house where they will be staying. In the movie Aziz gives Mrs. Moore the same warning in the mosque as in the novel about the possibility of leopards coming down from the Marabar Hills. At the tea given by Fielding in order that Adela and Mrs. Moore get to know some Indians, Professor Godbole, a Hindu, describes the Marabar Caves and makes them seem mysterious.

Returning now to Forster's novel, the author does an excellent job of indicating the fragility and instability of Adela's emotional state prior to her charge against Aziz of attempted assault in one of the Marabar Caves. Von Franz has noted that people are very easily influenced and can be made uncertain of their position when it is a question of their inferior function.[25] Also this function can be expressed in extreme ways. For a fortnight before the expedition to the Caves, Adela had been feeling apathetic and bored and had been living in a cocoon (an appropriate symbol for the transformation she will soon experience), for which she blames herself severely and in consequence feels compelled to utter enthusiasms which she does not feel (p. 133). It vexes her that she is not sublimely happy in the light of her being in India and being engaged (p. 133). As further evidence that she has not properly sorted out her feelings is her comment to Mrs. Moore at one point during their train journey to Marabar that they can't be far from the place where her hyena was. The accident in the car is, to her, a pleasant memory that has given her a good shake-up and taught her Ronny's true worth (p. 135). But, as I have already mentioned, Forster himself gives this incident quite a different interpretation that later proves to be correct. Adela continues to exaggerate her enthusiasm in contemplating how magnificent the sunrise over the Marabar Hills will be. But as if to underscore her insincerity, the sun rises without splendor, bringing a profound sense of disappointment with it (p. 137). An explicitly sexual metaphor mirroring Adela's concerns is employed in this passage as well: "Why, when the chamber was prepared, did the bridegroom not enter with trumpets and shawms, as humanity expects?" (p. 137)

Forster has created a provocative atmosphere of erotic illusion in which Adela partakes as the party approaches the Caves. For instance, there are some mounds by the edge of the track leading towards the hills. The villagers say both that they are graves and breasts of the goddess Parvati (p. 140). In addition, there is confusion that is never resolved concerning a snake. Adela thinks she sees a snake reared up, and Aziz says it is a black cobra. But when she looks through Ronny's field glasses, emblematic of inadequate rationality,[26] she discovers that it isn't a snake but a tree stump. Nevertheless, Aziz maintains that it really is a snake that has adopted protective mimicry (pp. 140-141). Critics Ted Boyle[27] and Keith Hollingsworth[28] have, I think, rightly noted the sexual symbolism involved. Clyde Reid, writing from a Jungian psychological perspective, points out that the snake can represent sexual and life energy.[29] To dream of, or by extension to fantasy about, seeing a snake can be an indication that one is too cut off from his/her instincts— precisely Adela's problem in not yet being able to recognize that she does not love Ronny.

But it is apparent that this awareness is forcing itself upon Adela's consciousness in the type of thoughts and dialogue with Aziz she has prior to entering one of the Caves. Forster describes her as thinking "What about love?" as she toils over a rock that resembles an inverted saucer (pp. 151-152). An instance of Jungian synchronicity (meaningful coincidence) occurs when she notices that the rock is nicked by a double row of footholds, and somehow that this question is suggested by them (pp. 151-152). The footholds remind her of the pattern traced in the dust by the wheels of the Nawab Bahadur's car. Adela's train of thought makes the reader think back to the episode of the car accident and the wrong conclusion that Adela has drawn from it until the present moment.

Adela's sudden discovery of her true feelings unsettles her, but in dealing with the situation she resorts to her typical way of handling difficulties—she wants to think it out, and in any case is not convinced that love is necessary to a successful marriage, an attitude that aptly illustrates her denigration of feeling matters. Forster says that after pondering these things, her emotions are well under control (p. 152), significantly just as they were after the car collision incident (pp. 88-89). Adela then proceeds to ask Aziz whether he is married, has children, and has more than one wife. She is quite unconscious of the fact that she has said the wrong thing to Aziz in asking the latter question—again another example of how her feeling function is undeveloped.

Adela goes into one of the Caves in a distracted state of mind, thinking with half her mind that sight-seeing bores her and wondering with the other half about marriage (p. 153). The stage is thus set for one of the crucial scenes in the novel during which Adela has a violent confrontation with her shadow and inferior feeling function.[30] Because Adela is not comfortable with her own sexuality and does not give her feelings their proper due, these aspects of her psyche have been largely repressed and have become major parts of her shadow, that part of the psyche that tends to be unconscious and acts as a repository of all the qualities of a person that the ego finds unacceptable or threatening. Human beings quite routinely project shadow contents on other people. Adela literally has observed a shadow near the tunnel of the Cave bottling her up— a verb equally applicable to her pent-up emotions (p. 193). Rationality proves to be ineffective in the situation when the strap of Adela's field glasses is broken as she hits at the shadow, and the glasses themselves are left behind in the course of Adela's flight from the scene (p. 155).

It is easy to understand why Adela might have a hallucination concerning Aziz as a would-be rapist. The reader has seen clearly that Aziz is an emotionally volatile person, who is very sensitive to how he is treated by other people, and who values such feelings as kindness and affection very highly. He thus becomes a perfect vehicle to carry

Adela's projection. Von Franz has made an observation that is highly relevant here. She says that "the inferior function is contaminated by the shadow in each type: in a thinking type it will appear as a relatively inferior or primitive feeling person."[31] Furthermore, she states that the "social representation of the inferior function is particularly fitting in that this function tends to have, in its negative aspect, a barbaric character. It can cause a state of possession."[32] Thus, it is no wonder that Adela imagines that the highly emotional Aziz—a native of a third-world, colonial country—has tried to force his attentions upon her in a physically violent way. Such a scenario corresponds to Adela's psychological weaknesses remarkably well. As Jungian Adolf Guggenbühl-Craig puts it, sexual fantasies can tell one a great deal about a person's process of individuation, what parts of the psyche need to be developed and made more conscious.[33] Thus, for Adela, it is necessary that she come to terms with her own eroticism and learn to evaluate and respect her feelings properly. It is not surprising, then, that Adela has hallucinated an assault made upon her since, as James Hillman states, when the psychological distance between people is too great, then as a substitute for this distorted relationship inferior feeling operates autonomously through ESP events.[34]

David Lean's version of the Cave scene in his movie is quite similar to Forster's treatment of it, although he changes a bit what Adela has to say. For example, when she stands on top of the hill and sees the panorama of Chandrapore below her, she comments that it is almost a mirage. Here one gets a sense of how her perspective is altering in relation to her concerns in this city, especially her relationship with her fiancé, Ronny. A more direct reference to her own dilemma of identifying her real feelings toward Ronny is her question to Aziz concerning whether he had loved his wife when he married her.

As if to drive home further the lesson to be learned from her experience in the Cave, both Forster and Lean have Adela run down the hillside in a panicked condition and in the process incur the embedding of hundreds of cactus spines in her flesh, symbolic of phallic penetration, according to one critic.[35] It appears that not only have Adela's feelings been at a low level of development but also her sensation function. Forster describes her senses as having been abnormally inert, and the only contact she had anticipated being that of mind (p. 193). The cactuses make her painfully aware of the physical side of reality, which she has habitually ignored.[36]

As shown earlier, von Franz alludes to the extremism in the functioning of one's inferior function, and Adela's behavior subsequent to the Cave episode aptly illustrates this observation. Forster describes her as vibrating between hard common sense and hysteria (p. 193). She also gives way to tears, for Adela, something vile, "a degradation more subtle than anything endured in the Marabar, a negation of her advanced outlook and the natural honesty of her mind" (pp. 193-194). Up to her old tricks as usual, Adela is always trying to " 'think the incident out' " (p. 194). But the fact that logic and rationality are ineffectual in this situation can be seen in both the symbolism of her discarded field glasses whose strap got broken and her fits of weeping (pp. 193-194, 196, 202).

Also she is plagued by an echo that recalls the noise she heard in the Cave. The echo is a suitable psychosomatic manifestation of the projection to which Adela has succumbed, resulting in her mistaken accusation against Aziz. Accordingly, while in conversation with Mrs. Moore and Ronny, when she voices the possibility that Aziz may actually be innocent and that she has made an error, her echo gets better. This improvement in her physical condition reflects the tentative withdrawing of her projection (pp. 202, 205).

Again as evidence that Adela's echo directly relates to her ability to accept responsibility for her shadow is the fact that it returns badly on the day of the trial (p. 212). While Adela sits in the courtroom, once more the thought runs through her mind about whether it is possible that she has made a mistake (p. 220). During her cross-examination by the District Superintendent of Police it is as if she relives as a kind of vision the events of the Cave expedition and realizes that she has wrongfully charged Aziz with assault (pp. 227-229). She admits her mistake and withdraws the accusation (pp. 229-230).

After leaving the court, she and Fielding are thrown together by the press of the crowd, and he offers his carriage to take her wherever she wishes to go (pp. 231-232). Some of the Indians seem to recognize Adela's heroism in saving Aziz at the expense of her own acceptability among her fellow countrymen. They garland her and even address her as Mrs. Moore (p. 233). This is a high compliment paid to Adela, since Mrs. Moore is revered by them as if she were almost a Hindu goddess (p. 225) about to have a cult following (pp. 256-257).

As evening approaches, Adela and Fielding converse about the Cave episode and both conclude that she had a hallucination and that she had been alone in the Cave the whole time (pp. 239-240). Adela comments that her experience was of the sort " 'that makes some women think they've had an offer of marriage when none was made' " (p. 240). Fielding believes that McBryde, the Superintendent of Police, played the role of exorcist for Adela in setting the matter straight. Adela is now completely free of her echo (p. 239).

In the movie version of *A Passage to India*, Lean adds some interesting touches of his own. As a tearful Adela is being driven in a car on her way to court, an Indian dressed as a monkey is on a tree branch. He then jumps onto the running board of the car and leers in the window at Adela. This happening immediately made me think of Lean's earlier temple scene in which a horde of monkeys chases Adela away and in tears she seeks Ronny.[37] The incident of the monkey-man makes the viewer wonder whether Adela will be any better this time at facing her true emotions when she testifies in court. As if to mirror the release of Adela's pent-up emotions when she cries upon nullifying her accusation against Aziz, a rainstorm occurs as the trial comes to an end. While Adela rides in the carriage with Fielding, she announces that her echo is gone, thereby symbolizing that by admitting her mistake at the trial she has unequivocally withdrawn her projection from Aziz.

After the Cave episode Adela appears to have much greater insight into the feeling side of her nature even if she concludes rather negatively that she is not fit for personal relationships (p. 197) and wonders whether she likes anyone (p. 260) or is capable of loving anyone (p. 212). But even though she does not want love, she wants others to want it (p. 263).[38] It becomes clear to her in trying to collaborate with Fielding in writing a letter of apology to Aziz, that turns out not to be moving, that she has no real affection for Aziz or Indians generally, whom cold justice and honesty without feeling do not satisfy (pp. 245, 260).

Adela's decision is to return to England, where she doesn't think she will do harm (p. 262), and to seek a career there and resume her friendships with people of her own type. In her recognition of her reserved emotional nature she seems to know that she is out of her element in India but would fit in quite comfortably in her native land. Fielding respects her as someone "no longer examining life, but being examined by it; she had become a real person" (pp. 244-245).

As opposed to Forster's final scene of Aziz and Fielding taking leave of each other, Lean ends his movie with Adela. She is sitting at home reading a letter that Aziz has written to her, asking for her forgiveness and expressing appreciation of her courage. Outside it is raining once again, symbolic of feeling situations in Adela's life. As Michael Sragow puts it, Lean's script has its own symmetry, ending as it begins with a curtain of rain and Adela's face.[39] It is as if her time in India was a primal dream. Her round trip passage to India—her hero's journey— has been completed.[40]

Notes

[1]E. M. Forster, *A Passage to India* (New York: Harcourt, Brace and World, 1924), p. 24. Subsequent references to this book appear in the text.

[2]Cf. also Bonnie Finkelstein, *Forster's Women: Eternal Differences* (New York: Columbia University Press, 1975), p. 128.

[3]Joseph Campbell, *The Hero With a Thousand Faces* (Cleveland: The World Publishing Company, 1956).

[4]Malcolm Cowley, ed., *Writers At Work: The Paris Review Interviews* (New York: Viking Press, 1967), p. 34.

[5]Carolyn Heilbrun, *Toward a Recognition of Androgyny* (New York: Alfred A. Knopf, 1973), p. 99.

[6]Chaman Sahni, *Forster's A Passage to India: The Religious Dimension* (New Delhi: Arnold-Heinemann, 1981), p. 14.

[7]Richard Schickel, *Time*, vol. 124, no. 27 (31 December 1984), 54-56.

[8]Marie-Louise von Franz, *Patterns of Creativity Mirrored in Creation Myths* (Zürich: Spring Publications, 1972), pp. 208-209.

[9]Erich Neumann, *The Origins and History of Consciousness*, trans. R.F.C. Hull (Princeton: Princeton University Press, 1971).

[10]Cf. also Louise Dauner, "What Happened in the Cave? Reflections on *A Passage to India* in V.A. Shahane, ed., *Perspectives on E.M. Forster's A Passage to India: A Collection of Critical Essays* (New York: Barnes and Noble, 1968), p. 62.

[11]E.M. Forster, "Notes on the English Character," *Abinger Harvest* (London: Edward Arnold, 1936), p. 13.

[12]Note the fertility symbolism in the mention of rain and the sexual aspect of the reference to mangoes. Aziz in a later conversation with Fielding offers to arrange for him a lady with breasts like mangoes (p. 120).

[13]Harlan Kennedy, "I'm a Picture Chap," *Ms.* 13 (March 1985), 30.

[14]Stanley Kauffmann, "On Films: The Course of Empire," *The New Republic*, vol. 192, no. 3 (21 January 1985), 26-27.

[15]James Hillman, "Senex and Puer: An Aspect of the Historical and Psychological Present" in James Hillman et al., *Puer Papers* (Irving, Texas: Spring Publications, 1979), p. 44.

[16]Hillman, "Senex and Puer," p. 45.

[17]Veronica Ions, *Indian Mythology* (London: Paul Hamlyn, 1967), p. 104; Benjamin Walker. *Hindu World: An Encyclopedic Survey of Hinduism* I (London: George Allen and Unwin, 1968), pp. 425-426.

[18]Debra Pilon, "Films: Passage to India," *HERizons: A Women's News Magazine*, vol. 3, no. 4 (May 1985), 40.

[19]Cowley, *Writers At Work*, p. 27.

[20]Sahni, *Forster's A Passage to India*, pp. 101, 106-107.

[21]Sahni, *Forster's A Passage to India*, p. 111.

[22]Sahni, *Forster's A Passage to India*, p. 111.

[23]Wilfred Stone, *The Cave and the Mountain: A Study of E.M. Forster* (Stanford: Stanford University Press, 1967), p. 307; cf. also Dauner, "What Happened in the Cave?"

[24]James Hillman, "The Feeling Function" in Marie-Louise von Franz and James Hillman, *Lectures on Jung's Typology* (New York: Spring Publications, 1971), p. 147.

[25]Marie-Louise von Franz, "The Inferior Function" in Marie-Louise von Franz and James Hillman, *Lectures on Jung's Typology* (New York: Spring Publications, 1971), p. 53.

[26]Ted Boyle, "Adela Quested's Delusion: The Failure of Rationalism in *A Passage to India*" in V.A. Shahane, ed., *Perspectives on E.M. Forster's A Passage to India: A Collection of Critical Essays* (New York: Barnes and Noble, 1968), pp. 73-74.

[27]Boyle, "Adela Quested's Delusion," pp. 73-74.

[28]Keith Hollingsworth, "*A Passage to India* The Echoes in the Marabar Caves" in V.A. Shahane, ed., *Perspectives on E.M. Forster's A Passage to India: A Collection of Critical Essays* (New York: Barnes and Noble, 1968), p. 46.

[29]Clyde Reid, *Dreams: Discovering Your Inner Teacher* (Minneapolis: Winston Press, 1983), pp. 43, 46.

[30]Cf. also Stone, *Cave and Mountain*, pp. 335-337, and Dauner, "What Happened in the Cave?" pp. 62-64.

[31]von Franz, "The Inferior Function," p. 54.

[32]von Franz, "The Inferior Function," p. 55.

[33]Adolf Guggenbühl-Craig, *Marriage Dead or Alive*, trans. Murray Stein (Dallas: Spring Publications, 1977), esp. pp. 79-93.

[34]Hillman, "The Feeling Function," p. 110.

[35]Dauner, "What Happened in the Caves?", p. 58.

[36]V.A. Shahane, *E.M. Forster A Passage to India: A Study* (New Delhi: Oxford University, 1977), p. 32.

[37]Cf. also Pauline Kael, "The Current Cinema, 'Unloos'd Dreams,' " *The New Yorker*, vol. 60, no. 48 (14 January 1985), 114.

[38]In fact, it is Adela's friendship with Fielding which leads to his being introduced to Mrs. Moore's daughter, whom he falls in love with and marries (p. 302).

[39]Michael Sragow, "David Lean's Right of 'Passage,' " *Film Comment*, vol. 21, no. 1 (January-February 1985), 27.

[40]Kauffmann, "The Course of Empire," 27.

The Women Flyers:
From Aviatrix to Astronaut

Elizabeth S. Bell

Aviation in its early days caught the spirit of the new century and was portrayed as the culmination of the courage, strength, foresight, and skill of those daring "knights of the airways," the aviators. The dream of flight, it seems, was couched in male terms. In fact, the chronicle of aviation, if we believe *The Oxford History of the American People*, is the story of "man's conquest of the air" (p. 894), told about male aviators. The scant mentions of women flyers, taking up a total of four lines of text in the entire 1153-page volume, deal with Ellen Church, "the pioneer hostess," and Amelia Earhart, whose death earned more words than the accomplishments of her life. This allocation of printed space constitutes an amazingly apt analogy, for throughout our century, women flyers have been seen as interlopers in what is most appropriately a male dominion.

But women had dreamed of flight, also; they, too, had longed for the taste of clouds on their lips and the challenge of meeting the void with their raw courage. The Anne Lindberghs and the Amelia Earharts tossed convention to the winds, both literally and metaphorically, and countered society's expectations for young women with a proposal of their own, one that accepted nothing less than an active part in the development of commercial aviation. In a 1928 article in *Living Age*, Lady Heath, then an assistant pilot with the royal Dutch Air Service and holder of a 1928 world altitude record for light planes, assured her readers that "not a few of the improvements and developments [in air travel] that have taken place in America are the direct outcome of the work of women" (p. 264). She further emphasized the increasingly important role of women in aviation, not only as pilots, but also as businesswomen interested in the technological and commercial facets of the growing air industry. The same year Lady Heath wrote that article, Amelia Earhart, for example, was a "director and stockholder of the Denison Airport at Quincy, Massachusetts, an instructor, pilot, and mechanic of the Denison Airport Corporation, and Vice-President of the Boston chapter of the National Aeronautic Association" ("Woman Hops the Atlantic," 8).

Nor were women to be remanded to the "safe" side of aviation. By the late 1920s and early 1930s, the period of time described by Antoine de Saint-Exupery in *Wind, Sand, and Stars* (1932) as devilishly dangerous for men pilots trying to establish mail routes across the Mediterranean Sea, women were engaged in adventures no less daring. In 1928 Lady Abe Bailey became the first woman to solo from London to Capetown, South Africa. Flying 8000 miles over ocean and unmapped land, Lady Bailey, who served as her own navigator and engineer, reported that her only problems arose when the Egyptian government seized her plane and refused to let her fly alone over the desert because as a woman she "ran a risk of abduction or even murder at the hands of fierce and fanatical desert Moslem tribes" (Wilkins, 457). In the 1930s, Beryl Markham was operating her own free-lance charter airplane service in East Africa where huge expanses of the continent remained uncharted and responsibility for ground mechanics, business, piloting, and navigating fell to her alone (Markham, 1942). These women and others like them were not to be relegated to the calm quiet life of the drawing room.

In our own part of the 20th century, this dream of flight can no longer be answered by variations on the Wright brothers; its particulars have changed. Today our visions, our expectations more closely resemble the voyages of the Starship Enterprise than they do the drawings of Da Vinci. We have landed men on the moon, explored through technology the surface of Mars, sent Voyager II into the far reaches of our solar system, and sparked a new generation of dreamers intent on making their fantasies reality. As with aviators, our early space flyers have been male; justly they have become the heroes of the final third of the 20th century. But they are only part of the venture, for again, women have dreamed of space exploration. Sally Ride, Anna Fisher, Judith Resnik are all women chosen by destiny—incognito as NASA—to carry on where their earlier counterparts left off. It is their opportunity to forge in our age the reputation for courage, daring, grace under pressure that their predecessors of fifty years ago formed for themselves.

Yet, the early aviatrices and the current women astronauts have more in common than their visions. In both the early days of aviation and the formative years of space travel, women have been assigned proscriptive roles, as wives, as mothers, as employees of suitable occupations. In the 1920s only the rare woman, or the poor one, worked outside the home. Woman's place was the home, and she left it at her own risk. Aviation, while it attracted many women, remained at the fringe of society; women were either discouraged from attempting it or their motives for wanting to fly, as well as their accomplishments, were impugned. In our own 1980s, even though more women work outside the home than ever before and pursue careers that offer greater opportunity for personal fulfillment than our grandmothers could have imagined, debate still continues on the felicitousness of this arrangement. Even as the "traditional family" is rapidly becoming a relic of an older time, it is still touted and revered as a cornerstone of the American way of life. Women may have a place in the boardroom, but—more often than not—they are still expected to run the home and take major responsibility for childcare. Serious pursuit of a career, especially one potentially dangerous, is frowned on for women.

Consequently, the pressures and prejudices that faced the first women flyers—Anne Lindbergh, Amelia Earhart, and others—parallel those faced by our most recent ones—Sally Ride and the other American astronauts. On one hand all of these women—and others like them—have dealt with the knowledge that they are breaking boundaries; on the other hand, they all record as well an irritation at the banalities with which the press confronts them and at the stereotypical female roles the public expects them to carry out even in the context of their historical achievements.

Written accounts and interviews with the astronauts provide an ironic *deja vu* when compared to those of the aviatrices, for all of these women share similar experiences: fighting to be allowed to become flyers, finding attention focused more on their gender or their traditional role than on their accomplishments, having to explain why they chose to counter the paradigm, and having to defend their accomplishments. These social and cultural elements, more than the physical or technological requirements of their occupations, represent the real barriers confronting all of the women flyers.

Societal attitudes which have resulted in limited access to their chosen professions have presented varying degrees of difficulty for these women. Amelia Earhart, for example, reports she had to be accompanied on her first flight by two male pilots because they decided that since she was a "girl, a 'nervous lady'," she might panic and try to jump from the plane. The second pilot's job was to catch her if she tried (Earhart, 1928). Were the pilots truly concerned about Earhart's mental state once she realized she was flying, or were they having fun at the expense of the woman who thought she could become one of them, a pilot? Ultimately it does not matter, for clearly they were demonstrating the prevailing attitude of the time toward women flyers. Anne Morrow, later to be Lindbergh, records in her diary that as a young woman, in college but still unmarried, she longed to fly. Certain that her father would be opposed to the idea—as he indeed was when he learned what she had been doing—

she arranged her first flights without his permission. Only his respect for Charles Lindbergh, whom he had recently met, kept him from stopping her once he found out (*Bring Me A Unicorn*, 1971).

Our own astronauts had similar problems, not with a literal parent, but with a patriarchal agency: NASA. Under President Dwight Eisenhower when NASA was deciding the qualifications astronauts should have, the decision was made that all astronauts must be military test pilots, an occupation denied to women. A formal hearing launched in the late 1950s by Gerry Cobb openly challenged this stipulation. While she was ultimately unsuccessful in her attempt to become an astronaut even though she was recommended for the job, she at least introduced the topic, and in the 1960s in preparation for the space shuttle program, NASA announced that the test pilot requirement was being dropped; scientists and others were, indeed, welcome as astronauts. In 1978, 20 years after Cobb's efforts, the first six women were selected to become astronauts amid public concerns that their training would have to be modified to fit the weaker physiques of females ("The Spacewomen," *NOVA*). In fact, Com. Robert Crippen, even as late as Sally Ride's first space flight, had to remind the public that NASA played no favorites in the physical or technical credentials of its astronauts: "She's flying with us because she is the very best person for the job. There is no man I would rather have in her place" (*Maclean's*, 27 June 1983). As we have learned, the fears that women would somehow weaken our space program were unfounded. Although the nature of their problems varied, from ridicule to misplaced concern to exclusionary definition, all of these women, regardless of the fifty years separating them, had to dispel the notion that women are emotionally or physically unsuited for the demands of aeronautics.

Yet even this has not been enough, for in our past even the accomplishments of women flyers have been belittled. Anne Lindbergh's ability to pilot an airplane was credited more to her husband's patience than to her skill. The *Post Dispatch*, as quoted in *Literary Digest* (12 April 1930), observes that "when one recalls how few women are able to learn such a simple thing as driving an automobile from their husbands, with whom they are in other matters (with the possible exception of bridge) able to get along perfectly, one begins to suspect that as a teacher Lindbergh must have had unusual tact and patience" (p. 39). The *Dispatch* expresses further astonishment that many of the Lindberghs' flying lessons lasted as many as four hours, when "Many flyers, however, believe that any lesson that lasts longer than between one and two hours is apt to prove a strain, particularly in the case of a woman" (p. 40). The patronizing overlay of these comments, leveled at one of America's most beloved women flyers, seems relatively banal in comparison with the barrage hurled at Ruth Elder, America's "bad girl" of the air.

The story of Ruth Elder demonstrates the extent to which women's accomplishments can be ignored or distorted. In late 1927 Elder, an extremely accomplished if showy pilot in her own right, attempted the first transatlantic flight by a woman, and on a route longer than the one Charles Lindbergh had earlier used. She occupied the position of co-pilot, and when problems developed during the trip, she took turns with the pilot in climbing outside of the cockpit, crawling along the fuselage during flight over the ocean in a vain attempt to dislodge ice that was weighting the plane down. Between soirees outside the plane, she calmly took her turn as pilot. Their efforts were unsuccessful, the plane ultimately crashed into the ocean, and Elder and her pilot were rescued by a Dutch oil tanker. Elder, who was wearing an inflatable suit which would allow her to stay afloat, urged the crew of the Dutch ship to save the pilot first, even though it meant that she would remain in the frigid North Atlantic longer. News reports of the event focused not on her courage or heroism, but on the dangerous vanity and foolishness that caused her to attempt the flight in the first place. She was chastized for endangering human life for no valid reason, but merely to show that a woman could fly the Atlantic, a task defined as "dramatic but not scientific" (Brooklyn *Eagle*, 1927). The Hearst papers hoped that after her failure "American girls will stay on the ground..." (Brisbane, 1927). Other papers intoned, "Men in the summer may strive to equal Lindbergh. Women should stay at home" (The *Irish News*, Belfast, 1927). Public attention was focused on Elder's style—color-cued flying suits, lipstick, flashy scarves, dashing good looks—rather than on her skill and bravery, and this focus on tangential issues gave credence to the denigrating of her very real accomplishments: although her flight was not completed she had broken the transatlantic distance record (*Liberty Digest*, 22 & 27 October 1927).

Tangential issues have always given women problems, especially when they deal with traditional stereotypes or conventional roles, as both the aviatrices and the astronauts have discovered. Marriage has presented all of them with frustrating encounters with press and public. Elder's husband was entreated to keep her at home. In addition she was criticized in several articles for using her maiden name in public and for not *announcing* that she was married. Her contention that she preferred to use her maiden name carried no weight with her critics. Charles Lindbergh was questioned on why he allowed his wife to accompany him on dangerous flights; to Anne Lindbergh's delight, he answered his critic by announcing that she was not his wife, she was crew. Indeed, she was co-pilot, navigator, and radio operator on all of their extended flights in the 1930s mapping and establishing commercial air routes over previously untraveled territory. Yet she was frequently ignored by the news media in their efforts to get substantive information from Charles. When Amelia Earhart was asked in an interview why her husband did not accompany her on her flights, her reply that if the choice were between her husband or 180 pounds of gasoline, she would rather have the fuel, raised some eyebrows and provoked some laughter, but its humor resided in the fact that her reply clearly showed an inverted scale of values for women.

In our own time, Sally Ride has been asked if her flight, earlier than that of her husband, had caused friction between them, while Anna and Bill Fisher spent several years from 1978 into the 1980s being interviewed on the effects of her selection as astronaut on their marriage. To complicate the matter, Anna Fisher had the audacity to become pregnant, not announcing the fact to NASA until several months had passed. She missed only a few weeks of training, gave birth to her daughter on a Friday and returned to work and training on Monday, and earned an unforgettable place in history—or at least in contemporary women's magazines—as the first "Mother in Space." Whatever she accomplishes as astronaut, it will be as wife and mother that she is recorded. Shannon Lucid, who already had three children at the time of her selection as astronaut in 1978, responded with irritation at the effect of gender-based stereotypes on four years of questions from reporters: "We do the same work as our male colleagues, yet nobody asks them about their families, or how their kids feel about their work" (Williams, 45). Societally we grant to men the right to have both a professional life and a personal life that do not overlap; too often as a society we still grant to women only a personal/professional life that we see as interwoven and inseparable.

In both eras, the women flyers have chafed at the attention focused on their traditional roles. In *North to the Orient* (1935), Anne Lindbergh expressed frustration at interviews—especially from women reporters—which provided Charles with questions about route, equipment, technology, and her with questions about what she packed for lunch. She was, after all, the navigator and radio technician; she, too, knew of the dangers and problems of the flight. Amelia Earhart, also, found herself being asked more about her comfort and her diet during flights than about the technical issues involved. In our own time, who can forget the interview in which Sally Ride was asked, "In emergencies, how do you handle the situation? Do you weep?" Her response,—surprised laughter and "Why doesn't Rick get questions like this?"—points up a rather obvious conclusion: Rick as a male doesn't need to overcome stereotypical assumptions of incompetence or hysteria. Sally, Amelia, Anne, Ruth, Anna, etc., as females do.

So why do these women continue to dream and work at making their visions come true? All of them respond in very much the same terms, communicating some of the spirit of adventure they all share. Flying, they agree over the years that separate them, is fun. It was Ruth Elder's reason for taking to the air, even amid the abuse she received from the public: "I like to live and I like fun, and one day when I saw a plane fly over Lakeland I thought to myself, 'that's living; that's fun'.... I was thrilled by aviation from the first moment that I stept [sic] in a plane" ("American Super-Girl and Her Critics," 56-67). Although the situation was vastly different and rapport with her audience much more pleasant, Sally Ride echoed Elder's sentiment almost fifty years later when she described her space flight as "fun. In fact, I'm sure it was the most fun that I'll ever have in my life" (*Current Biography*, 1983, 29). "Freedom" is another word that frequently appears in the writings of these women, freedom from restraint as well as freedom from boredom. Among the women flyers of both ages, part of the appeal of flight is that it is like no other sensation, creating in its participants a human enjoyment of its transcendental qualities. Anne Morrow Lindbergh combined her poet's soul with her flyer's sense of adventure to capture some of this magic: "Suddenly I felt the real sensation of going up—a great lift, like a bird, like one's dreams of flying—we soared in layers. That lift that took your breath away—...I know, now, why aviators are inarticulate. The bare facts alone are transferable; anything else is just so much froth on the surface of the realities" (*Bring Me A Unicorn*, 105, 234).

But the search for adventure, as necessary as it is for anyone who attempts to break the boundaries of the physical earth, is not enough to explain the actions of these pioneer flyers. All of these women have demonstrated a commitment to humankind that is part and parcel of their love of flying. Whether it is Lindbergh's flood rescue missions in China, Markham's midnight flights with medical supplies to lonely outposts in East Africa, or Sally Ride's technical achievements in space engineering and astrophysics on board the Challenger, these flyers have added to the welfare of their fellow beings. Lady Heath spoke of the promise aviation held for women of her generation: "To fly is to live, and to live is to want to do some good in the world. Here, then, is a great opportunity for us women; and the more of us who avail ourselves of it the greater the benefit that will accrue...throughout the length and breadth of the world" (Heath, 265). Others—Earhart, Markham, Bailey, Seddon, Ride, to name only a few—have responded to the opportunity flight allows for expanding humanity's knowledge of the cosmos. It is fitting that Judy Resnik's words at the time of her selection as astronaut express this facet of the women flyers, for—hauntingly like Amelia Earhart—she ended her life in the fiery explosion of space shuttle *Challenger* in the pursuit of her dream: "I feel less like Columbus and more like Galileo. Progress in science is as exciting to me as sitting in a rocket is to some people" (Gwynne with Morris, 74).

These women fly—in air or in space—because having recognized it as a possibility, they will except it as nothing less than a reality. All record a commitment to flight as joy, as occupation, as mission. Theirs is the dedication necessary to face the challenge of breaking societal paradigms and uncodified, informal strictures against abandoning traditional female roles.

Our age, seemingly so different from the past and obviously so advanced in technology, which *appears* to have substantively changed the prevailing perception of woman's place in society, shows remarkably little advancement in human concerns. On an everyday, operative level, we are still defining women in more restrictive, more conventional terms than their talents and ambitions warrant. As the experiences of our women flyers indicate, the boundaries broken by Lindbergh, Elder, and Earhart must be attacked again by their metaphorical grand-daughters. Granting this, Anne Lindbergh's entreaty to a friend at the time she announced her engagement to Charles, provides both advice and reminder to her modern counterparts, indeed to all women who attempt the unconventional: "If you write me and wish me conventional happiness, I will *never* forgive you. Don't wish me happiness...wish me courage and strength and a sense of humor—I will need them all" (*Bring Me a Unicorn*, 228).

References

"American Super-Girl and Her Critics." *Literary Digest.* 95 (29 October 1927): 52-57.

Earhart, Amelia. *20 Hrs. 40 Min.* 1928. New York: Arno Press, 1980.

"Flying Higher, Faster." *Southern Living.* 13 (June 1978): 102, 104.

Gwynne, Peter, with Holly Morris. "Sextet for Space." *Newsweek.* 92 (14 August 1978): 74-75.

Heath, Lady. "Women as Aviators." *The Living Age.* 335 (December 1928): 263-265.

"Husband and Wife Teams in the Flying Game." *Literary Digest.* 105 (12 April 1930): 39-40.

Lindbergh, Anne Morrow. *Bring Me a Unicorn.* New York: Harcourt, Brace Jovanovich, 1971.

———. *Listen, The Wind!* New York: Harcourt, Brace and World, 1938.

——— *North to the Orient.* New York: Harcourt, Brace and Co., 1935.

Markham, Beryl. *West With the Wind.* 1942. San Francisco: North Point Press, 1983.

Owen, Russell. "Ruth Elder's Revolt." *Nation.* 125 (23 November 1927): 509-510.

"Ruth Elder's Ocean Flight." *Literary Digest,* 95 (22 October 1927): 9.

"Sally K. Ride." *Current Biography.* 44 (1983): 27-29.

"Spacewomen." *NOVA.* PBS 1983.

Weinhouse, Beth. "Space Age Mother." *Ladies' Home Journal.* (May 1985): 136, 202.

Wilkins, Harold T. "Champion Airwoman Wins 8000 Mile Race." *Popular Mechanics.* 50 (September 1928): 457-459.

Williams Janis. "Make Way for the Ladies in Space." *Saturday Evening Post.* 254 (September 1982): 42-45, 108.

"Woman Hops the Atlantic." *Literary Digest.* 97 (30 June 1928): 8-9.

A Romantic Feminist:
Margaret Sullavan in *Only Yesterday*

T. J. Ross

Love—like what a mother feels for her child
Marilyn Nash in *Monsieur Verdoux*

I know of few films of the thirties surer to elicit a more positive and engaged response from student (or film society) audiences today than *Only Yesterday*, a romantic melodrama produced by Universal Studios in 1933. This kind of melodrama, in which the film's director, John Stahl, specialized, is more familiarly known as the woman's picture, or "weepie," and simply as a weepie, *Only Yesterday* remains both exemplary and irresistible. Its heroine meets the essential requirement for a weepie in possessing an indomitable capacity for both romantic love and mother love: her death scene, with her son and her lover both standing by, can still leave audiences misty-eyed. And as generally holds true in such instances, our tears are as much tears in tribute as in sorrow, for by the end of her story, the heroine of a woman's picture will have one-upped everyone in sight so that what we behold at the moment of her death is not, as in the case of the isolated gangster hero, with his back to the wall, a *coup de grace*, but rather, an eventful moment in which an individual's experience coheres and adds up to a fate. As George Morris has written, in one of the few articles on Stahl, "Death as a transcendent, not necessarily negative, experience recurs with varying intensity throughout Stahl's work."[1]

Another champion of Stahl, Andrew Sarris, remains however, a bit nervous in face of what he takes to be the film's dated and "mindless worship of child-cult (a spiritual disease especially endemic of the thirties)"[2] Yet whether we see the passions of mother love as "diseased" or intransigently "natural," this kind of passion is essential to the film's premise and point and the film's premise, as embodied in the style of its heroine, continues to move us for the way it touches on matters to which audiences remain sensitive. With the passage of time *Only Yesterday* proves to have been ahead of its time; in its slant on sexual politics the film remains indeed provocative.

Certainly the film proved eventful for the actress making her screen debut in the leading role; there was no question that her death scene marked the birth of a star. The plot of the film is as extravagant and mordant as one would expect; yet the demands of the plot touch on something in the performer that serves to sustain her, this first time before the camera, in fashioning a definitive screen image. My chief concern in these remarks is with Sullavan's screen image and with the manner by which she molded that image. It is the "screen presence" that we may note here taking shape and finally thrown in relief by the shadings and contours of the plot.

The plot itself depends on a juxtaposition of feminist assumptions with a fatalistic mood and this blend of feminist assertion with a romantic fatalism determines Sullavan's manner. She acts a character who is shown to be equally self-sufficient and equally at home in both private and public realms. And given the public events affecting her life, we come to see her not only in personal terms but also as a representative 'figure of her times' whose story reflects the spectrum of social and historical events that comprise, so to say, the march of her times. In this respect, the film retains, to a surprising degree, the spirit of the non-fiction source which provides its title and point of departure. In his best-selling work of popular sociology, Frederic Lewis Allen dealt with a generation whose key experiences were bounded by World War I and the stock market crash. These events bridge the two nights of love the heroine spends with the chief "man in her life": the first, on the eve of America's entry into the war; the second—twelve years later—on a New Year's celebration ushering in 1929. And like the book, the tone of the film is reminiscent, taking us in flashback to the heady times when—when the heroine, like the century, was in her teens.

The film opens in present time with a quick shot on a calendar to establish the date: October 29, 1929. The camera then glides to the floor of the stock exchange where it singles out an anonymous figure. From a distance which keeps him anonymous, we follow this figure as he has his shoes shined and then, leaving his coat behind, makes his way to the men's room. From behind the door, we hear the shot with which he ends his life.

As a crowd gathers, we cut to another crowd at a Manhattan penthouse where the guests and hangers-on anxiously await the arrival of their stockbroker host. The mood is set when one of the guests exclaims, in a line that will later be echoed by the heroine, "In a market like this a moment is a lifetime and a second an eternity." In the course of this long take, which allows for a survey of the intrigues and desperate negotiations taking place in various corners of the room, a maid answers the phone to say, "Mr Emerson is not here." As she speaks, the doors of the penthouse lift, close by, open to reveal Mr. Emerson who, with this theatrical flourish, enters the scene. Like the faceless man at the exchange, news of whose death he brings, Mr. Emerson too, we soon learn, is coolly intent on suicide. And like the other man he sticks to form, remaining well-mannered and impassive as he cuts through the crowd to shut himself in his study. On his desk he finds the letter that will renew his will to live in giving him, in his word, a "future." The letter provides both the film's flashback device and point of view, putting us inside an experience that interlocks with the life of a generation and at the same time is uniquely anchored to a passion in the grand manner.

John Boles, who plays Jim Emerson, the object of the heroine's passion, is himself clearly not cut out to play Tristan to anybody's Isolde. He gives no hint of emotional depths that might correspond to the psychic force that compels the heroine. He stands for the average successful man of his time and as such he is completely representative. He is the best you can expect. In this role he is akin to the men in the lives of the heroines of, say, Ibsen or Antonioni. Ibsen's stuffy bankers and morose ministers or Antonioni's glum architects and cold stockbrokers—these are presented as the best on offer. Nor, like the heroines of Ibsen or Antonioni, does the Stahl heroine look for anything more. A well-mannered stooge like Boles is enough to set her ablaze. In tune with the conventions of romantic love, love happens at first sight: which is to say, the force of feeling aroused in the heroine is like the compulsive force aroused in a woman at first sight of the child she has given birth to. What counts, irrespective of the quality of the motivating object, is the birth of love. And it will be the heroine's decisions that perforce determine the ensuing action.

In its intensive high notes, the soap-operatic weepie attains a grand-operatic energy and resonance. As grand opera deals with royal or bohemian worlds, the Stahl weepie deals in the main with characters of the upper middle class with secure bank accounts and identities. Stahl's people are neither victims nor rebels. The premium rather is on a style equal to the demands of both social convention and personal dignity. The heroes—John Boles, Charles Boyer, Adolphe Menjou, Robert Taylor—tend to be stoical, easygoing, and slightly repressed. In this, they match Stahl's own directorial style: as Universal's top director, he was noted for bringing to the conventions of the woman's picture a tact and intelligence that guaranteed works of a sustained dignity in tone and characterization. What held true for Stahl held true equally for Sullavan, whose own style and intent matched his: thus their collaboration in *Only Yesterday*, while it fairly meets audience expectations, also undermines (and so allows for greater dignity in treatment) a main premise of the genre: that a woman's relation to society—her social identity—was gained through and depended on her relation to a man.

Wit entails surprising juxtapositions and the wit of this film inheres in its combining, as noted earlier, the travail of a grand passion with a feminist point of view. Rather than cancelling one another out, both aspects are held in a tension that gives the film its edge. It is this paradoxical edge that seems most to engage present-day audiences of the film.

II

When we first behold the hero, he is shown moving down the center of the frame as he cuts a path to his room and the fateful letter on his desk; a complementary early shot in flashback of the heroine reveals her stepping from a doorway into a ballroom to make her way up the center of the screen toward a man in uniform perched at the far end of the floor. The action that follows is initiated by her when she first addresses the soldier. She had earlier swapped dance programs with a friend in order to be able to claim him for a waltz. After the waltz, they leave the hall to stroll toward a moonlit lake, where they disappear among the shadows. Their pace as they move toward the lake front is slow and deliberate; when they reappear, their pace is faster and more brisk. Before re-entering the emptied hall, they pause for the man to adjust the belt of his companion's dress which had been flapping loosely.

This sequence, typical of the director's tact and economy of means, is not played as a seduction; throughout the couple act in concert— even as, more than a decade later they will again act in concert when, once again, the hero will be unaware of the full implications of his role. The heroine's own independence of mind is reflected in the anti-war speech with which she attacks her mother's jingoistic attitude. Their quarrel anticipates their subsequent conflict over the heroine's pregnancy. Committed to bearing her child, she embarks for New York, noting that "New York is the only place to live." As the hero leaves for the war, the heroine departs for the adventure and combats of the city.

A montage sequence juxtaposes shots of Captain Emerson leading his men in battle with shots of Sullavan in hospital in her battle to give birth. This does not mean the film rests on a standard celebration of the maternal principle with the maternity ward established as the woman's proper turf. Rather, we have the presence of Billie Burke as the aunt with whom Sullavan takes up residence and who refers to her niece's pregnancy as"...something that just happened—a biological circumstance." She further points out, as she prepares to bob the heroine's hair: "Women have now cut more than their hair. We can get jobs now, and what's more, we've kicked the bottom out of that old fraud, the double standard." Although she would soon fall prey to typecasting as a rich nincompoop, Burke here well enacts an autonomous, confident woman; and it is her views rather than those held by Sullavan's mother that the film clearly endorses.

Sullavan joins Burke in running a chain of clothing stores, an enterprise in which both thrive. In her personal life Burke is involved with a man (played by Reginald Denny) so much younger than she that she feels qualms about "robbing the cradle." It is in fact evident that Denny, who suits her on the sexual plane, appeals as well to her maternal instincts. In all of which Sullavan assures her aunt there is nothing to object to. The aunt marries her young man. Throughout the film she is presented as a character who has satisfactorily co-ordinated her social, sexual, professional—and maternal—interests.

As a story of a grand passion, the heroine's in contrast is a story of imbalance. Yet her passion marks an aspiration, an aspect of being, which proves to energize rather than block her pursuits. She has no problems in establishing herself in a career and in raising a child outside of marriage. Since their one meeting, she had not heard from the child's father. When she next sees him, he is leading his troops down Fifth Avenue on their triumphant return from the war. Before her ardent rush at him, he remains polite, failing to recognize her. Here we arrive at the weepie's obligatory humiliation scene. The film is without background music and the more brilliant for that: certainly in this scene we no more need musical nudgings than we need much dialogue. The emotional charge is transmitted entirely by Sullavan whose features in close-up register a sequence of shocks going from unbelief to understanding to humiliation.

When her aunt remarks that, after all: "He only saw you that one evening," the heroine retorts, in a recall of the film's opening line on the stock market: "One evening—a lifetime for me." And then the chance for a replay when, at a New Year's celebration at the St. Regis on the eve of '29, Sullavan crosses glances with a man at another table who had been ogling her. In every respect the moment is a 'high': the high point in mood, in the plot, and in Sullavan's performance as she half smiles in bitter triumph and fatalistic acceptance. Just as Ingrid Bergman would through her career hold the patent on a stance of quivering composure; or Crawford on the set jaw and eyes that glared like headlights,

Sullavan, from here on, would hold the patent on the taut half smile, a smile beguilingly reinforced by the quaver in her voice.

What is chiefly implicit in Sullavan's manner is "class" in the sense of instinctively impeccable style: she could always come out one-up without leaving anyone else feeling put down. The scene in the St. Regis of a pickup without a word spoken is carried off indeed in high style. And throughout it is the heroine who sets the evening's tone and terms.

"I've had two moments in my life like this" she says, on entering the man's apartment.

"I'm jealous of the other" is the response.

"You needn't be."

On her departure at break of day, she insists on remaining anonymous. "Let's leave it like this: perfect." Perfect surely for a plot fashioned in the heyday of the narrative film: in consequence of this second meeting, the father will be united to the child born of the first. And perfectly in keeping too with the characters Sullavan would go on to play, from *So Red the Rose* through *Three Comrades* to *No Sad Songs for Me:* characters all the more insistent on "perfection"—on style—through their fatalistic sense of the odds. Whether she wins or loses, for the Sullavan heroine it is always in the style of her choice. Nor does passion ever sweep her away; it serves rather as the integrating principle of her style. It also gives to her character a certain opacity and thus sustains the figure she cuts in the world.

As to the figure she cut in the world, rarely did it fit a staunchly middle class mold; more often she played characters a touch Bohemian in their life style like the jaded actress of *Shopworn Angel*; or the displaced Southern belle of *So Red the Rose*; or, in two of her best known films, *The Mortal Storm* and *Three Comrades*, figures displaced by the force of events on the eve of World War II. In contrast, she is constrained to the point of numbness and least convincing as the housebound patient Griselda of *The Shining Hour* and hardly a match for Joan Crawford who, with her energetic stride, walks away with the film.

It is rather as an uprooted figure fashioning a style equal both to the odds and to her own standards that Sullavan won her audience. In her autobiography, *Haywire*, Sullavan's daughter, Brooke Hayward, holds back from acknowledging her mother's achievement as a star. Hayward shows small interest in the rapport Sullavan enjoyed and could count on with her audience. Thus the daughter remains indifferent to what her mother represented to largely immigrant and working class audiences: the kind of "class act" that transcends social class and in consequence challenges social conventions. The character Sullavan projected from the screen was very much 'her own person.' It may be that Sullavan's own temperamental bias toward a more quirky, Bohemian mode of life than she would allow herself in her determination to build for herself and her children an upper middle class existence of picture book perfection led to conflicts she could not finally handle. This must remain a matter of conjecture. More certain is the responsiveness of audiences to a style which comes across as heroic precisely for its representation of "grace under pressure." Not only yesterday's audience but today's as well.

Notes

[1]George Morris, "The Man Who Understood Women" in *Film Comment* (May-June 1977), Vol. 13 No. 3, p. 26.
[2]Andrew Sarris, "Films in Focus," *Village Voice,*, April 29, 1986, p. 55.

Bradley and the Beguines; Marion Zimmer Bradley's Debt to the Beguinal Societies in her Use of Sisterhood in her Darkover Novels

Anne K. Kaler

Charles Williams in his work *The Figure of Beatrice* sees Dante's use of Beatrice as the "greatest expression of the way of approach of the soul to its ordained end through the affirmation of the validity of all those images, beginning with the image of a girl" (8). As Beatrice was to Dante, as Laura was to Petrarch, as Lady Poverty was to Francis of Assisi, as the girl in the Liffey was to Joyce, men have consistently used the image of the ideal woman to express their human strivings toward the Godhead.

But what do women writers use? What do modern women writers use to be an inspiration for their heroines? What universal figure can an author use to inspire women to attempt those higher goals usually reserved for men—autonomy, journeying to expand horizons, a Faustian craving for knowledge, and final reconciliation and union with the Godhead. An author like Marion Zimmer Bradley has few figures from which to choose; while she must preserve the masculine energy of the hero, she cannot use a male muse for fear of offending her audience's post-women's liberation views on equality. Because, as she says, she "likes to distinguish between history and fantasy," her choice is further complicated by her statement that she does not see any " 'evidence' of a pre-existing, primordial 'matriarchial' society" (*Free Amazons of Darkover* [FA] 13). Conversely, she cannot use the classical Amazon as the answer because she could not "write the usual story substituting a mighty Amazon for the hearty hero. Women, in general, do not go on quests in the manner of male heroes" *(Sword and Sorceress* [SS] 9). What historical or literary figure then is there for the doyenne of Darkover to use to establish that happy balance of masculine and feminine aspects in each reader that provides the necessary "valor [that] has neither race nor color [nor] gender" (SS 13), for the heroic fiction of her extensive Darkover series?

Borrowing a bit from medieval convents, a bit from the Amazon warriors, and a lot from medieval women's societies, Bradley fashions an ideal composite figure or muse for her heroines to follow—that of a women's collective society known as a sisterhood. By having both masculine and feminine elements combined into one concept of sisterhood, the sisterhood extends itself out to become a recognizable paradigm of duality of the human personality: the practical sisterhood of the Free Amazons or Renunciates for the masculine outward journey and the Dark Sisterhood for the feminine inward journey of the soul.

In her introduction to *Free Amazons of Darkover*, Bradley admits that the origin of the Free Amazons came from a dual source: a dream she had and from the literary necessity to provide conflict and change for the male protagonist in the 1962 *The Planet Savers*. Borrowing the Sisterhood of the Sword from her fellow novelist Patricia Mathews, she created her Sisterhood of Avarra as a "counterforce" to the male sense of brotherhood, only to find that the Free Amazons and the Sisterhood of the Sword, "at the end of *Two To Conquer* [were] beginning to merge" (FA 13) into one complex and composite concept. While Romilly in *Hawkmistress* joins the Sisterhood of the Sword, the concept of the Free Amazon society did not fully develop until the 1976 *The Shattered Chain* [SC] and the 1979 *To Keep The Oath*. The further exploration of the practical nature of such sisterhoods takes place in the 1983 *Thendara House* [TH] at the demand of the "many readers who wanted to know more about the everyday life within an Amazon Guild House" (FA 13); the mystical inward journey ended in the 1984 *City of Sorcery* [CS], where the major heroines join the Dark Sisterhood. Other spin-offs of Bradley's use of sisterhoods occur in her massive 1984 *The Mists of Avalon*, which incorporates the Celtic version of the Arthurian legends through a mystical island sisterhood of Druidic priestesses and in her new 1985 series of Zadieyek of Gyre, significantly titled *Warrior Woman*. So intriguing is her concept of sisterhood that anthologies of stories about Darkover heroines and warriors are still being written by other authors under Bradley's editorship.

Such a concept of sisterhood might tempt a lesser author to make a feminine Utopia at the expense of a masculine dystopia: Bradley's strength is that she does not do that. "The value of heroic fiction" she says in the introduction to *Sword and Sorceress,* is "that it forces us to confront the heroic within ourselves. I don't think this need is limited to men, or to women. Stories limited to men's affairs are only half the story. Stories limited to women's affairs are, equally, only half the human truth" (13). This is not to say that the blending of imaginative fantasy and history occurs easily. She rejects the existence of a Utopian matriarchial culture as fanciful wishing and an historical Amazon community as doubtful, yet so detailed is her rendering of women's communal living that she must have had some yet unidentified source other than her fertile brain. While she acknowledges that "every culture without exception seems to have had shamanesses or healing sisterhoods... [and that] even in the Middle Ages...women choosing to opt out of their society were allowed to go into convents" (FA 13), this is too easy an answer as any study of medieval convents will show. For, while there are similarities between medieval conventual living and the Darkovan Free Amazons, there are so great a number of dissimilarities that the answer must lie in still another form of female communal life, closer to the Darkover Renunciates, one closer in both practice and in thought.

Convents in the Middle Ages did not provide shelters for all the women who chose to "opt out of their society" because the dowries charged by such cloistered convents were often beyond the reach of the average family. Often the convents became the refuges for the wealthy and noble women alone; while they became choir sisters educated to sing the Divine Office in Latin, their servants became lay sisters who did the menial work and who had daily contact with the outer world. As a result of such financial inequalities, many convents became such social arenas that reformers, like Teresa of Avila and Clare of Assisi, tried to restore the simpler, penitential life first intended by the founders. As Ernest McDonnell notes, only a semi-religious like Mary of Oignes could bring a "new type of *conversio* free from monastic dependence [but one] submissive to ecclesiastical law" (59); thus he sees that, while the "convent was thus the natural and obvious alternative to marriage [although] the admission fees were prohibitive, a *medium vitae genus inter monasticum et saeculare*" (85) had to provide another solution for the unattached woman.

Thus what Bradley's Free Amazon society most resembles is not the typical cloistered convent of the Middle Ages but rather the twelfth century penitential movement of secular women religious, the Beguines, that movement of secular women living a semi-cloistered life but earning their own individual livings, participating in the communal life of the Beguinage, a common life "halfway between the rules of religious orders and the freedom of laymen" (McDonnell 4).

The Beguinage was not a substitute for a convent; while some convents were too expensive for all women to enter, they still flourished alongside the Beguinage because their economic and social structures were different while their religious purposes were similar. Whereas the cloistered nuns had personal and liturgical prayer, asceticism, and manual labor as their major aims, the early Beguines had a more apostolic life in mind, a life later supported by the mendicant and penitential movement of the Franciscans and Dominicans. As Joseph Strayer comments in *The Dictionary of the Middle Ages,* "the manual labor of mendicancy in the midst of the world must have seemed closer to the models provided by Christ and the apostles than did the lives of the cloistered nuns [so that] joining in a beguinal community, unattached women could pool their economic resources, find mutual protection, and gain a sense of identity" (158-60).

From these three reasons—economic security, mutual support and protection, and a sense of identity—a fourth flows naturally and is developed by Bradley as mysticism—that of deeper spirituality of the inward journey after the economic and social needs are answered. This is seen in Bradley's three heroines—Magda, Jaelle, and Camilla—and their increased use of *laran,* which deepens each heroine's spirituality until they all join the Dark or Grey Sisterhood, the mystical and final phase of the heroines' search and the counterpart of the final unitive step in mysticism.

It was the economic as well as the religious conditions in Northern Europe in the twelfth century that gave birth to this unique female movement. The desire for economic autonomy forced both the Beguines and the Free Amazons to earn their living in a male-dominated world where their femininity is questioned repeatedly. Here the difference is not between the masculine and feminine roles—the tomboy or the housewife—but rather, as Bradley expresses it, the heroine's quest lies in the integration of the individual as individual, separate from the usual restrictive ties placed on women in any society. A Free Amazon's apparent sacrifice of her femininity then becomes meaningful. Living the Oath of Renunciates so akin to the code of medieval chivalry, the Free Amazon warrior protects the weak and vulnerable while earning money for her guild house. Jaelle hires herself out as a travel guide, especially for women traveling alone; Camilla is a warrior and bodyguard. Ironically, the Free Amazon's skills in the martial arts rival the growth by mythical rites-of-passage ordeal of the boy-hero into manhood—both must learn to use their new powers only to defend themselves, never as an aggressive act to gain power. In a male-dominated world, the woman warrior must use her deceptively small size to outmaneuver the larger male. Her skills are swiftness, not strength; she must, like the boy hero, learn to trust in her own inner strength as the only source on which to rely. Only when she is in complete accord with her own nature is she most powerful. When the feminine compassion for the weak and the masculine strength to defend them blend, she becomes a fully integrated human. The women's communal society provides a nurturing arena for such growth.

Bradley improves on her sources without compromising her ideals: she attributes the source of her first Amazon character of Kyla in *The Planet Savers* as a licensed mountain guide (FA 13) to Arlene Blum's *Annapurna*, the true story of women's first attempt to scale mountains in spite of male opposition; the later characters of Jaelle and Rafaella are also travel provisioners and mountain guides, despite jealousy from their male counterparts. The same male hostility in the marketplace existed for the Beguines. From contemporary records of guild transactions. Ernest McDonnell shows that the many lawsuits which were enacted against the Beguines for establishing a pseudo-guild forced "the beguine who left the convent, if she wished to resume work, [to] submit to the usual apprenticeship" (274) of the male-dominated textile guild.

The structure of the medieval guild may have contributed to the increased appeal of the Beguinage for an unmarried woman, for in many guilds a married man could not be an apprentice or a journey-man, a factor which postponed or prevented marriages. This, linked with a male population already decimated by war and natural causes, may have caused an imbalance in population so that the women who were left unmarried were also left without economic support. Often they were apprenticed to guilds because their families could not pay dowry for their marriage or for their entry into a convent. Thus, according to McDonnell, "if a girl was unable to make a rich marriage...she became a beguine" (85). The Beguinage provided a satisfactory compromise in its time, just as women's communes do in more modern times, and just as the Free Amazon Guild houses provide an alternative to the Towers and the normal chain-binding marriages of certain Darkover societies.

While the secular life of the Beguines allowed them to practice a vital apostolic life which included the "nursing, weaving, spinning and embroidery...funerary services, washing, and housework for others" (Strayer 160), the Beguinage itself provided a half-way house between the strictly cloistered nuns and the secular life in a time when an unattached woman had little status or safety. Clare of Assisi had to establish a cloistered community in the twelfth century Italy to satisfy her society's demands for propriety, although her first desire was to follow Francis' nomadic mendicancy. Her Northern European counterparts had been settled in Beguinages for a century before but no such societies existed in southern Europe at the time; indeed, Dante himself takes a dim view of the one Beguine he includes in his work. Even to as enlightened and educated a person as Dante, the thought of an unprotected woman, earning her own living, was intolerable. Such a woman had no choice: she had to marry or become a cloistered nun, shut off from the world and its cares and pleasures. But the Beguines could do what cloistered nuns could not: with their purpose stated by McDonnell to "foster piety, practical or contemplative, to hold aloof from the dangers of the world without stopping ordinary work" (5), they were able to serve the people with their skills, especially those pertaining to women. Bradley's Free Amazon guild house concept and the Bridge society provide a similar link between the opposing worlds of Terra and Darkover. In *Thendara House* some of the Renunciates are chosen to learn Terran skills most needed by women: midwifery, maternal care, birth control, hygiene. For example, Jaelle knows when she is pregnant by counting "a small calculating device of [colored] beads [to] keep track of her woman's cycles by the movements of the moons" (138). Marisela, who is of the grey Sisterhood and who dies, is a midwife. Bradley details the medical practices each guild house member possesses and stresses the others' occupations almost as soon as they mention their names and affiliations.

Another strong link between the fantasy women of Bradley and the real women of the Middle Ages is the economic independence that enabled women to control a larger part of the Northern European textile industry; Chaucer's Wyf of Bath is no exception as a woman in the English-Flemish textile trade and, even to the present day, cloistered nuns have used lace-making and fancy embroidery as a source of income. While cloth-making is not stressed in the Thendara Guild House, the women of Darkover, Renunciate and non-Renunciate alike, are involved in household maintenance because Darkover is a primitive world. When Magda first enters Thendara House, she is shamed because she cannot contribute to the house's economy except in the most menial way, since she cannot cook, sew, weave, dye, or garden nor can she master midwifery, "farriery, metalworking and forging, veterinary medicine, dairying, chessemaking, animal husbandry or bootmaking" (41).

Clothing, however, plays a deep part in the life of the two groups of women. Although scholars have discounted the idea that the origin of the word "beguine" came from St. Begga or from Bishop Lambert "Le Begue" or the Stutterer, Old French has a word "beguine" from "baga" meaning a hood. Almost consistently, Bradley stresses the hood as a part of the Amazon costume, a not unexpected necessity on a cold planet. The most likely origin of the word "beguine" is probably taken from the indeterminate color ("bege" or "beige" in French) of the natural fibers of the homespun cloth, favored by those mendicant penitential societies such as the Franciscans because it aligned their lifestyle with that of the poor and it distinguished them from the relatively expensive white (i.e. processed or bleached fabrics) or dyed black habits of the Benedictines, Dominicans, and Augustinians. Francis of Assisi's father was a cloth merchant; Francis' rejection of his father's values included his stripping off his rich wardrobe to adopt the homespun gown of the poor, a robe still preserved in its original grey-brown state. On the other hand, other semi-religious like Margery Kempe, the religious scamp of the fourteenth century, who was criticized for wearing white clothes since those who reserved for the clergy, did not adopt the homespun habit. While early nuns did not wear distinguishing habits, in time the orders of nuns established a certain mode of clothing as suitable and, although the beguines had no set color or cut in clothing, they probably wore the same "drab homespun" (Strayer 158) fashioned into recognizable scapulars and hoods, as did the general populace. When Jacques de Vitry, the Augustinian bishop, supported the Beguine Mary of Oignes, the Beguines were wearing a "uniform grey dress to distinguish them from others" (Beck-Fink 245).

While Bradley seldom mentions specific colors (except in fancy clothes), her heroines are garbed in similarly unprocessed, natural colored clothes, not for reasons of poverty but for comfort and practicality. Thus, the "typical Amazon dress [of] low boots of undyed leather, fur-lined trousers, a fur smock...with heavily embroidered leather jackets and hoods" (FA 10) emerges as a sensible series of garments for working women on a cold planet. In *Thendara House*, while Magda slowly sees the comfort and sense in her new Darkovan clothes, her counterpart Jaelle not only objects to the tight and revealing clothes she must wear in the Terran society but also to the uniformity of their dress.

Uniformity of housing is also a point Bradley considers. Each of the guild houses has its own flavor, its own charisma, each being a separate self-sustaining community of varying numbers of women. Where a strictly cloistered Carmelite convent is limited to twenty-one nuns, other convents could house any number of nuns within its walls. Unfortunately, while exact records of the early Beguinages have been lost and only records of the thirteenth and fourteenth century ones remain, the earliest Beguinages probably varied from ten to twenty women in size and were a "number of small houses grouped about the church or hospital...and shut off by a wall from the outer world" (Schaff-Herzog 28). When Magda first sees Thendara House, it is described as a "walled building, windowless and blind to the street" (18), just as the Beguinages were formed by having the inside of the cottages facing inward to a courtyard, a primitive way of assuring no windows opened onto the street.

Bradley is keenly aware of the similarity between the Free Amazons and medieval nuns. In *Thendara House*, she has the Terra Intelligence Chief Cholayna question Magda about her joining the Renunciates. "What was it you called them—Renunciates? Sounds like an order of nuns, what do they renounce?" (12). Whereas the cloistered nuns renounce all doings with the temporal world to concentrate their energy on the next world, the Oath of the Free Amazons binds them only to renounce the need to be dependent upon men for protection or support. Like the Beguines who had businesses to run, children to raise, and family and social affairs to manage, the Amazons desire autonomy and self-identity—economic, physical, emotional. They have no need for an individual man to defend them; their Guild House structure provides the society for mutual protection and support and the training in self-defense. Like the Beguines, Bradley's Amazons recognize that in numbers there is strength.

Both sets of women took vows or oaths, affirming their commitment to their beliefs. While nuns took solemn vows of poverty, chastity, and obedience, the Beguines apparently took only the simplest promises, ones from which they could easily be dispensed. Like nuns, the Beguines were bound to chastity during their stay but could leave at any time to marry. In contrast, for Bradley's Amazons chastity is voluntary, restricted only by their Oath of the Renunciates "to give myself to no man save in my own time and season, and of my own free will and desire" (FA 18). This predictable difference between the nuns' total renunciation of the use of sexual pleasure and the Free Amazons' use of sexual pleasure as a legitimate right is dictated by an author's need to accommodate the modern sexual mores of her audience and by her need to repopulate her universe. For nowhere is the Amazon community held up as perfectly self-sufficient (as it is in Joanna Russ's works, for example) because the integration of the elements of the heroine's personality necessitates a balance between masculine and feminine. Men are needed for pleasure, for sexual release, and for the begetting of new life. In practice, the Free Amazons keep their female children with them but surrender their male children, either at birth or five years old, to an accepting household, that of the father or another near relative. No nuclear family structure exists in Bradley's Free Amazons or in the Beguines' shared communal living, which, one supposes, included communal child care. In the annals of religious women, saints and foundresses of orders, there are many married women, whose children came with them or were raised by obliging family members. Just as virginity is no pre-requisite for Bradley's Free Amazons, neither was it or is it a pre-requisite for either the Beguines or for nuns, while chastity certainly was for the latter groups.

Although Bradley handles problems of lesbianism in other novels written under pseudonyms, her solution to the sexual difficulties of a community of women in the Darkover series is the establishment of a freemate marriage. This first occurs in her novel *World Wreckers* in which she used a "freemate Couple (probably, though not explicitly, lesbians, to balance the sexual identity crises of the male character." (FA 9). Freemate marriage between women binds both to legal rights and obligations to foster the other's children. While it is identical to marriage without the *de catenas* or chain-binding laws, it does not necessarily imply lesbianism. Within the Darkovan society, there are no restrictions on homosexual relationship: indeed, in the Free Amazons, it is almost expected in a woman's growing up and, when several minor characters renounce men so strongly as to bind themselves to other women, it is seen as a stage of sexual development rather than as an end in itself. Some mature women come to their freemate marriages with prior knowledge of men but with a desire to be united with a particular woman. Such is the case with Magda and Jaelle who become freemates to protect their children's futures and, as a result of their mutual participation in *laran*, are linked in a bond "closer than family, closer than sex, closer than her own skin" (CS 319). Magda, who is half-Darkovan and half-Terran, feels herself to be a "Renunciate at heart—I think I would always have been one, had I known such a choice existed.... I have never had any women friends at all. I was always trying so hard to be one of the boys that I never paid any attention to what other women did...until I met Jaelle" (TH 13, 4). Even Camilla, the *emmasca* who has been made genderless by the difficult operation, does not have her leanings stressed because her personality is so well balanced between masculine and feminine that she sees affection as more important than sex. She is so sympathetic that she is able to say that "I know that men are very like women—only not, perhaps, so free to be what they are. It's a pity there's no Guild-house for them" (CS 55-6).

Another factor Bradley employs is the testing periods common to most organized religious groups: three to nine months for postulancy, a canonical year-and-a-day for the novitiate, and three to eight years until final profession. In *The Shattered Chain*, Magda, having been forced to swear the oath of the Free Amazons to save her husband's life, decides to honor it by living as one of them obeying the strict enclosure of being "housebound" in the Thendara Guild House for six continuous months. While this roughly parallels the postulancy period in medieval religious orders, the testing period of the Beguines is not known because no records have come down to us (an interesting comment in itself of the fragile existence of women's communal life outside a recognized religious order.) It is likely that such a testing period was similar to that of the trade guilds and the religious orders, without the formality of the stages being named as postulant or apprentice, novice or journeyman.

The entry into religious life is duly noted as a crises in Bradley's novels. When Keitha flees to Thendara House for protection from her abusive husband, she must publically take an oath that she is doing it of her own free will. While religious still commit themselves in public ceremonies before the bishop for final vows, a simpler set of initiatory questions is asked of each entrant before they are allowed over the threshold—usually a formula of the "what do you desire" ritual. Bradley incorporates this in the final questions that Kyntha of the Sisterhood asks the travellers in the *City of Sorcery*: "What does thou seek? . . . What is thy truest will?" (CS 420-2). Another proof of the author's intimate knowledge of acceptance into religious communities is Keitha's formalized cutting of her own hair to signify her desire to adopt the short practical haircut of the Renunciates' hair style. Nuns traditionally cut a lock of their hair in public, not only to signify their death to the world, but also to make the wearing of their veils and headpieces easier. Likewise, Jaelle in her brief marriage with Peter resents her longer hair because it deprives her of the "distinctive Renunciate cut which proclaimed her independence of any man" (TH 138).

The lengthy chapter in *Thendara House*, in which Magda's shortcomings as a prospective Renunciate are bandied back and forth until three sisters agree to support her, is similar to the Chapter of Faults in religious institutions, in which religious ask forgiveness for their sins against each other and the community. The acceptance that Magda feels when even her "enemy" Rafaella defends her assures her of her vocation and matches, as Strayer says, the Beguines' purpose to "live in communal houses and encourage each other to do good by mutual exhortation" (158).

While the Beguines started as a penitential movement of secular women, they were soon caught up in the mystical fervor of the Middle Ages, caused in part by the increased popularity of the language arts, which encouraged self-reflective journals. Where twelfth and thirteenth century writings for nuns, such as *The Ancrene Riwle* and the works of the English mystics Juliana of Norwich and Margery Kempe are well known, earlier European writings of mystics, such as Mechthild of Magdeburg, Beatrice of Nazareth, Mary of Oignes, and Hildegard of Bingen, influenced the major European mystics, Meister Eckhart and Ruysbroeck, as well as secular writers such as Dante. Unlike pious haliographical stories of miracle workers in the *Legenda Aurea*, one necessary element to determine a true mystic is that his or her life story continues beyond his or her lifetime, usually as an autobiography or as book of devotions which detail the soul's striving to reach the Godhead. Hildegard of Bingen, a twelfth century Benedictine abbess, transcribes her thirty-six visions into illustrations in her work *Scivias*, centering on the need of the soul of "greening power" (Fox 30); Teresa of Avila uses the garden and gardener; Mechthild, Christ as the heavenly Bridegroom and Streaming Light; Meister Eckhart, the underground river; Gertrude the Great, the Sacred Heart of Christ.

The one such image Bradley invents is *laran*, that telepathic power of communication inherent in some of the Darkover clans, which is a primitive form of mystical powers which sees any "extraordinary gifts and visions" (Beck-Fink 376) as mystical. She blends the natural mysticism of the Celtic peoples with the entire concept of religious mysticism and with that mysticism of the Beguines in particular. Starting the *Darkover Landfall*, Bradley has Judy Lovat define her dream lover in mystical terms: he comes during the mind-altering Ghost Wind to say that their "minds were open to one another...the most total love and sharing any human beings could know...he told me—our people's minds were like half-shut doors" (127) The mystics often see the Godhead as complete communion, an absorption of the lesser being into the love of the higher being. So also Judy's lover is beyond the senses—"It's like hearing someone's voice and knowing it by the sound...as if he were standing beside me, touching me, and then it fades again. A moment of reassurance, a moment of—of love, and then it's gone" (128). To non-mystics the experience seems a hallucination or madness; to Judy and her *laran*-bearing descendants, it is a part of their nature.

Just as the true mystic uses his body and his writings as an expression of his contact with the Godhead, Judy and the other Darkover mystics must possess a physical means to conduct the energy of the *laran* Where words are not enough to convince non-believers of *laran*, symbols must take their place because they speak to the soul intuitively and directly without the interference of the reasoning process; to the non-mystic, the symbol must often have a physical manifestation. Bradley uses the matrix jewel as a symbol and as a means to achieve the telepathic and mystical union. Where the mystical union with the Godhead became an unalterable part of the mystic's personality and existence, so also does the jewel become an integral part of the Darkover *laran*-bearers. Father Valentine, the former priest, theorizes to Judy that "perhaps the jewel is attuned to whatever is in your mind that makes you YOU" (128). When he goes to inspect it, Judy refuses to let him touch it because it hurts her, "as if it were part of me" (128). Just as the mystic cannot allow the divine madness to be taken from him or her without destroying the personality, the distorted character of Dezi in the later book *The Forbidden Tower* is horribly mangled when he tries to obtain his brother's matrix from the otherworld, so driven is he when his own matrix jewel is destroyed.

That the jewel is intended as a substitute for symbols of organized religion is made doubly clear when Father Valentine rejects the "sacraments or priesthoods from a world that's only a memory," fearing that those "rituals...will quickly dwindle down into superstitions" (125). When Judy admits she took off her cross to replace it with her matrix jewel, he sees it only in a pragmatic, scientific way: "a jewel to enhance telepathy [although] telepathy can't just exist, it must have some natural phenomenal basis" (128). Later a priestess-teacher in *The Heritage of Hastur* describes *laran* as "certain energy centers in the body...[which] everybody has...but in a telepath they are stronger and more...perceptible...like an extra pulse beat, here above your brow...[and] there's one at the base of your throat" (332).

What causes the *laran* to become evident to the early space ship survivors is the mysterious Ghost Wind which changes their personalities, much as the Holy Ghost (as He was called in pre-Vatican II days) or the Holy Spirit is seen in the Gospels as a Wind or Fire which changes the personalities of the apostles from fear into heroic action. The description of the Annunciation of Christ's birth employs the same terminology of the mystical Spirit-Wind: "the Holy Spirit shall come upon you and the power of the Most High shall overshadow you" (Luke 1:35).

Throughout the novel, there is a persistence of mysticism which is particularly Celtic. When Judy is readying herself to visit Valentine, she overhears a girl from the New Hebrides singing "one of our island songs...about a fairy who fell in love with a mortal man...and wanders...still looking for him, wondering why he never came back to her" (124). Valentine refers to her "fairy lover" (128) but when convinced that she has really been impregnated by an alien of the "gentle people" (127), his mind makes a "curious near-blasphemous" leap to the concept that perhaps God is sending a "Child...a strange child, not quite man...on this strange world...[and that perhaps] the Child I worshipped all these years was not some such strange alliance" (129).

Father Valentine is or was a priest of the St. Christofer of Centaurus of the Reformed Catholic Church; The Saint or holy Christofer is easily explained. St. Christopher, until his dethronement by the Bollandists, was the patron of travellers because of his legend of the origin of his name—the Christ-bearer, the man who carried the Christ child across a river. That a space voyage would have St. Christopher's priest as a "Christ-bearer" to the stars and as a patron for the protection of the space ship is not unexpected until one considers the second part of the name—Centaurus. As well as being the name of a guiding star in our galaxy, the word "centaur" connotes a double image of a mythical animal, half-man and half-horse, one who is Half-God and half-human as Christ is, or one who is a mixture of two races as Judy's child will be, or just as Magda herself is in the later novels. In addition, there is even significance in the name of the patriarchial horsemen from the Caucasus, mistakenly named centaur because their furry chaps blended into the pelts of their horses, who conquered the matriarchial tribes of western Europe, including the Druidic Celts. On Darkover, however, the patriarchial Reformed Church of Centaurus, which expected to conquer new worlds for their "Christ," is reduced to ineffectiveness by the Celtic aristocracy of the Hastur-Comyn lines with their female leaders and keepers and the matriarchial force of the Free Amazon guild house structure.

Bradley's Celtic background appears in other forms. The majority of people on the doomed space ship—those who become the ancestors of the Darkover natives—are Celtic in their looks (the striking red hair and the dark coloring of the aristocratic Hastur and Comyn lines that rule Darkover) and even in their names—Alistair, Ewen, etc.. The leader Rafael MacAran, father of Camilla's child, is aptly named "son of Aran" after those furthermost islands of western Ireland and the bastion of Celtic/Iberian culture. Thus, the word used for these inbred telepathic ability or unexplained mysticism is a form of MacAran's name—*laran*, or, as it would be in French, *l'aran*, the Aran of people of Aran. Another possible source may stem from the *lares* of Roman times, whose secondary meaning was the beneficient spirits of the dead who commune with the living, a power than *laran* gives to its bearers in the form of the Otherworld or Overworld communication system.

For the individual in the Darkovan world, the development of *laran* has potential mysticism as its base. The purgative self-denial of the Keepers of the Towers strongly imitates the asceticism and the exclusive chastity of religious orders, as in the character of Leonie, the Keeper of the Arilinn Tower, who almost destroys Damon and Callista of the Forbidden Tower with her obsession about chastity (FT). While the individual character suffers the physical, emotional, and mental drain inherent in the use of *laran* needed to produce effects, the *laran*-bearers must suffer this purgation step to cleanse the body and soul for higher experiences, just as the mystics and the medieval religious did. Only when she and Jaelle are near death in the cave does Magda first use her *laran* to make contact with the Grey Sisterhood, those "shadowy figures, dark-robed women...[whose] words dissolved into the calling of crows," mistaking them as hallucinations of her feverish mind. In the last novel, *City of Sorcery*, Camilla foregoes her life-long denial of her *laran* to find and save Magda in an action that rips open the old wounds of her brutal childhood; only the old warrior's suffering at the death of Jaelle enables her to achieve finally her quest for the Grey

Sisterhood in her usual direct fashion: "where do I start looking for this wisdom. In your city? Take me there... Do your duty, my sister, that I may do mine" (CS 420-1). Magda recognizes that choosing to be one of the Grey Sisterhood involves sacrifice: "Magda felt a sharp pain at her heart. Jaelle had gone before her, with Marisela. Now Camilla had outstripped her and was to be taken from her." (CS 421). Novel after novel stresses this point; it becomes a Beowulfian *leit motif* that suffering and denial of the self, the purgative step of mysticism, alone leads to the illuminative step and to the unitive final union.

While Magda feels that her "own awareness of mental processes had increased a thousand-fold when she began to explore her *laran*" (CS 60), she discovers through the death and return of Marisela that only those with *laran* can go into the Grey Sisterhood of full communion, on earth or after death. Joseph Campbell's works record this death and return of the typical hero as the duty of the hero. When the heroic death of Magda's freemate Jaelle and the decision of Camilla to join the Dark Sisterhood force Magda to her final decision to join them, she knows it means her own passage through the death of self into the unknown, a strong component in the mystical union. When Magda comments that "'the real me, the truest me, is Darkovan. Yet too much Terran to be true Darkovan...[I] had never really belonged anywhere" (TH 17), her final decision is more understandable because it culminates in her choice of a higher lifestyle, participation in a mystical Sisterhood, which forces her to leave the world behind to concentrate on another world in the company of sympathetic friends. She has been in training for this decision for a long time and the entire last book leads, in symbolic fashion, toward this decision on the mountain top. In turn, each of the others finds what she is looking for—Jaelle receives freedom from her limited *laran* abilities and from daily responsibility; Camilla, the neutered woman, finds the answer as to why she, who was to have been a Tower priestess with her Hastur heritage before she was brutally raped by men, had to become a bitter *emmasca* denying her powers and living as a man. The answer which comes from one of the Grey Sisterhood who calls her by her long-denied Hastur name is paradoxical: "few of thy sisters have had such trials. How shall the fruit grow unless the blossoms are pruned from the tree?" (CS 346). Hildegard of Bingen expresses the same paradox in her image of greenness as necessary to the soul: "now bear in mind that the fullness you made at the beginning was not supposed to wither?" (Fox 32).

While Bradley purposely leaves nebulous the process of dying or of Magda's achieving acceptance into the Sisterhood, she expresses her perception of the final unitive meeting as being "encompassed in an instant love-feast of greeting, made up of all the kisses and embraces, and tenderness they had ever known, without time or limits of the body and it lasted...a long time...an intensity of loving communion" (CS 71). Where Bradley uses the religious terms of "communion" to describe that the intensity of this union which Magda feels is greater than the bond with her freemate Jaelle or even than the physical love she feels for Camilla, the medieval mystics used sexual terminology to describe their final unitive state with the Godhead as a way of explaining mystical experiences. Teresa of Avila speaks of Her Divine Lover as piercing her heart with swords, John of the Cross, of a hot spear in the genitals; Catharine of Siena, of her mystical marriage; Hildegard, of Christ as the moisture of "Greenness Incarnate" (Fox 32). In mysticism, then, the sexual images of the union of masculine and feminine designate the completeness or union of the created with the Creator into a new relationship. As the modern analyst of the mystics, Mircea Eliade, comments, "the experiences of the Light...bring a man out of his worldly Universe or historical situation and project him into a Universe different in quality, an entirely different world, transcendent and holy" (Fox 33).

Just as the mysticism flowed directly from the twelfth century nuns' and Beguines' recommitment to the spiritual life, so Bradley has her Free Amazon society evolve its mystical counterpart from the earthly practical society of women into the Grey and Dark Sisterhoods. Just as some orders of nuns or sisters have a sub-group of contemplative members who are "cloistered," so also does Bradley conceive her Dark Sisterhood as a rarefied and esoteric sorority within the Guild of Free Amazons and separate from those *laran*-bearers in the Towers. The Grey and Dark Sisterhoods are best distinguished by Marisela; "The Sisterhood are those who serve Avarra; we on the plane which we call physical life, and they, the Dark Ones, on the plane of existence known as the overworld" (CS 58). Thus, while the Dark Sisterhood may best be considered analogous to the Communion of Saints in the Christian Church, they, like the saints, seldom interfere in human activities because they see the larger picture; they cooly debate Jaelle's and Magda's destiny: "This time we will save them... But remember, it is not a personal compassion for any individual. It is only that this is a point where destiny intersects with the humane thing to do. We would all rather save lives, but we cannot interfere" (TH 402). In the later novel, the Sisterhood claims that it has "only one aim; that in the fullness of time, everyone who comes to this world shall become everything that he or she can be or do or accomplish. Perfection is for the individuals, one at a time" (CS 353), a goal reiterated by mystics, religious, and Beguines alike.

In contrast, the theme of the discordant sisterhood, the villainous force in the *City of Sorcery*, is that "the end of every quest is to become what you are and this means power" (CS 371): The Dark or Grey

Sisterhood, on the other hand, believe that "the end of wisdom is to know and to refrain from doing" (CS 371), a paradox to the practical Free Amazon Guild but an understandable goal for the mystical Sisterhood. Magda at the end of this novel questions if her joining of Camilla and Jaelle in the Sisterhood is "the end of a quest? Or a beginning? Did all quests end like this, the final step upward to the pinnacle of a mighty mountain which gave way to reveal a new and unknown horizon?" (CS 432). Here Bradley ties together her major themes: Magda, searching for love and acceptance, describes her arrival in terms of a heroic quest and of a religious journey, terms quite familiar to medieval mystics who embodied their concept of the Godhead as a garden or a journey or a mountain or a cloud or a lover.

Even the names Bradley uses are significant and have power in themselves as when the adventurers are not allowed to name the city of sorcery nor the leader of the wicked sisterhood, a possible throwback to the Jewish prohibition against uttering the name of God. Such power in names continues in Bradley's choice of character names. As the legally named Terran Magdalen Lorne and the Darkovan Margali n'ha Ysabet, Magda is named after the Regent Lady Bruna's freemate wife Margali, who entered such a marriage to protect her unborn son's inheritance; Magda herself forms a freemate marriage with Jaelle to protect both of their daughters. With the Terran form of her name, Magdalen Lorne, establishing the "lonely" or "forlorn" aspect of her character, Magda's name is most reminiscent of the Biblical echoes of the name: Magdalen is a form of Magdala, the Hebrew words for "fish towers" or "dried fishes". Both references work when Magda is cast in imitation of the matriarchial concept of the Near-Eastern fish goddess worship of Astarte, Isthar, Isis, and Aphrodite, especially since Magda is part Terran and is connected with the earth, which seen from the heavens has its blue seas as its most noticeable feature. Like her Biblical ancestress, Mary of Magdala, Magda is released from her seven demons of sexual and religious passions by the intervention of a higher love in her life; also, like Mary of Magdala who supposedly retired to a cave to leave the world of men for mystical pursuit of the Otherworld, Bradley's heroine ends her purgative journey in a cave, that most feminine of symbols and an entrance befitting the Dark Sisterhood. More importantly, her Terran names which shortens to Magda is suggested by that most famous of all beguines, the mystic Mechthild of Magdeburg. Just as Mary of Magdala is identified by the town, Magdalen Loren is the "Magda" searching for the "burg" or city of sorcery, finding rest only in the dark Sisterhood as her ancestress Mary found rest only in the non-sexist kingdom represented by Christ.

In complement to the water image of Magda stands the desert or dry image of Jaelle, who comes from the "Dry Towns" of Darkover. Bradley's use of the name of Jaelle neatly weaves the desert-living Israelite heroine Jael, the wife of Heber the Kenite in Judges 5:17-22, who pounds the tent peg through the temple of her people's enemy Sisera, with the Darkovan's Jaelle's occupation as a tent-provisioner. Deborah's canticle which cites Jael as a "tent-dwelling" woman reinforces this linking of Jaelle and Jael as tent-dwellers capable of defending themselves and their nations. Even when Sisera's mother longs for the "spoils of dyed stuffs, embroidered, two pieces of dyed work embroidered for my neck" (Judges 5:26-30), the love of finely embroidered clothing of Bradley's Amazons serves to connect them as weavers and embroiderers, both conventual and Beguinal occupations.

The third person in the inevitable feminine Jungian triad is the warrior Camilla, the *emmasca*, whose name has several connotative echoes within the Darkover series and from earlier literature. She is named for the lover of the blessed Cassilda in the Darkover series and for the Earth-born specialist who must bear unwanted children because the space-ship survivors must reproduce in Bradley's novel of the origin of Darkover, *Darkover Landfall*. Like this early Camilla, the later warrior suffers an unwanted pregnancy. Over three books she withholds her origins from the reader, as well as from her friends, until Magda's increased sensitivity taps into Camilla's nightmare and the story becomes known. Kidnapped by pirates and raped, the young Elorie Lindir of the Alliard clan has her breasts cut off and her unwanted child ripped from her womb by her ravishers, a mutilation which forces her clan to reject her as unfit for her hereditary office as tower priestess. Her real name then contains one of the Hebrew words for God, "Eloi", the Aramaic form which Christ used in his final cry from the Cross. In literature, Camilla's name echoes that of the virgin warrior queen of the Volscians whose death in the Trojan War is detailed in Vergil's *Aeneid*; she also carries the Latin name for a freeborn girl, one who is an attendant at a sacrifice. Camilla, to preserve her integrity and sanity after the brutal rape and subsequent rejection by her Hastur clan, has "sacrificed" her femininity and her *laran*-ability by her *emmasca* operation which rendered her sexless. Since Bradley borrows heavily from religious sources, her Camilla may also have derived from St. Camillus, a sixteenth century soldier and gambler who tended the wounded on the battlefields.

While cloistered nuns changed their names to signify a new life in faith, because of the scarcity of female saints' names, often the names chosen were masculine, so that, while they might be "brides of Christ", they often bore the name of an earthly man, albeit a holy one. Often such names were preceded by the name of Mary, the mother of Jesus,

to balance out the masculine-feminine polarity. There is no record as
to whether Beguines had name changes but one can suppose they retained
their father's surnames, while addressing themselves by their baptismal
or feminine names. Traditionally, all religious sisterhoods address each
other as "sisters" to stress the binding nature of their commitment to
communal life. Bradley follows this example by having the Renunciates
consider themselves as sisters, although they do not ordinarily address
each other as such; however, when her former enemy Rafaella clears
the way for Magda to join the Dark Sisterhood with Camilla and Jaelle,
Magda hears her "rough...words...[of] pure love; what Rafaella had
said was *sister*" (CS 422).

Besides the use of the word "guild" itself for the Free Amazon Guild
House, another religious aspect is in the use of the name "Lauria" for
the Guild Mother of Thendara House, the most strongly detailed of the
guild houses. A "laura" is the general name for a monastery in the Eastern
church, characterized by small cells grouped around a central church,
the monks living a communal life but inhabiting separate residences.
The word "laura", as used by *The Catholic Dictionary*, describes the
"Beguinage, resembling in this the ancient *laura*...not a convent but
a collection of small houses...surrounded by a wall, and with a chapel
in the centre" (73). The existing remains of the Beguinages in Louvain
follow this general plan. Bradley's city of sorcery is not described but
the path to it is "the pinnacle of a mighty mountain...a new and
unknown horizon" (CS 423) and it is spoken of as having outer gates
and as being devoid of "riches and jewels" (CS 421).

Bradley's earliest Sisterhood was caused by the necessary union of
the priestess-healers of Avarra, the dark mother of birth and death, and
the mercenary warriors of the Sisterhood of the Sword in the 1962 *The
Planet Savers*. The name of Avarra may be a corrupted form of the "Ave
Maria" name of the Christian Virgin Mother of Jesus, Mary; Magda,
for example, sees Avarra in a dream drift "before her eyes again, her
compassionate face, her hands outstretched as if to touch Magda's
face...Magda suddenly felt a great peace and contentment" (TH 93).
Mystics like Bridget of Sweden and medieval painters, like Da Vinci
and Fra Angelico, reiterate this compassionate quality of the Virgin
Mother. The prayer called the "Ave Maria" itself bears out this dual
role of the woman: the first part praises the life-giving nature of Mary,
ending with the phrase "blessed is the fruit of thy womb, Jesus"; the
second part beginning "Holy Mother of God" describes the death-dealing
aspect—"pray for us sinners,   now and at the hour of our death". The
name of Avarra thus considered seems too handy to be coincidental for
an author of Bradley's stature. Even the name of Evanda, since she seems
to be the goddess of light and of growing things, may be Bradley's blend

of the dual names of Eve and Adam. Thus once again, the mythological need to blend the polarities, such as in the Mary-Eve duality of the medieval period, appears in the natural flow of a writer's mind, with her invention of the middle ground of the Free Amazon society as her modern answer to the ancient problem of "what do women want?"

What then do women want? The same things men do—autonomy, equality, independence, adventure. Idealized heroines do not scrub pots. Bradley's heroines do so occasionally. But they find more pleasure in those quests normally saved for men. Representing, as they do, the realistic middle ground between the idealized heroine and the fallen woman, Bradley's heroine's are doers, much in the tradition of female saints who were doers—founding convents, chastising popes or defying Roman emperors. If Dante's Beatrice is man's major concept of what a channel to God must be like, she has to be reduced to a cool classical literary pleasantry, for the history of the Middle Ages teems with examples of working women, who found their own way to God and who occasionally dragged others to the Godhead.

While Dante, like many male writers before and after his time, focussed his energy on a single female source, his immediate predecessor, the mystic Francis of Assisi, had multiple feminine sources; the Virgin Mary, Mother Church, Clare (his first cloistered follower), his own mother, and his favorite, Lady Poverty. The analogy is not as far-fetched as it may seem. Dante was so influenced by Franciscanism that he became an active member of the secular order, founded by Francis for the lay people who insisted on following his apostolic and pentitential lifestyle. (It is now called the Secular Franciscan Order and has millions of members worldwide.) By choosing Beatrice as a spiritual channel to the Godhead, Dante reverted to the more classical use of the feminine as the muse, rather than following the Franciscan way of life which encourages both men and women to work toward the same perfection. Although he mentions a multiplicity of women in his works—saints, sinners, religious, seculars, even Beguines—Dante deprives himself of a variety of feminine influences. And, although Dante was dedicated to the *metanoia* of Franciscanism, one suspects that it was his wife who lived the more penitential life for keeping the family going while he was in exile for his political beliefs.

Bradley, refusing to be forced into writing female versions of such narrow male ideals of women, presents a very real solution to the polarity that has artificially separated women into the Mary-Eve figure. Her women are women—individual, autonomous, independent, with a long unrecognized and unrecorded history behind them, one significant part of which is the Beguinal society of the medieval period. In her search for a satisfactory role model, Bradley uses more than a generalized concept of medieval conventual and Beguinal life in her Darkover series. She uses direct religious sources from the strong twelfth century feminist economic and mystical movement of the Beguines and of the vibrant Franciscan penitential movement to form her Free Amazons. Instead of using one single feminine source, her heroines find their ideal spiritual guide in a group of women, who, though little known in English literature, have descendants in most religious and economic societies. Like the Bridge society and the Free Amazons themselves, the concept of Beguinal society with its practical economic measures, communal living, mutual support, and religious basis may have provided a handy example for Bradley to incorporate into her Darkover series as a solution to the basic problem of the female writer writing in a male world. For what role models do women have to imitate? How can a heroine make her way in the world of men while retaining her integrity and autonomy. As neither chastely cloistered nuns nor married women bound by male dictates, the historical Beguines supply the sense of autonomy and the mystical aspect that allows Bradley to develop effectively her Guild of Free Amazons in general and her characters' deepening grasp of their own integrated personalities, their potential for mysticism, their autonomy and their sense of themselves. In short, they are women— no more and no less.

Bibliography

Beck, Hans Georg. *et al. From the High Middle Ages to the Eve of the Reformation*, translated by Anselm Biggs. New York: The Seabury Press, 1980.

Bradley, Marion Zimmer. *City of Sorcery* New York: DAW Books, 1985.

_____ *Darkover Landfall*, Boston: Gregg Press, 1978.

_____ [with the Friends of Darkover] *Free Amazons of Darkover*. New York: DAW Books, 1983.

_____ *Forbidden Tower, The*. New York: DAW Books, 1977.

_____ *Hawkmistress*, New York: DAW Books, 1983.

_____ *Heritage of Hastur, The*. New York: DAW Books, 1975.

_____ *Planet Savers, The*. New York: Ace Books, 1962.

_____ *Sharra's Exile*. New York: DAW Books, 1978.

_____ *Shattered Chain, The*. New York: DAW Books, 1976.

_____ *Spell Sword, The*. New York: DAW Books, 1974.

_____ *Sword of Aldones, The*. New York: Ace Books, 1962.

_____ *Sword and Sorceress: An Anthology of Heroic Fantasy*. New York: DAW Books, 1984.

_____ *Thendara House*. New York: DAW Books, 1983.

_____ *Warrior Woman*. New York: DAW Books, 1985.

Dictionary of the Middle Ages, The. ed. Joseph Strayer, Vol. 2. New York: Charles Scribner and Sons, 1983.

Fox, Matthew. *Original Blessing: A Primer in Creation Spirituality.* Santa Fe, NM: Bear and Co., 1983.

—— *Illuminations of Hildegard of Bingen, The.* Santa Fe. NM: Bear and Co., 1985.

McDonnell, Ernest W. *The Beguines and Beghards in Medieval Culture.* New York: Octagon Books, 1969.

The New Schaff-Herzog Encyclopedia of Religious Knowledge. Vol. II, Grand Rapids, MI: Baker Book House, 1977.

Salmonsen, Jessica Amanda. *Amazons.* New York: DAW Books, 1978.

Williams, Charles. *The Figure of Beatrice.* London: Faber and Faber, 1943.

Donna Trenton, Stephen King's Modern American Heroine

Carol A. Senf

For the past ten years Stephen King has been an enormously popular writer, and part of the reason for that popularity is the fact that his books feature ordinary human characters with whom the reader can readily identify. Moreover these ordinary people become heroes and heroines because they confront unspeakable horrors with courage and conviction.[1]

By far the strongest of King's heroines is Donna Trenton in *Cujo*.[2] To establish her as a modern American heroine, King does two things: First he places her in a realistic environment and shows her confronting the same problems that face ordinary human beings today; second he deliberately contrasts her with the dependent women of earlier Gothic literature and horror films,[3] the women her son Tad thinks of when he dreams of warning her about the monster in his closet: *"Be careful, Mommy, they* [monsters] *eat the ladies! In all the movies they catch the ladies and carry them off and eat them!"* (p. 7, King's italics). Though Tad never confesses his fears to his mother, Donna is aware of the tradition of female weakness and passivity. A former librarian, she repeatedly compares herself—sometimes facetiously but more often seriously—to a damsel in distress and her husband to the knight who will rescue her. In fact, King reveals that Donna must abandon the notion that the heroine is someone to be rescued. Only then can she attempt to save both her son and herself from the rabid Cujo, a monster that King emphasizes is a symbol for all the evil forces against which human beings must struggle, only then can she become a suitable representative of the modern, more assertive woman.

In a similar fashion, Charity Camber, a working class version of the trapped American woman, accepts responsibility for herself and her son and escapes from a brutal and abusive husband. A lesser version of the heroine, Charity is also a strong and courageous woman with whom twentieth-century readers can be proud to identify.

Although King is often identified as a writer of supernatural horror because of his early novels, *Salem's Lot* and *The Shining*, his emphasis on ordinary human life is clear from the very beginning of *Cujo*, which he prefaces with the following quotation from W. H. Auden's "Musee des Beaux Arts":

About suffering they were never wrong,
The Old Masters: how well they understood
Its human position; how it takes place
While someone else is eating or opening a window or just walking dully along...

By choosing this quotation, King emphasizes the human rather than the superhuman; and he distances himself still further from his early novels in the rest of *Cujo*. Reinforcing the ordinary quality of human suffering is the first page of the novel, which identifies the monster in Castle Rock, Maine, as a sick human being:

He was not werewolf, vampire, ghoul, or unnameable creature from the enchanted forest or from the snowy wastes; he was only a cop named Frank Dodd with mental and sexual problems. (p. 3)

King is obviously playing with the readers' expectations. However, the figure of Frank Dodd, a sick and destructive human being rather than a vampire or a haunted house, will appear again and again in the novel, sometimes linked with Cujo, another example of an evil that occurs within the natural world:

Screaming, he got both hands under the dog's muzzle again and yanked it up. For a moment, staring into those dark, crazed eyes...he thought: *Hello, Frank. It's you, isn't it? Was hell too hot for you?* (p. 272, King's italics)

Despite Sheriff Bannerman's reference to Dodd's return from the grave, however, King expects the reader to recognize that Cujo and Dodd are both examples of evil within the natural world, not supernatural Evil.

In addition to being about natural evil, *Cujo* is about women. Although Bannerman, Joe Camber, and Gary Pervier are men victims of Cujo and Vic Trenton is practically destroyed by the death of his son, *Cujo*—more than King's other novels (with the possible exception of *Carrie*) focuses on women's experiences. From the first paragraph, which catalogues Frank Dodd's six victims—all women or young girls— to the last, the novel scrutinizes the lives of women in twentieth-century America.

Danse Macabre, a work in which King combines autobiography with his analysis of the horror tradition, reveals that King understands the complexities of women's lives, especially the ways their lives are influenced by their relationships with men. For example, comments on the movie *Alien* illustrate his awareness of men's condescending attitudes to women:

> The Sigourney Weaver character, who is presented as tough minded and heroic up to this point, causes the destruction of the mothership *Nostromo*...by going after the ship's cat. Enabling the males in the audience, of course, to relax, roll their eyes at each other, and say either aloud or telepathically, "Isn't that just like a woman?"[5]

Furthermore King is aware that men's attitudes to women range far beyond gentle condescension to fear and outright hostility; and his discussion of the movie *The Stepford Wives* comments on men's hostility to liberated women. In fact, King is aware that he shares some of these fears:

> If *The Stepford Wives* concerns itself with what men want from women, then *Carrie* is largely about how women find their own channels of power, and what men fear about women and women's sexuality...which is only to say that, writing the book in 1973...I was fully aware of what Women's Liberation implied for me and others of my sex. The book is...an uneasy masculine shrinking from a future of female equality.... Carrie White is a sadly misused teenager.... But she's also Woman, feeling her powers for the first time....[6]

Aware of male fears of women, King is able to use this understanding in his books. Carrie's extraordinary power is unleashed in one terrifying night that destroys an entire town, but *Cujo* reveals that women terrify men even with less extraordinary strength. Arriving on the scene after his wife has finally overcome Cujo, Vic Trenton wants to escape rather than offer her comfort for her ordeal:

> He didn't know what he had expected, but it hadn't been this. He had been afraid, but the sight of his wife...standing over the twisted and smashed thing in the driveway, striking it again and again with something that looked like a caveman's club...that turned his fear to a bright, silvery panic.... For one infinite moment, which he would never admit to himself later, he felt an impulse to throw the Jag in reverse and drive away...to drive forever. What was going on in this still and sunny door yard was monstrous. (p. 289)

Especially perceptive here are King's recognition that men rarely admit their fear of women openly and his use of the word "monstrous" to describe one man's response to a woman's exhibition of power. He knows that such exhibits are so rare that they inspire awe and terror.

Although *Cujo* culminates with Donna's horrifying ordeal and her need for exceptional courage, most of the novel takes place within the minds of Donna and Charity as they face more ordinary problems. Douglas Winter observes of the novel that its "storyline evolves about two marriages," and that both of these "marriages are in jeopardy."[7]

Of the two Charity is less interesting, and King spends less time on her because her problems are less psychologically complex. This is not to say that her problems are not serious—in some ways more serious than Donna's—for Charity is married to a physically abusive man:

Joe had used his hands on her a few times in the course of their marriage, and she had learned.... Now she did what Joe told her and rarely argued. She guessed Brett was that way too. But she feared for the boy sometimes. (p. 46)

Most of the sections that involve Charity focus on her attempts to show her son a better way of life, one that is physically very different from their life with Joe. Escaping even briefly from Joe requires both luck and skill—the good luck of winning the lottery and skill in the courage to approach her husband. In fact, King reveals that she could "sometimes gain the upper hand just by seeming brave. Not always, but sometimes" (p. 81). King also lets the reader know that these moments of bravery are risky, however, for the Camber marriage, like so many other marriages, is essentially unequal: "Joe could go places alone or with his friends, but she couldn't, not even with Brett in tow. That was one of their marriage's ground rules" (p. 48).

Joe's power over Charity stems both from his greater physical strength and from the economic advantage of having money to spend as he chooses. Probing Charity's mind after she wins the lottery, King reveals to the reader how economic dependence on their husbands affects women:

Lady Luck had singled her out. For the first time in her life, maybe for the only time, that heavy muslin drape of the everyday had been twitched a little, showing her a bright and shining world beyond. She was a practical woman, and in her heart she knew that she hated her husband more than a little, but that they would grow old together, and he would die, leaving her with his debts and...perhaps with his spoilt son. (p. 70)

In short, five thousand dollars isn't enough to provide her and Brett with more than a brief escape.

If King had stopped his portrait here, the reader would be left with a kind of caricature of an unliberated woman who is trapped by economic dependence and fear of physical power. However, King recognizes that many women are not able to take charge of their lives because they are also trapped by powerful internal compulsions, in Charity's case by love for the man who continues to victimize her:

Was she going to kid herself and say that she did not, even now, in some way love the man she had married? That she stayed with him only out of duty, or for the sake of the child (*that* was a bitter laugh; if she ever left him it would be for the sake of the child)?...That he could not, sometimes at the most unexpected moments...be tender. (pp. 114-15, King's italics)

Passages like this one focus on the kinds of complex emotional issues that King's ordinary characters face every day and negate a criticism so often leveled against popular writers like King—that they create nothing but caricatures. Moreover, it negates Chelsea Quinn Yarbro's specific criticism that King cannot "develop a believable woman character between the ages of seventeen and sixty."[8] Both Donna and Charity are believable human beings because they confront the ordinary problems faced by the readers. The character of Charity, however, is more clearly modeled on an older notion of the heroine as a person to be rescued by someone else, by circumstance, or by luck. Less heroic than Donna, Charity escapes from her husband largely because of luck rather than because of skill and self knowledge. Nonetheless, at the end of the novel, she is a confident and independent woman who is working to achieve her own goals. Such independence and preparation for her son's college education could not have happened while she was married to Joe Camber.

If Charity is believable, strong, and almost heroic, Donna is an ordinary woman who becomes the modern American heroine. Middle class and college educated—a librarian married to an advertising executive—Donna is also much more articulate about her condition as a woman and about everything that being a woman means.

Despite these differences, King very carefully highlights significant similarities in the two women. The first of these similarities is the fact that Donna, like Charity, is aware of her physical limitations. Although Donna is a large woman—five-eleven and "an inch taller than Vic when she wore heels" (p. 39)—and an athlete, she is easily physically intimidated by both Steve Kemp and Joe Camber; and King's careful relating of Donna's thoughts also reminds us of how women are—more often than men—influenced by their physical condition:

Falling off the back porch when she was five and breaking her wrist.
     Looking down at herself...when she was a high school freshman and seeing to her utter shame and horror that there were spots of blood on her light blue linen skirt.... Holding Tad in her arms, newborn, then the nurse taking him away; she wanted to tell the nurse not to do that...but she was too weak to talk....(p. 218)

Furthermore, though her husband is not the kind of man to employ physical force, King makes it clear that Vic is in control, for Donna "hadn't wanted to come to Maine and had been appalled when Vic had sprung the idea on her" (p. 43). Such details suggest that the Trenton marriage is unequal and that Vic makes the important decisions.

King, who is exceptionally sensitive to material culture in the twentieth century further reveals the inequality in their marriage by focusing on the cars they drive, an emphasis that clearly reveals Donna's economic dependence. Vic drives an expensive imported sports car, a Jaguar, while Donna drives one of the least expensive automobiles ever produced in Detroit, the Ford Pinto. In this way King reveals that Vic is a man who likes to pamper himself; and, when he shows that Vic is totally aware of the media attention to the dangers associated with driving the Pinto, he also reveals that such pampering may be at the expense of his family. Ironically, however, Donna and Tad don't die inside a burning Pinto. Donna survives, and Tad dies of dehydration when Cujo traps them inside the Pinto during three of the hottest days of the year.

Furthermore, like Charity Camber, Donna feels trapped though her feelings of entrapment are only partially due to lack of money. A former professional, Donna contemplates going back to work. However, she ultimately labels it a "ridiculous notion, and she shelved it after running some figures on her pocket calculator" (p. 43). Here—as elsewhere—King uses financial worries to emphasize ordinary problems, the kind of problems a reader might face. However, despite the reference to money here and elsewhere in the novel—Vic's new advertising agency is having financial difficulty, for example—Donna's problems are not lack of money, but the fact that she has too much time on her hands—time to worry about her loss of identity. Donna recognizes the problem:

She started to sharpshoot at Vic about little things, sublimating the big things because they were hard to define and even harder to articulate. Things like loss and fear and getting older. Things like being lonely and then getting terrified of being lonely....Feeling jealous because his life was a daily struggle to build something...and her life was back here, getting Tad through the day. (p. 44)

Donna's later heroism is foreshadowed when King shows that she can't escape the loneliness in the ways that are acceptable for women: volunteer work, "hen parties," and soap operas. A doer and a confronter rather than an escapist, Donna tries to fill her life in traditionally acceptable ways—through housework and through caring for her son. She realizes, however, that this work won't last because "every year the world gets another little slice of him" (p. 91). Ultimately her loneliness and sense of frustration lead her to a disastrous affair with Steve Kemp, a man as physically brutal as Joe Camber and certainly more psychologically abusive.

The affair with Kemp is an illustration of Donna's weakness—of her tendency to drift until someone else provides her with a solution. On the other hand, the scene in which she ends the affair even though he threatens to rape her in her own kitchen foreshadows the final climactic scene when she decides that she cannot depend on someone else:

She had been afraid to use her loudest voice, and had done so only when it became absolutely necessary. Because that was where civilization came to an abrupt, screeching halt. That was the place where the tar turned to dirt. If they wouldn't listen when you used your very loudest voice, a scream became your only recourse. (p. 42)

Ironically, although Donna fears the absence of civilization, she will discover herself only when she has rid herself of civilization and its expectations for women. Screaming at Kemp, she discovers her power over him: "And if I get a chance to tear your balls off or put one of your eyes out, I won't hesitate" (p. 42). It is a power that women rarely achieve.

Trapped by Cujo in the Pinto, which becomes a symbol of her entire life as a dependent, Donna slowly begins to take control of her life. At first, clearly expecting to be rescued—by Vic, by the mailman when he comes to the Cambers, by anyone—she remains like the old style passive heroine:

She didn't know why no one had answered the SOS she had been beeping out. In a book, someone would have come. It was the heroine's reward for having thought up such a clever idea. But no one had come. (p. 158)

Alone in the Pinto, with only her four-year-old son for company, Donna becomes a new kind of heroine, a woman who takes control of her life rather than waiting for someone—the proverbial knight—to save her. In fact, Donna begins to realize during the ordeal that she is a new kind of woman:

That had been the first time she had really believed—believed in her gut—that she was going to grow up and become a woman, a woman with at least a fighting chance to be a *better* woman than her own mother, who could get into such a frightening state over what was really such a little thing.... (p. 186)

Finally, forced again by external circumstances to take matters into her own hands, Donna contrasts herself to the heroines of earlier literature, the traditional damsels in distress:

The time had come, and Donna knew it.... No one was going to come. There was going to be no knight on a silver steed riding up Town Road No. 3—Travis McGee was apparently otherwise engaged.

Tad was dying. (p. 284)

Reminding the reader again that *Cujo* takes place in the real world, King has Donna's victory over Cujo come too late to save Tad.[9] The little boy dies while his mother is battling the monster; and Donna, who had earlier saved his life when his tongue blocks his windpipe and who finally overcomes the monstrous dog, cannot bring him back to life. It is thus a hollow victory. Her marriage in jeopardy and her son dead, Donna has lost all the things that supposedly provided meaning for traditional heroines. Realizing, however, that the modern heroine must not be afraid to confront life, readers should feel purged by their vicarious participation in her victory. As Donna herself recognizes before she leaves to do battle, this ability to confront one's problems is all that matters:

Had this terrible vigil been only a matter of hours, or had it been her whole life? Surely everything that had gone before had been a dream, little more than a short wait in the wings? The mother who had seemed to be disgusted and repulsed by all those around her, the well-meaning but ineffectual father, the schools, the friends, the dates and dances—they were all a dream to her now.... Nothing mattered, nothing *was* but this silent and sunstruck dooryard where death had been dealt and yet more death waited in the cards.... The old monster kept his watch still.... (p. 285)

King seems to realize here that his readers—especially his women readers— are ready for a new kind of heroine, a woman who is prepared to leave behind triviality—the constant dusting of pottery knickknacks that Donna equates with women's lives—and confront the unspeakable with courage and conviction.

Recognizing his readers' needs, Stephen King makes Donna Trenton a new kind of heroine. First, he presents her as an ordinary human being, one troubled by the same kinds of problems that confront ordinary human beings, and he shows that such an ordinary human being can live with dignity and courage. Finally he has this ordinary person confront an exceptional—almost superhuman—adversary.

Stephen King has become an immensely popular writer, and part of that popularity is undoubtedly his ability to write a suspenseful story. However, another—and probably more important—reason for his popularity stems from his ability to create characters with whom the readers can readily identify. Although most of his novels focus on men characters, *Cujo* scrutinizes the problems that confront twentieth-century American women. Donna and Charity are ordinary women, one middle class, well educated and articulate; the other, working class, uneducated, and less introspective. Despite seemingly overwhelming odds, each woman manages to take control of her life. Donna especially in her display of courage becomes a new American heroine, a strong woman with whom women in the twentieth century can be proud to identify.

Notes

[1]Most of the writers who discuss King in *Fear Itself: The Horror Fiction of Stephen King*, ed. Tim Underwood and Chuck Miller (New York: Signet, 1985) comment on his realism.

A writer himself, Peter Straub introduces the volume by observing the way King uses "the real stuff of the world, with marriages and hangovers, with cigarettes and rock bands and junk food and rooming houses" because King is "a writer first, and then a writer of horror and fantasy." (p. 9)

George Romero comments that King knows all about us:

> Stephen King's books provide similar total experiences for me and, I think, for most who read them. He knows the same people I know, he's been to the same gas station, the same Seven-Eleven, he listens to the same rock and roll that's on my local AM band, and I know damn well he's been to an amusement park not too far from my hometown. (p. 257)

Douglas E. Winter observes that the horror in *Cujo* is "not supernatural":

> It is woven from the dark strands of the American social fabric: decaying marriages, economic woes, malfunctioning automobiles and junk food....we are obsessed with fear, running scared of our daily lives, where we can no longer trust the food we eat, the neighbor's dog, or even ourselves. Money, love and death are the framework of our fear, and King reminds us of their everyday presence with incisive, relentless effect. Fear strikes at the supermarket. (p. 245)

Don Herron suggests that King's obsession with horror is a way of emphasizing the horror of everyday life:

> Horror springs in King's stories from contemporary social *reality*, and I'd like to say it is this quality more than any other which has made King a bestseller. King doesn't take vampires seriously, and neither do most of his readers, but you would have to be a fool or a saint not to recognize and react to the pervasive horror in everyday life. Just turn on the evening news. (p. 92)

[2]Stephen King, *Cujo* (New York: Signet, 1982). All references to *Cujo* will be included within the text.

[3]King's discussion of both literary forerunners and classic horror films in *Danse Macabre* clearly reveals his awareness of the tradition in which he is working.

[4]Winter, "The Night Journeys of Stephen King," in *Fear Itself*, p. 245.

[5]Stephen King, *Danse Macabre* (New York: Berkley Books, 1982), pp. 76-77.

[6]*Danse Macabre*, p. 170.

[7]Winter, p. 245.

[8]Chelsea Quinn Yarbro, "Cinderella's Revenge—Twists on Fairy Tale and Mythic Themes in the Work of Stephen King," in *Fear Itself*, p. 65.

[9]Douglas E. Winter observes in *Stephen King: The Art of Darkness* (New York: New American Library, 1984) that King himself found the conclusion to *Cujo* too horrifying:

> Indeed, King has said that if he were ever to rewrite one of his published novels, it would be *Cujo*; and his original screenplay adaptation of the book saw Tad survive—an ending that was adopted in the 1983 motion picture directed by Lewis Teague. But the pessimistic stance of the novel was in King's words, "almost demanded." (p. 102)

Woman as Hero
in Margaret Atwood's *Surfacing*
and Maxine Hong Kingston's
The Woman Warrior

Mara E. Donaldson

Margaret Atwood's *Surfacing* and Maxine Hong Kingston's *The Woman Warrior* are contemporary female *Bildungsromane*. They exemplify patterns of personal transformation which are strikingly similar to and significantly different from the pattern of the heroic quest in Joseph Campbell's *The Hero With A Thousand Faces*.[1]

The similarities have been discussed elsewhere and the patterns of personal transformation in Atwood and Kingston have been identified as heroic quests.[2] This essay, therefore, will examine the important *difference* between the quest patterns of the two novels and that of Campbell's study. Indeed, *Surfacing* and *The Woman Warrior* reveal an alternative pattern of heroic transformation, a new symbol of the female hero. The essay will also explore the significance of this alternative pattern of transformation for the Christian theological tradition regarding sin.[3]

Heroes in general have traditionally been male.[4] Thus, studies of the similarities between the quest patterns of the women in these novels and Campbell's hero show that women as well as men can be heroes. But the gain of identifying female transformation as authentically 'heroic' pays the price of loss of the particular character of the *female* hero's transformation.

Campbell's hero undergoes a process of separation, through initiation, to return which Campbell interprets as a personal transformation from egoism to self-willed submission (30, 391). The hero who begins his journey is arrogant; the one who returns is humble. The pattern of moving from arrogance to humility parallels the dominant Augustinian interpretation of sin as *hubris*, or pride.

The pattern and emphasis which emerges in *Surfacing* and *The Woman Warrior* offers a different image of transformation. The female hero's journey also involves a process of separation, initiation, and return, but her personal transformation is from self-negation to self-affirmation, from lack of pride to self-pride. Thus, we discover in *Surfacing* and *The Woman Warrior* a potentially new symbol, the female hero, which is suggestive for the understanding of sin recently proposed by feminist theologians as a movement from self-negation to self-pride, not *vice versa*.[5]

I

Joseph Campbell gives us the classic definition of the hero's quest in *The Hero With A Thousand Faces*. His discussion is based on his work in comparative mythology and on psychoanalytic theory, especially the work of Sigmund Freud and C. G. Jung and its contribution to dream interpretation.[6] According to Campbell, myth and dreams house universal archetypes, equally valid for both men and women. The hero is the "man or woman who has been able to battle past his personal and local historical limitations to the generally valid, normally human forms" (19-20). The hero's mythological journey is described as a three-fold process of separation-initiation-return, which Campbell calls the monomyth: "A hero ventures forth from the world of common day into a region of supernatural wonder: fabulous forces are there encountered and a decisive victory is won: the hero comes back from this mysterious adventure with the power to bestow boons on his fellow man" (30). Campbell's hero, then, is first of all a '*winner*,' a successful warrior, and second, one who is not defined by other persons. The hero is the one who defines, who acts, who orders. These observations become significant when we consider the classical counterpart to the hero, the heroine. Heroines traditionally play supportive roles. They are defined either in relation to the hero or in terms of sex roles, while the hero is defined in terms of his quest. The hero/heroine distinction points to sex-role differences within mythic narrative itself.[7]

However, the three-fold process of the adventure is, according to Campbell, universal beyond sexually determined distinctions. The first phase, separation or departure (49-95), begins with the call to adventure and is described by Campbell as a "form of self-annihilation" (91). The hero leaves a world which is familiar and moves into a realm which is unfamiliar, mysterious, unconscious. In the language of myth, departure is characterized as descent into the well, into the forest, into the "belly of the whale" (90-94).

The period of initiation, the second phase, is a period of purification. It is a "process of dissolving, transcending or transmuting the infantile images of our personal past" (101). In the language of myth, this is the period where the hero battles dragons, solves riddles and outwits ogres. Crucial to this phase of initiation is the meeting with the Queen Goddess (109-126) and the murder of or atonement with the Father (126-149). For the male hero, this is the familiar Oedipal pattern: Oedipus slays his father, marries his mother, and for a period rules wisely. The mystical marriage with the Goddess "represents the hero's total mastery of life, for the woman is life, the hero its knower and master" (120). And the atonement with or murder of the Father, Campbell argues, "consists in no more than the abandonment of that self-generated double monster—the dragon thought to be God (super-ego) and the dragon thought to be Sin (repressed Id)" (130).

When the quest has been accomplished the hero must return, in the final phase, to the world with some elixir or boon for the restoration of society (197). Not all heroes survive the impact of crossing the return threshold, but that is what must be done to complete the adventure. In the language of myth this is the time of the return of the Golden Fleece, the time of wisdom and salvation.

Who is the hero at the end of the quest? Campbell states, "The hero is the man of self-achieved submission" (16). Thus, the circular schema of the journey is misleading: The hero is not the same at the beginning. This self-achieved submission is for Campbell the victory of the "self" over the "ego."[8] "Man is that alien presence," Campbell states, "with whom the forces of egoism—must come to terms, through whom the ego is to be crucified and resurrected, and in whose image society is to be reformed" (391).

The external, literal process of the hero's journey becomes a metaphor for the universal, internal quest for self-awareness. As we have seen, for Campbell, the hero's quest is universally applicable. Universal here refers to 1) the process itself—separation, initiation, return—and 2) the pattern of the journey—the movement from arrogance and egoism to humility. Campbell presupposes the existence of an individual ego, an ego which hinders or prohibits genuine self-understanding. The infantile, arrogant ego must be purified or annihilated in order for the mature self, the humble self, to emerge. It is not clear that the struggle Campbell describes is universal; it does represent one pattern of transformation, however. If there is a universal element in Campbell's discussion, it must be the process of the journey as separation, initiation, return and not the pattern of the journey. In order to derive a different pattern we turn to Atwood's *Surfacing* and Kingston's *The Woman Warrior*.

II

Margaret Atwood's *Surfacing* is a recent example of a feminist quest for self-awareness. Others have discussed the quest motif in *Surfacing*, including Josie Campbell and Joan Leonard who specifically argue that Campbell's typology of separation-initiation-return is central to understanding the novel.[9] More recently, Carol Christ in *Diving Deep and Surfacing* distinguishes between "two dimensions" of the quest— the spiritual and the social.[10] "Women's spiritual quest," Christ states, "concerns a woman's awakening to the depths of her soul and her position in the universe", while a woman's "Social quest concerns [her] struggle to gain respect, equality and freedom in society—in work, in politics, and in relationships with women, men, and children."[11] Although the spiritual and the social are both parts of the quest, *Surfacing* emphasizes the spiritual quest, and as we shall see below, *The Woman Warrior* stresses the social quest.

Critics of *Surfacing* have artfully demonstrated how the explicit, external search for the narrator's missing father becomes an implicit, internal search for herself. Having identified the structure of the narrator's quest as heroic, we must be attentive to the content of the quest as it differs from the male hero's quest. The transformation in *Surfacing* is not from egoism to self-achieved submission but from submission to affirmation.

The narrator's external journey begins when she receives a letter telling her that her father is missing. She leaves the city with Joe, her current lover, Anna, her best friend of four months, and Anna's husband, David. The first phase of her journey, separation, occurs literally when she leaves America and returns to her childhood home in Canada. Though it is a return home, she is a stranger. As the narrator explains: "Now we're on my home ground, foreign territory" (14). The initial search for her father becomes a search for her denied past. She has disassociated herself from her mother's death, and she has repressed a more recent event in her past, too painful for her to remember. In her quest she is assisted by two 'gifts,' one from her father and one from her mother. With these gifts she is able to find her father and accept the truth about her past.

She begins her initiation, the second phase, when she discovers several primitive cave drawings that had belonged to her father. These lead her ultimately to the underwater caves from which her father had taken the drawings. As she is diving to find these caves, she thinks she sees her father's body floating up at her from the bottom of the lake (167-173). The shock of this vision forces her to remember the event in her past which she has kept hidden from herself, from Joe, and from her family. She has had an affair with a married man, and has had an abortion. But because she cannot accept the abortion she has constructed a story about her past marriage, divorce, and the child she has left in the city. For her the story is true. Early on she says about the search for her father,

> If he's safe I don't want to see him.
> There's no point, they never forgave me,
> they didn't understand the divorce; I don't
> think they even understood the marriage,
> understand it myself (34).

The shock of seeing the apparition in the lake marks the end of one phase of the narrator's initiation. The second gift, from her mother, completes a second stage. After the narrator sees what she thinks is her father's body, she returns home to Joe, Anna and David. There she finds in an old album of her mother's a picture she had drawn as a child. She describes it saying, "on the left was a woman with a round moon stomach: the baby was sitting up inside her gazing out. Opposite her was a man with horns on his head like cow horns and a barbed tail" (185). She perceives the picture to be a message, a gift, from her mother, but she cannot understand its meaning. When Joe, Anna and David return to the city, the narrator hides from them so she can remain alone on the island. During this time alone, she becomes more and more like the moon goddess of her painting, experiencing the rituals and powers of the wilderness surrounding her home. Her whole world becomes alive with gods and forces that are powerful. She finally sees a vision of her mother feeding the jays in their garden and then a vision of her father who has been transformed into one of the creatures of the cave drawings (218).

If the first phase of her initiation is recognition and remembering, the second phase is reconciliation. She comes to accept her parents, their lives, their humanness, their deaths. As she puts it, "When I wake in the morning I know they have gone finally, back into the earth, the air, the water, whatever they were when I summoned them" (219).

The result of her days of solitude is her acceptance of her own power. This is the elixir or boon with which she returns from her journey. "This above all, to refuse to be a victim. Unless I can do that I can do nothing. I have to recant, give up the old belief that I am powerless and because of it nothing I can do will ever hurt anyone" (222).

The mythological journey, then, begins in *Surfacing* as the literal quest for a missing father, and becomes a metaphorical quest for selfhood. This journey is one of descent and return. This descent is radically transforming. She must accept the abortion and more importantly accept her responsibility for it. "Whatever it is, part of myself or a separate creature, I killed it. It wasn't a child but it could have been one, I didn't allow it" (168). Up to this point she has been a passive observer in the event and in her life. She sees herself as powerless and has accepted a world in which she is the victim. In short, hers has been a kind of self-willed submission, a vicious cycle she must break. It is all the more necessary, then, that in the last section of the novel, following her discovery of her mother's gift, that she discover and celebrate her own power. She feels this power as she imagines giving birth to a new child, a new creation (191).

Although she has no guarantee that her future will be better than her past, she at least can begin to take responsibility for that future. Her internal journey has been from self-submission and passivity to self-awareness and celebration. She has not struggled to subdue the egoism, central to Campbell's monomyth, but has struggled to give birth to an ego-self which is separate and independent from the expectations of others. Thus, the narrator in *Surfacing* emerges a female hero, whose external journey reveals an alternative vision of heroic transformation.

III

If the mythic journey in *Surfacing* is primarily spiritual — "the hero's awakening to the depths of her soul,"[12] then the journey in Maxine Hong Kingston's *The Woman Warrior* is primarily social. To the initial description of the social quest (p. 6) Christ adds, "in the social quest a woman begins in alienation from the human community and seeks new modes of relationship and action in society"[13]. In her autobiography Kingston struggles to overcome her alienation as a Chinese-American girl in Stockton's Chinatown. Her alienation is two-fold. First, as Chinese she is socially alienated from the dominant American culture, and second, as female she is alienated from her own Chinese culture. She remembers hearing such comments as, "there's no profit in raising girls. Better to raise geese than girls" (54). In order to transform the non-heroic reality of her life, she becomes the Woman Warrior in her fantasy. Kingston's mythic journey is finally the affirmation of her identity as a Chinese woman in a dual culture which continually negates it.

As in *Surfacing* where the literal and the mythic are juxtaposed, in *The Woman Warrior* there is a constant juxtaposition of the non-heroic, everyday life and Kingston's heroic, mythic interpretation of those literal events. The juxtaposition of the non-heroic and the heroic is demonstrated in the first two sections of the book. In the first, "No Name Woman," Maxine's mother tells her the story of her aunt, her father's only sister, who committed suicide by drowning herself in a well after giving birth to an illegitimate child. Her father no longer speaks of her because of the disgrace she brought to the family. Her aunt's story is the first of Kingston's "ghosts." She tries to imagine some dignity for her aunt:

Perhaps she encountered him in the fields or on the mountain where the daughters-in-law collected fuel. Or perhaps he first noticed her in the marketplace. He was not a stranger because the village housed no strangers. She had to have dealings with him other than sex... His demand must have surprised, then terrified her. She obeyed him; she always did as she was told.(7)

Maxine's mother tells her this story when she first begins to menstruate. It is bad enough to be a girl but she must not humiliate the family!

Yet her mother also tells her the story of Fa Mu Lan, the girl who took her father's place in battle: "She said I would grow up a wife and a slave, but she taught me the song of the warrior woman, Fa Mu Lan. I would have to grow up a warrior woman" (24). Kingston describes the mythic adventure of the warrior woman in the second section, titled "White Tigers." The retelling of the story of Fa Mu Lan becomes in the novel the retelling of Kingston's own quest for identity. At the age of the seven, Kingston becomes Fa Mu Lan who follows a bird high into the mountains. The bird leads her to a hut where she meets her teachers, an old man and woman. After a day and a night with them, they offer to train her to become a warrior. She is given a choice: " 'What do you want to do?' " the old man asked, " 'You can go back right now if you like. You can go pull sweet potatoes, or you can stay with us and learn how to fight barbarians and bandits' " (27). She remains with them, separated from her village and from her family.

Her initiation takes fifteen years. She must first learn how to be quiet and then how to master her body:

The two old people led me in exercises that began at dawn and ended at sunset so that I could watch our shadows grow and shrink and grow again, rooted to the earth. I learned to move my fingers, hands, feet, head, and entire body in circles. (28)

At the end of her first phase of her training, the woman warrior is sent on a survival test on the mountain of the white tigers. Upon her return she spends eight more years learning dragon ways. "Tigers are easy to find, but I needed adult wisdom to know dragons" (34).

Finally, the time comes when she is ready to return. She has become the Woman Warrior. "When I could point at the sky and make a sword appear, a silver bolt in the sunlight, and control his slashing with my mind, the old people said I was ready to leave" (39). Her time with the old people has been a time of learning skills and learning to control her power as a woman warrior. She has not been denied her womanhood however. As the woman warrior, she has a husband and a child. She is ready to fight and is victorious in avenging her family and village. When the fighting is finished and her public duties are completed, she returns to her husband and son to take up her family duties. "I will stay with you, doing farmwork and housework, and giving you more sons" (54).

The myth of the woman warrior contrasts sharply with Kingston's Chinese-American girlhood, a girlhood caught between the traditions (the ghosts) of the past, old world China, and the exigencies of the present. For example, she tells the story of a drugstore delivery boy making a wrong delivery to the laundry. Her mother takes the mistake as a curse on her family and sends Maxine to the drugstore to make them stop the curse. " 'You get reparation candy,' she said, 'You say, You have tainted my house with sick medicine and must remove the curse with sweetness.' He'll understand " (197-198). The druggist does give her candy but not because he understands but because he feels sorry for her.

Kingston attends both an American school and a Chinese school. The tensions between the traditions emerge again. For three years in grade school she will not talk and covers her drawings with black paint. She has a zero IQ in kindergarten because she had not learned to speak English. When she does begin speaking, she takes out her frustrations on a classmate in the sixth grade who recites in class but refuses to talk (200-211). Following her unsuccessful attempts to get her classmate to talk, Maxine becomes mysteriously ill and spends the next eighteen months in bed.

Her early fear is being sent back to China where she thinks she will become a slave. So she makes herself as unattractive as possible. She is messy, clumsy, rebellious. According to one villager, Maxine has the voice of a "pressed duck" (223), the result of her mother cutting her tongue (the frenum) when she was very young (following an old chinese custom to keep her daughter from being tongue-tied). This fear, however, is replaced by another. Maxine becomes terrified that she will be married off to the first man who wants her. When a mentally retarded boy starts following her around at school and then to the laundry, Maxine is certain her parents are planning to marry her off to him so that they can find husbands for her sisters. She finally rebels, confronting her mother with her "telling-list," the two hundred things she has kept bottled up inside (234). The confrontation is a painful one between the mother, caught in the old, and the daughter, struggling for dignity and identity in the new.

Maxine leaves for college and though her fears of being sent back to China or of being married off fade, the quest for identity remains. "I continue to sort out what's just my childhood, just my imagination, just my family, just the village, just movies, just living" (239). Kingston ends her autobiography with her version of the story of Ts'ai Yen, a Han poetess captured by barbarians and taken from her homeland. Haunted by the songs the barbarians play on their flutes, Ts'ai Yen creates her own bittersweet songs about China and her family. After twelve years she is ransomed and brings the songs back with her where at least one is passed down in translation. Ts'ai Yen, the poetess, is both Kingston, the writer, and Fa Mu Lan, the woman warrior.

Although Kingston does not describe her actual girlhood as one of transformation or as heroic, she finds affirmation of herself in the images of her imagination. Her journey, like that of Atwood's narrator and Campbell's hero is one of separation, initiation, and return. But the actual pattern of the journey is closer to Atwood's narrator than it is to Campbell's hero. Like the narrator in *Surfacing*, Kingston's struggle is for a self which is authentic and creative. In *Surfacing* the denial of self is rigidly constructed in the narrator's story of her false marriage and pregnancy; her discovery and affirmation of self comes with her acceptance of her past, the celebration of her natural powers, and from the image of the new creation—the child—within her. Kingston's struggle for selfhood consists in breaking through cultural expectations which doubly bind her. Her struggle is to learn to discriminate among the ghosts of her past. Her discovery and self-affirmation comes from learning to distinguish among the 'ghosts' and from her creativity as a writer. Fa Mu Lan is the woman warrior of her childhood; Ts'ai Yen is the woman warrior actualized in her writing.

IV

I have argued in this essay that a close reading of *Surfacing* and *The Woman Warrior* yields a heroic pattern which differs in pattern and emphasis from the heroic pattern in Campbell's work. Campbell's monomyth emphasizes the transformation from pride to humility; *Surfacing* and *The Woman Warrior* emphasize an alternative pattern of transformation—from self-denial and humiliation to pride and self-affirmation.

Normative claims such as Campbell's have been attacked for some time by feminists who argue that the value judgments implicit in such claims reflect only one perspective—the male—present in Western culture. In this final section, I am interested in particular in the critique made by feminist theology and in the ways an appreciation of the symbol of the female hero can assist a feminist theology of sin.

In 1960, Valerie Saiving   pointed out the dominance of one

perspective in her critique of Anders Nygren and Reinhold Niebuhr's concepts of sin and love. She argued that their positions reflected the "widespread tendency in contemporary theology to describe man's predicament as arising from his separateness and the anxiety occasioned by it to identify sin with self-assertion and love with selflessness."[14] Such theologies do not adequately account for the experience of women whose denial of self, both culturally conditioned and self-imposed, lead to a different understanding of sin. For Saiving the sin of women is better understood as "triviality, distractibility, and diffuseness; lack of an organizing center or focus; dependence on others for one's own self-definition...in short, underdevelopment or negation of the self" (37).

Saiving's argument has since been expanded and developed. Two examples are representative of the shape and direction of the theological discussion. First, in recognizing the difficulty of defining "women's experience," Judith Plaskow uses an anthropological approach to define a perspective on "women's experience" which concentrates more on "the interrelation between cultural expectations and their internalization"[15] than on innate biological differences, a weakness she sees in the Goldstein analysis. Plaskow then analyzes the theologies of sin and grace in Reinhold Niebuhr and Paul Tillich. Her emphasis throughout is on the importance of the *social context* of sin and grace and on the necessity for theology to integrate women's experience into its reflections. Their error, Plaskow argues, is that they moved away from their understanding of structures to theologies which lost the concreteness of human experience in general and women's experience in particular.

Susan Nelson Dunfee's article is a second example of the shape of the feminist critique since Saiving. Dunfee begins with an experiential assertion—"A woman knows guilt for most of her life."[16] Such a core experience, she argues, again negates the Christian emphasis on sin as pride, for women are not bound by their pride but by their "hiddenness," their lack of pride. Thus, women are doubly bound "because self-assertion is equated with the sin of pride, the knowledge of her desire to be a self is often experienced by a woman with guilt and anxiety" (322). Although Dunfee is also critical of Niebuhr's theology of sin, she does find in his theology the nascent condition for a theology of sin as hiding which speaks more directly to women's experience.

The strength of the Saiving, Plaskow, and Dunfee arguments lies in their assessment of an important problem within the Christian interpretation of sin as pride. Each articulates a perspective largely ignored within the tradition and thus calls us to reexamine that tradition for alternative interpretations. The feminist critique of sin as pride, therefore, leads to a model for understanding an alternate vision of sin as self-denial. Within this strength, however, resides a potential weakness. The analyses of Saiving, Plaskow, and Dunfee tend to lead to a competing system of concepts no less satisfying or universal than the theologies of Nygren, Niebuhr or Tillich. The tendency to abstract from biological, anthropological, or experiential evidence is a weakness because, like the theologies which they criticize, they, too, lose a sense of the particular and the concrete. Beginning with and remaining attentive to the symbols of transformation as they are born in the narratives of our time holds onto the concrete and the particular.

Initially, the heroic journeys in *Surfacing* and *The Woman Warrior* appear similar to the hero's journey in Campbell. And they are similar to the extent that they involve separation, initiation and return. The differences in the patterns are, however, striking and allow us to see the female hero as a new symbol. Just as Campbell's hero reflects and embodies one perspective on experience which parallels a theological tradition which defines sin as pride, so also does the symbol of the female hero reflect and embody another model of experience. Thus, like the male hero, the symbol of the female hero mediates an experience— and a theological perspective which claims that such a denial of self is also sinful.

My method throughout the essay has been descriptive rather than prescriptive. That is, I have described dominant characteristics of male and female heroes and not absolute ones. The female hero as she emerges in *Surfacing* and *The Woman Warrior* is no more universal or normative than is Campbell's hero. But the point is not finally that the sin of pride is only a male sin and the sin of self-denial only a female sin. The point is rather that the dominance of one perspective limits our understanding and acceptance of the other as legitimate. And both fail when they ignore the symbols of transformation born and nurtured in particular narratives. The imposition of the pattern of transformation of the *male* hero from pride to humility onto the process of separation, initiation and return in Campbell's monomyth may prove to be misrepresentative not only of female experience, but also of much of contemporary male experience. This is suggested in contemporary literature, in particular, by the noticeable lack even of *male* characters who fit the model of Campbell's traditional male hero. Thus, the birth of the female hero may provide a heuristic model which breaks through the stereotypes of 'male' and 'female' which bind the former no less than the latter. Its. theological significance may begin to show at least one manner in which feminist theology is clearly more than a theology of the feminine.

Notes

[1]Margaret Atwood, *Surfacing* (New York: Popular·Books, 1972); Maxine Hong Kingston, *The Woman Warrior: Memoirs of a Girlhood Among Ghosts* (New York: Vintage, 1977); Joseph Campbell, *The Hero With A Thousand Faces* (Princeton: University of Princeton Press, 1973). Quotations in the text will be identified by page numbers. Thanks to those who read and commented on earlier drafts of the essay—Robert Detweiler, Betsy Lunz, Robert Paul, and Robert Scharlemann. I especially appreciate the comments and editorial assistance of Wayne Floyd who was particularly helpful and supportive at the end of the project.

[2]Josie P. Campbell, "The Woman As Hero In Margaret Atwood's Surfacing," MOSAIC XI (1978): 17-29; Joan Leonard, "Language and the Heroic Quest in Margaret Atwood's *Surfacing*," Unpublished essay presented at the Southeast Regional AAR meeting, Spring, 1981; Carol Pearson and Katherine Pope, *The Female Hero in American and British Literature* (New York: R. R. Bowker Co., 1981), pp. 193; 205-211; 238-239.

[3]To say that the hero's quest is analogous to a theological tradition assumes a relationship between myth, symbol and literature which has been influenced by Paul Tillich's discussion of symbol and myth in *The Dynamics of Faith* (New York: Harper & Row, 1957), pp. 41-54; Paul Ricoeur's discussion of symbol and reflection in *The Symbolism of Evil* (Boston: Beacon Press, 1967), pp. 347-357; and by Carol Christ's discussion on ˙women's stories and self-understanding in *Diving Deep and Surfacing: Women Writers on Spiritual Quest* (Boston: Beacon Press, 1980), pp. 1-12.

[4]The dominance of the male as hero is seen not only in Campbell's study but in general in the introductions to heroes in such studies as Edith Hamilton's *Mythology* (New York: The New American Library, 1969) and Thomas Bulfinch's *Mythology* (New York: Dell Publishing, 1959). The Amazons and the Valkyries are perhaps the best known exceptions to the hero-as-male rule, but as yet we know very little of their individual quests. It is difficult, therefore, to conclude just how much of an exception they are.

[5]Valerie Saiving Goldstein, "The Human Situation: A Feminine view," *Journal of Religion* 40 (1960): 100-112 (Ms. Saiving has changed her name since the article first appeared; references in this essay are from the reprint of the article in *Womanspirit Rising: A Feminist Reader in Religion*, eds. Carol P. Christ and Judith Plaskow, (New York: Harper & Row, 1979), pp. 24-42); Judith Plaskow, *Sex, Sin and Grace: Women's Experience and the Theologies of Reinhold Niebuhr and Paul Tillich* (Washington, D.C.: University Press of America, 1980); Susan Nelson Dunfee, "The Sin of Hiding: A Feminist Critique of Reinhold Niebuhr's Account of the Sin of Pride," *Soundings* LXV (1982): 316-327.

[6]Florence Sandler and Darrell Ruck in their article, "The Masks of Joseph Campbell," *Religion* 11 (1981): 1-20 argue that Campbell, especially in *The Hero With A Thousand Faces*, was greatly influenced by Heinrich Zimmer, the German Indianologist, whose work he edited in the 40s and 50s.

[7]Pearson and Pope, *The Female Hero*, pp. 4-5; Joanna Russ, "What Can A Heroine Do? or Why Women Can't Write," *Images of Women in Fiction: Feminist Perspectives*, ed. Susan Koppelman Cornillon (Bowling Green, Ohio: Bowling Green University Popular Press, 1972), pp. 3-20.

[8]In seeing the hero at the end of the quest as an integrated whole capable of transforming society, Campbell is using C. G. Jung's distinction between the *ego* and the *Self* archetype. Realization of the Self is for Jung the major goal of the process of individuation. See C. G. Jung, *Two Essays on Analytical Psychology (The Collected Works of C. G. Jung,* Bollingen Series 7), p. 238.

[9]Josie Campbell, "Woman," op. cit., p. 20; Joan Leonard, "Language," op. cit., p. 5. See also, "Margaret Atwood: A Symposium," *The Malahat Review* 41 (1977).

[10]Christ, *Diving*, op. cit., p. 8.

[11]Ibid.

[12]Ibid.

[13]Ibid.

[14]Saiving, "The Human Situation," op. cit., pp. 25-26. Page references are included in the text.

[15]Plaskow, *Sex*, op. cit., pp. 2-3. Page references are included in the text.

[16]Dunfee, "Sin," op. cit., p. 316. Page references are included in the text.

"New" Women in Old Stories: Silhouette "Intimate Moments"

Diane M. Calhoun-French

In a 1984 article which appeared in the American Library Association's *Openers*, Joe Parisi divided popular romance fiction into three categories—sweet, spicy, and steamy—based on the novels' sexual explicitness. According to Parisi, Silhouette's new "Intimate Moments" series clearly falls into the final category. Now, while I certainly concur with that observation, it was not the novels' promise of a new level of eroticism which most intrigued me when I perused several volumes on the drug store racks. What fascinated me were the details about the novels' heroines given on the back cover, specifically, descriptions of their occupations.

Women's romance fiction, especially the Silhouette series, has for some time accommodated itself to the truth that many women do work, but, more often than not, the heroines have pursued fairly traditional careers as singers, dancers, artists, doctors, lawyers, social workers, and the like. Rarely do the main characters in Silhouette's newest series engage in such mainstream female occupations. Instead, "Intimate Moments" gives us—among others—a land developer, a movie studio president, a female jockey, a charter yacht captain, the designer of Navy fighter planes, a coal company president, an airline owner, a real estate tycoon, and—my personal favorite—an automobile repossessor. Needless to say, I was both fascinated that the heroines should have such jobs as these and curious to know how the writers treated such non-traditional career women. What follows are some conclusions about the authors' attitudes toward women in such situations and their perceptions of how careers for women affect the stock and trade of women's fiction: male/female relationships.

By the way of background, "Silhouette Intimate Moments," begun in 1983, is the latest series published by Silhouette Books, which labels itself "America's Publisher of Contemporary Romance." Four new novels in the series appear every month and may even be purchased by

114

subscription. In a letter to the reader in Volume I of the series, the editor promises not only the "increased realism, deeper characterization and greater length" of "Silhouette Special Editions" and the "increased sensuality" of "Silhouette Desire," but novels that are "longer than the usual, with all the depth that length requires. More sensuous than the usual, with characters whose maturity matches that sensuality. Books with the ingredient no one else has tapped: excitement."

A consideration of this brief "prospectus" brings me to my first observation: that careers are *used* in these novels—and I mean that word pejoratively—first, to provide a superficial dimension of excitement such as an occasional shipwreck or battle might in women's historical romances, and second, as an undeveloped index to the heroine's maturity, the fact of which serves as the editor's moral justification for increased and broadened sexual activity.

We rarely see the heroines' lives as shaped by their experiences on the job, nor do we see them encountering the day-to-day conflicts that accompany responsibilities such as theirs. Indeed the only dimension of complexity in the heroine's working world is introduced by the hero whose animal magnetism makes it impossible for her to do her job.

This fact stems from what is the most important message "Intimate Moments" authors are delivering to their readers: that serious male/female relationships and *serious* female careers cannot co-exist. While the endings of these novels pay lip service to the notion that females can be both satisfied and satisfying wives as well as effective executives and the like, the events of the novels argue otherwise. Women choose careers because they have been frustrated in their relationships with men or to avoid such relationships altogether and they are successful in those careers only as long as they are not confronted by men with whom they could become seriously involved.

Let me illustrate these ideas at work in three novels: Kristin James' *Dreams of Evening* (1983), the first novel in this series; Brooke Hastings' *Interested Parties* (1984); and Parris Afton Bonds' *Widow Woman* (1984).

The heroine of *Dreams of Evening*, Erica Logan, is a hotel manager who, when her establishment is brought out by a large corporation, finds herself confronting in its new owner the man by whom she has had an illegitimate child ten years earlier after a short but oh-so-intense summer relationship. We learn as she reflects on the intervening years that "As the time passed, she grew to despise Antonio Cruz. He had lied to her and abandoned her, and she built up a fierce hatred of him and all men. They were either callous, careless creatures like him or self-righteous condemners like her father, and she was determined to live like her aunt, a dedicated career woman, able to support herself and her child" (pp. 60-61). And anyway, with her job, we are told, she has neither any time for nor interest in men. It is important to the plot that Erica has made her judgments about men—and thus a career—based on erroneous information. In fact, the hero had not abandoned her at all; instead he had been duped into believing she was ready to abandon him. Not only is Erica's career presented as a mutually exclusive alternative to a serious romantic involvement, but it is threatened by the reappearance of Tonio, whose sexual advances she cannot refuse. She awakes from their lovemaking one day after his arrival at the hotel "with a flash of shame.... For almost ten years she had hated him from the depths of her soul, yet his expert hands and mouth had brought her to abject surrender within minutes.... She would have begged him to take her if she had been capable of speech" (p. 86). Aware that she cannot withstand the temptation working with him will subject her to, she resigns, aware that the odds of getting another such ideal job are against her.

The heroine of *Interested Parties* is Kate Garvey who is, the novel's back cover explains, "in the business of 'making' men"—that is, training them to win elections. While there is no suggestion that Kate has become a top-notch political consultant after a frustrated love affair, she does wonder if her career is "a way of avoiding emotional entanglements" (p. 187) and acknowledges to herself "that the only time a man could top her list of priorities was when she was trying to elect him to something" (p. 19). Like Erica Logan, Kate finds her job-effectiveness jeopardized by a man who generates a "physical reaction...so embarrassingly intense that she has to remind herself that she [is] in Washington on business" (p. 9). As the novel unfolds and she is forced to take politically expedient action to which the idealistic hero objects— he is an academic, by the way, who has been cajoled into running for U.S. senator—she begins to feel "almost corrupt" (p. 86) and by the novel's end she has "lost her taste for her work" (p. 235) completely.

Cass Garolini, the "Widow Woman" of Bonds' novel, has one career behind her as the story opens and is forced into another as its events unfold. We learn that she has—at twenty-seven—just recently retired, a spectacularly successful international model. Her decision to pursue a career—like Erica Logan's—is the product of a disastrous romantic relationship: a failing marriage to an alcoholic pianist whose extravagant lifestyle she was forced to support. This fact notwithstanding—that marital circumstances forced her into her job—the author insists that successful career women make unsuitable mates. Near the end of the novel, the hero, an investigative reporter, confronts Cass with the "truth" that she was implicated in her husband's decline and death: "Your New York acquaintances and business associates were quite willing to reveal that Mario was deeply infatuated with you, with your beauty.... That as your career soared, Mario doubted his own abilities and turned more and more to alcohol...that your desire for your own success drove him to kill himself with drinking and a fast, sordid life" (p. 213).

For our purposes, Cass's second career is more interesting than her first. At her father's death, she assumes the position he has vacated (again, out of financial necessity); she becomes the county sheriff. And once more, as in the other novels I've mentioned, we find that her ability to discharge her responsibilities is compromised—very nearly destroyed—by the uncontrollable passion she conceives for a hypnotic stranger whose "overpowering virility" (p. 133) she is unable to ignore. Attending the Law Enforcement Academy—a condition of her employment—Cass "barely [hears] the lectures.... Instead her mind too often [drifts] to thoughts of Cade, visions of his well-honed body, memories of his glances, his touch" (p. 172). More importantly, her sexual desire for the hero jeopardizes her chances at being elected to the position of sheriff for a full term. Unable to run the farm which her father has left her by herself, she hires the hero as a live-in laborer. Overwhelmed by her lust for him, Cass allows herself to sleep with him, not once but several times, and thus opens herself up to charges of immoral, even unethical conduct, since the hero has been involved with strikers Cass has been asked to arrest. The questions of exactly how the heroine would have dealt with such charges and whether she would have been elected in spite of them are neatly sidestepped when the hero announces in the nick of time, "The Widow Woman is going to be my wife" (p. 248).

As I have mentioned, these novels end with the heroines happily married—or on the brink of being so—and just as happily employed. However, in each instance it is clear that their careers are grossly subordinate in importance to their marital relationships and usually to their husbands' careers as well. At the end of *Widow Woman* Cass Garolini has been elected sheriff—thanks, of course to the hero's making an "honest woman" of her. And, while he has supposedly sacrificed his wanderlust to make it possible for her to maintain her position, she quite willingly offers to move if there's "somewhere else [he'd] want to live" and only withdraws her invitation when he reminds her, "I can write my novels anywhere" (p. 250). As we have seen, Kate Garvey has become disillusioned with her work as a political consultant by the end of *Interested Parties* and while she will continue to work—and in politics—she tells the hero, "You'll have to offer me a job." "You have so many talents, I don't know how to use you," he replies. "You can handle the political end of the office if you want to, but you'd also do a first-rate job on legislation.... Then again, Miss Garvey, maybe I'll just lock you in an office with nothing but a bed in it and assign you the job of keeping the senator happy" (p. 248). And, finally, in *Dreams of Evening*, Erica

Logan *will* return to hotel operations-but in the company which her husband owns *and* as his subordinate.

The tenuousness—temporariness—of these heroines' authority as career women whose responsibilities inevitably include supervising men is underscored by two final observations I'd like to make. The first concerns the presence of two other types of men in the novels besides the hero: one group whom we see the heroines managing to relate to successfully on a purely professional level and another group who, although involved with the heroine, do not pose a threat to her professionalism. The first, those around whom we see the woman doing her job, are inevitably presented as slightly less than male—"the effeminate-looking young man" (p. 6) who is Erica Logan's front-desk clerk, for instance, or the "effete" (p. 64) young men Cass Garolini has worked with in Manhattan. The second, more interesting group, are men with whom the heroines have had casual or steady relationships but to whom they are incapable of becoming seriously attached—men such as Eric Reinhart, the only son of the country's most prominent and wealthy family in *Widow Woman,* or Jerry Savich, a pediatric surgeon in *Interested Parties.* What is significant about these men is that they constitute, by description *and* position, the *typical hero* of women's fiction a decade or so ago. What this strategy does, of course, is to allow the authors to insist on one level on the professionalism and emotional autonomy of their heroines while simultaneously affirming their underlying thesis: that even the most successful career woman cannot remain so in the face of a *real man.*

I would like finally to suggest that in many novels in the "Intimate Moments" series the central fact of the heroine's being somehow "over" the hero by virtue of her profession is undercut from the very outset by what can only be termed strange contortions of plot which pit the heroine's authority against the power of the hero—always to her disadvantage. In *Love Me Before Dawn,* a novel I have not mentioned, for example, the main character is designing a prototype for an airplane when she becomes romantically entangled with the man who is to test it. While she has control over the craft he is to fly, it is he whose behavior and opinions will largely determine whether her design is accepted. In *Interested Parties,* Kate Garvey is clearly "in charge" of the image presented by the candidate whom she is trying to elect, but it is also he, like the test pilot, who determines whether or not her efforts will succeed. And in *Widow Woman,* Cass may be the sheriff but it is Cade Montoya who exerts real influence with the strikers it is her duty to subdue.

The underlying import of these novels is clear, I think. Women can have careers—but *only* in the absence of or at the expense of satisfying romantic—or even satisfying sexual—relationships. Moreover, whatever *authority* they might have by virtue of their positions is neutralized by the real *power* of *real* men. This message is disturbing, partly, of course, because it is delivered at all, but even more because it is delivered in ways the unsophisticated reader cannot perceive. While purporting to present *new* women as idealized fantasy figures for their readers, "Intimate Moments" are really recounting the *old* lies. And, unfortunately, in this sensuous and glamourous new wrapper, they are perhaps more appealing than ever before.

Scarlett O'Hara:
A Paradox in Pantalettes

Ann E. Egenriether

Scarlett O'Hara, the central figure in Margaret Mitchell's *Gone With the Wind*, is the quintessential American heroine. More than any other female character in American fiction, Scarlett embodies many concepts associated with the American success story; and, as a result, she has captured the imagination of readers and film buffs over the last five decades. Like Hester Prynne in Nathaniel Hawthorne's *The Scarlet Letter*, Scarlett endures great hardships and triumphs over them; like Carrie in Theodore Dreiser's *Sister Carrie,* Scarlett is an opportunist who uses every available resource to further her goals. Unlike Hester or Carrie, Scarlett actively pursues her desires, makes her own decisions (for better or worse) and assumes responsibility for her actions. Whereas Hester and Carrie passively accept whatever Fate hands them, Scarlett determines her own destiny. To paraphrase *King Lear*—Scarlett is more acting than acted upon.

As the nonpareil of American heroism, Scarlett must of necessity be a paradox. Scarlett is a heroine not merely in that she survives the devastations in her life, but because she survives, triumphs and flourishes in the world of men. Scarlett succeeds by virtue of her willingness to play according to rules established by men, and she is not above bending those rules with her considerable feminine charm and wiles to her own advantage. Scarlett is a paradox, for she can only survive by working and thinking like a man, yet as a woman she is acutely aware of the importance of maintaining social approval and avoiding censure. With such conflicting emotions, to survive foremost, to succeed, and to appear the ever-refined Southern belle, Scarlett becomes the quintessential American heroine: she can reconcile her paradoxical desires and she grows in the process.

The process of Scarlett's growth into maturity and her road to success are long and difficult. Born into the antebellum Southern planter aristocracy, Scarlett is a pampered princess with every wish and whim gratified. The only difficulties in her secure world are maintaining her demure appearance before the watchful eyes of her mother and the sharper ones of Mammy and the constant trial of keeping a dozen beaux on the string simultaneously. The former task is much more problematic, for it pits Scarlett's inherent robust, high-spirited nature against the decorous demands of being a lady. She engages in a constant battle of wills between "her mother's gentle admonitions and the sterner discipline of her mammy" to conform to the proper behavior, but "her eyes were her own" (1) and they mark a fierce and unbecoming streak of independence.

Scarlett possesses this independence at a time and in a place where women were considered to be helpless, clinging creatures in need of protection. Social convention decreed, among other things, that women conform to standards of behavior which placed little value on feminine naturalness and ability. Scarlett realizes early in her life that she is an anomaly—her basic personality contrasts sharply with the expected behavior of ladies. For her role model, Scarlett sees her mother, Ellen, as "the embodiment of justice, truth, loving tenderness and profound wisdom—a great lady. Scarlett wanted very much to be like her mother. The only difficulty was that by being just and truthful and tender and unselfish, one missed most of the joys of life" (41-42). Scarlett learns the outward trappings of gentility from her mother because it enables her to become popular with the young swains of the County; her real self, more closely resembling her Irish father's boldness and brashness, penetrates issues and relationships no more than surface deep.

From her parents, Scarlett inherits both her father's obstinancy and willfullness and her mother's sweet face and figure, as well as the comfort and security of a rich planter's life. From her parents, Scarlett also inherits her love of the land, Tara. As her father, Gerald, tells her, "Land is the only thing in the world that amounts to anything,...for 'tis the only thing in this world that lasts, and don't you be forgetting it! 'Tis the only thing worth working for, worth fighting for—worth dying for" (24). From neither of her parents, however, does Scarlett inherit the ability to survive in a world where all comfort and security are lost. When the Civil War breaks out, Scarlett faces a world in which nothing stands between her and desolation but her own determination to survive and a shrewd mind, adaptable to radical change.

In the early years of the war, Scarlett views life as exciting. Though she is newly widowed, the war enables Scarlett to participate in life again instead of being immured in mourning. With the help of Rhett Butler, Scarlett begins to flaunt the strict Southern conventions of proper behavior and the war affords her many opportunities to perpetuate her role as a Southern belle. The horrors of war never touch Scarlett very deeply until her family and Tara are jeopardized. When Atlanta falls, Tara is used as a headquarters for the Yankee forces. Scarlett returns to Tara to find her mother dead, her two sisters dangerously ill, her father mentally incompetent, the slaves gone, food and clothing scarce. All the security of her youth is eradicated in a matter of days and Scarlett must assume the burden as head of the household. Scarlett realizes that she alone is now the bulwark against which Tara and the family rests. With her return to the devastation of Tara, Scarlett forever leaves her girlhood behind her:

Tonight was the last time she would ever be ministered to as a child. She was a woman now and youth was gone.... Her burdens were her own and burdens were for shoulders strong enough to bear them. She thought without surprise...that her shoulders were strong enough to bear anything now. (288)

For the role of provider and protector Scarlett is poorly prepared. Nothing and no one in her old life could have helped Scarlett to anticipate the challenges and hardships of this new world. Only her sheer will to survive and to save her family and Tara enables Scarlett to face the grim realities of her new life. When foraging in her neighbors' garden for food, Scarlett remembers:

...things and people who were dead, remembering a way of living that was gone forever—and [she looked] upon the harsh vista of the dark future... Her head was raised high and something that was youth and beauty and potential tenderness had gone out of her face forever. What was past was past... The lazy luxury of the old days was gone, never to return. And, as Scarlett settled the heavy basket across her arm, she had settled her own mind and her own life. There was no going back and she was going forward...[She vows], "As God is my witness as God is my witness, the Yankees aren't going to lick me. I'm going to live through this, and when it's over, I'm never going to be hungry again. No, nor any of my folks. If I have steal or kill—as God is my witness, I'm never going to be hungry again." (293)

From this point on, Scarlet adapts herself like a chameleon to changing circumstances in order to survive: she undertakes the grueling task of running Tara, she attempts to entrap Rhett Butler into marriage, and failing that, succeeds in catching Frank Kennedy for a husband, she starts her own lumber business, and along this difficult road Scarlett strays far from the teachings of her mother to meet the never-ending challenges of the war-torn South.

    What comes as a rude shock to Scarlett is the realization that she is so ill-equipped to deal with the demands which her new life makes upon her. Born and reared into a life of ease and leisure, Scarlett must now direct her energies to the ceaseless and tedious tasks of homemaking and farming. Where once she never turned to her hand to any labor, now Scarlett turns the earth with plow and hoe to survive. Scarlett learns quickly out of desperation to work hard, but she cannot quite comprehend why and how such changes have occurred in her life. She laments in despair"

"Nothing, no, nothing [Mother] taught me is of any help to me! What good will kindness do me now? What value is gentleness? Better that I'd learned to plow or chop cotton like a darky."... She did not stop to think that Ellen's world was gone and a brutal world had taken its place...and she changed swiftly to meet this new world for which she was not prepared.(297-98)

For Tara, Scarlett willingly changes and her sole goal, after basic survival of the family, is to protect Tara. When the Carpetbaggers raise the taxes on Tara after the war, Scarlett faces her worst crisis. Without the tax money, she will lose Tara; if she loses Tara, she loses more than just the land: she will lose an idealization, a living symbol of the accomplishment of her forebears, her own past life, and her own hopes and dreams for the future; her heart and soul would be torn from her should Tara be taken away. Tara, therefore, is worth any sacrifice Scarlett must make.

It is this desperation which sends Scarlett back to Atlanta to raise the tax money from Rhett Butler. Her methods to entrap Rhett are all feminine when she appears at the jail decked out in her new finery made from her mother's drapes, but her determination and calculation are all masculine. She weighs her options with Rhett, takes a gamble that he will, contrary to his professed sentiments, marry her, and when that gambit fails she does not scruple to offer to become his mistress to save Tara. Ironically, Scarlett fails with Rhett because she relies too much on her own will and "masculine" determination to make her plan work and not enough upon her own natural coquetry. In fact, Rhett admonishes Scarlett about her tactics being too masculine and counterproductive:

"When you are trying to get something out of a man, don't blurt it out as you did to me. Do try to be more subtle, more seductive. It gets better results. You used to know how, to perfection. But just now when you offered me your—er—collateral for my money you looked as hard as nails. I've seen eyes like yours above a dueling pistol twenty paces from me and they aren't a pleasant sight. They evoke no ardor in the male breast. That's no way to handle men, my dear. You are forgetting your early training." (403)

When Scarlett does not succeed in her scheme with Rhett, she has no qualms of conscience in using Rhett's advice to snare her own sister's beau, Frank Kennedy, and marrying him. She takes the most direct route to achieve her ends with Frank: with a frightening singleness of purpose she flatters "that old maid in britches," plays the helpless but brave little woman and successfully disguises her determination under the face of demureness until she has Frank secure. Scarlett does not balk at doing anything distasteful, unpleasant, unprincipled or even immoral to further her goals of saving Tara, but all the while Scarlett uses her femininity as the lever she needs to win—paradoxical methods which are quite effective.

Though Scarlett saves Tara from being sold out for taxes, she soon discovers that this is only one crisis she will face in the post-war South. Reconstruction brings worse terrors than the war itself and Scarlett realizes that the only bulwark between her and destitution is money. Raising the tax money was merely a stopgap: Scarlett needs to build a secure fortress against the uncertain future. In her new husband, Frank, Scarlett seizes an opportunity for financial security. After the war, Frank started a general store with war surplus goods and he considers opening up a lumber yard as a sideline. Scarlett immediately sees the tremendous opportunities for money-making in the lumber business with the building boom in Atlanta after the war. Scarlett's grasp of mathematics, her vision of a growing Atlanta and her own boldness propel her into a course of action to become financially independent, even from her husband. In going over Frank's store accounts Scarlett discovers both his business ineptitude and her own abilities. She muses to herself:

"Just imagine Frank trying to operate a sawmill! God's nightgown! If he runs this store like a charitable institution, how could he expect to make money on a mill? The sheriff would have it in a month. Why, I could run this store better than he does! And I could run a mill better than he could, even if I don't know anything about the lumber business!"

A startling thought this, that a woman could handle business matters as well as or better than a man, a revolutionary thought to Scarlett who had been reared in the tradition that men were omniscient and women none too bright.... She had been brought up to believe that a woman alone could accomplish nothing, yet she had managed the plantation without men to help her.... Why, why, her mind stuttered, I believe women could manage everything in the world without men's help.... With the idea that she was as capable as a man came a sudden rush of pride and a violent longing to prove it, to make money for herself as men made money. Money which would be her own, which she would neither have to ask for nor account for to any man. (426-27)

With her mind made up, Scarlett sets about the most direct route to accomplish her desires and she cares not at all about the disgruntled mutterings and shocked faces of her family and friends. She decides to collect on Frank's delinquent accounts and to borrow money from Rhett Butler. With money in hand, she purchases the sawmill to start her lumber business. Scarlett further disregards convention after buying the sawmill by running it herself. She neither consults Frank about the purchase of the mill nor does she turn it over to him to manage. Scarlett goes into business for herself and she compounds her audacity by succeeding at it. She steps out of woman's traditional role, first by working at all, then by working in an unwomanly way: instead of earning her way by her needle or baking or painting, she enters the rough world of men. And in this business world, Scarlett adapts herself very well: where once she seemed all fluttering timidity,

> now her reactions were all masculine. Despite her pink cheeks and dimples and pretty smiles, she talked and acted like a man. Her voice was brisk and decisive and she made up her mind instantly and with no girlish shilly-shallying. She knew what she wanted and she went after it by the shortest route, like a man, not by the hidden and circuitous routes peculiar to women.... Scarlett was guided by no one but herself and was conducting her affairs in a masculine way which had the whole town talking about her. (441)

Finally, in making a success in her business Scarlett poses a threat to any Southern gentleman who has not likewise succeeded.

In succeeding in her lumber business, however, Scarlett never loses sight of her femininity. In fact, she capitalizes on her womanliness:

> The fact that she was a woman frequently worked in her favor, for she could upon occasion look so helpless and appealing that she melted hearts. With no difficulty whatever she could mutely convey the impression of a brave but timid lady, forced by brutal circumstance into a distasteful position, a helpless little lady who would probably starve if customers didn't buy her lumber. But when ladylike airs failed to get results, she was coldly businesslike and willingly undersold her competitors at a loss to herself if it would bring her a new customer. (457)

With impunity, Scarlett engages in sharp business dealings and lies about her competitors, because she knows the code of the Southern gentleman will protect her. No gentleman would ever speak denigratingly of a Southern lady without serious consequences to himself. Thus, Scarlett makes a great financial success at her business by combining her feminine charm and grace with masculine directness and decisiveness.

In her quest for financial security Scarlett does achieve her goal: her sawmill and lumberyard thrive under her direction and she even marries Rhett Butler who is very wealthy, thus forever securing herself from financial worry. In the process of attaining money, however, Scarlett undergoes a number of changes, not all of which are positive. From the time she returns to the desolation of Tara, Scarlett is forced into the role as head of the household, a rapid and radical change from the pampered princess of the plantation. As Scarlett scavenges for food, hoes and chops cotton, kills a Yankee marauder, attempts prostitution, sells herself into a loveless marriage and builds up her business in a man's world, she sacrifices a part of herself. For Scarlett are lost her innocence and all ties with the past. Scarlett abandons the gentle teachings of her mother because they have no place in her new world; she alienates herself from family and friends because she gains her ends in ways they consider unwomanly and against the Southern code. Scarlett is different from her peers and she cannot understand why. As Rhett tells her, "All you've done is to be different from other women and you've made a little success at it. As I've told you before, that is the one unforgivable sin in any society. Be different and be damned!" (469). Through the terrors of Reconstruction, Scarlett learns that nothing is more important than money and the security it brings—not family or love or public approbation. Scarlett mistakenly believes that after she wins the security which she so obsessively seeks, she will have the leisure and inclination to "permit herself to be kind and gentle, as Ellen had been, and thoughtful of other people and of the proprieties too.... She would be a lady in the true Southern manner, as her mother had been" (467). Scarlett thinks that only money makes a lady and she scoffs at those who do not grasp this. Scarlett divorces herself from her old life and greedily embraces the new. In the process, however, she alienates herself from that old life, those old allegiances.

Scarlett achieves her dream of success but the cost she pays is being alone. Her parents are dead, old friends distant, her children strangers. Where once Scarlett scorned the opinion of her friends and neighbors, now she regrets not having those same people about her to share old memories, to refight old battles, to belong once again with her own people who knew her life, her struggles and her triumphs because they were also their own. Scarlett is alone and realizes too late that she has only herself to blame for her present loneliness. Scarlett does recognize, however, that she is not totally bereft of the comfort and companionship of old friends; indeed, Melanie and Rhett were always there behind her:

> For years she had had her back against the stone wall of Rhett's love and had taken it as much for granted as she had taken Melanie's love, flattering herself that she drew her strength from herself alone. And even as she had realized earlier in the evening that Melanie had been beside her in her bitter campaigns against life, now she knew that silent in the background, Rhett had stood, loving her, understanding her, ready to help. (708)

Scarlett learns finally that love is more important than money, that Rhett is her real refuge and security. But Melanie is dead and Rhett is leaving her to find his own peace. Scarlett ultimately achieves her dream of security, but more importantly she acquires knowledge and a certain wisdom about herself and what her life means.

As *the* fictional American heroine, Scarlett O'Hara meets life with all of its vagaries headlong. Though raised to expect life filled with comfort and leisure, she faces war, famine, poverty, Reconstruction and death with an indomitability which always matches and frequently surpasses that of the men in her world. Scarlett battles for success in her world by employing the tactics and strategies of a hard-headed entrepreneur overlaid by the shimmer of lady-like gentility. She makes a success of her life because she is first willing to sacrifice everything short of Tara to attain her goals, and secondly, because she grows and matures in the process: by the end of the novel, Scarlett understands that material success pales if she is alone. Scarlett can finally admit to herself that, "Rhett is my soul and I'm losing him. And if I lose him, nothing else matters! No, not friends or money or—or anything. If only I had him I wouldn't even mind being poor again. No, I wouldn't mind being cold again or even hungry" (715). With such an insight into her own psyche, Scarlett perhaps gains the truest mark of a Southern lady (and one which ever escaped her), she cares about some one else with no thoughts of her own aggrandizement. Scarlett finally learns to love Rhett as a mature woman. Scarlett travels an arduous road towards success, the success of a woman in a man's world and of a mature woman— a paradox in pantalettes.

Works Cited

Mitchell, Margaret. *Gone With the Wind*. 1936; rpt. New York: MacMillan Co., 1964.

Anonymous Heroines:
Black Women as Heroic Types
in Robert Gwathmey's Art

Charles K. Piehl

The popular and critical success as well as the controversy surrounding the book and the subsequent film *The Color Purple* have brought attention to the largely neglected issue of the place of the black woman in society.[1] Alice Walker's novel and the recent scholarly work of Jacqueline Jones emphasize the double burden black women carried in a society dominated by whites and males.[2] Even though Walker and Jones give considerable attention to oppressive conditions in the lives of many black women, neither author ignores the fact that these same burdens also contributed to the development of a sense of common endeavor as women sought sources of strength and support. Since many of these women worked in isolation in rural areas, they looked to their work, their families, and very often other women for meaning in their lives. These also were the places they found their heroes.

Scholars have argued that the concept of the hero has changed dramatically in the twentieth century as the triumphal and romantic heroism of previous eras has been found wanting in an age of mass destruction and disillusionment. The heroic ideal seemed either irrelevant or dangerous in its traditional form, and the search for a true democratic hero yielded questionable results. "If a hero is defined as an event-making individual who redetermines the course of history," wrote Sidney Hook during World War II, "it follows at once that a democratic community must be eternally on guard against him."[3] By midcentury the anti-hero was in vogue and heroism appeared to have retreated into the world of media fantasy.

Anonymous Heroism

Despite the alleged crisis of heroism in the twentieth century, people continued to long for heroes and heroines and occasionally find them, even in this anti-heroic world. One need only look at the way in which social groups, attempting to build a common spirit among their members, have sought to identify heroes to serve as models for others to emulate. Efforts to uncover stories in notables of black and women's history, to name two examples, have served as part of a hero-building process in addition to being attempts to remedy past neglect and to set the historical record straight. Such efforts have been particularly common in groups whose members have been rendered anonymous by historical indifference. A recent feminist survey of art addressed this problem by proclaiming in its title the *Anonymous Was a Woman*.[4]

The identification of anonymous heroes is not entirely new, for they have been found in identifiable heroic "types" in which the characteristics of countless anonymous heroes or heroines are consolidated into a mythical but nonetheless recognizable category. Such heroic types can be found throughout American history, from the founding settlers of the seventeenth century, through the cowboys of the nineteenth century, to the currently popular entrepreneurial hero of the high technology world. As Richard Hofstadter and others have reminded us, the myth of the yeoman farmer carried a potent political message in the late nineteenth century. A latter day version of the concept of the virtuous and independent republican which emerged in the eighteenth century, the yeoman farmer served as a heroic type, a model of the anonymous hero that lived in the minds of people even if never precisely in reality.[5]

Gwathmey's Art

Despite the pervasiveness of heroic types in popular thought, the predominant heroes of American history have been male and white. The paintings of the Virginia-born artist Robert Gwathmey (b.1903) offer an opportunity to examine the visual presentation of anonymous black women as heroines worthy of recognition by blacks and whites, males and females at a time when heroism was believed to be declining. He attempted to identify for a wider audience a heroic type which had long been recognized in the black community but which was recognizable more widely only in caricatures such as the Mammy.

Gwathmey's work from the late Thirties to the present rejected the depiction of heroism as found in the mythology of the Old South or in the Lost Cause of the Confederacy. This mythic heroism had been a staple of Southern art of the kind that Gwathmey, a white man, had seen while growing up in Richmond during his formative years. He later recalled visiting the Confederate Museum, the only place in the city where art was displayed to the public, and seeing nothing but "Pretty bad portraits of...Confederate generals."[6] While there certainly were other types of Southern art about which Gwathmey did not know, the kind that reflected the dominant political and social view was what Southerners knew best.

Years later, with a federal government commission to paint a mural in a new post office in Eutaw, Alabama, Gwathmey confronted the strength of this visual mythology. As his commission stipulated, he inquired through the postmistress into the social and historical background of the community. He received a reply that stressed the antebellum and Confederate glories of the community's white population, implying that such were the sources of appropriate images to use in the mural. Not surprisingly, Gwathmey incurred some displeasure from the white community in the Eutaw area when *The Countryside*, his mural depicting five fieldworkers, two of whom were recognizably black, was installed in the post office lobby in 1941.

Gwathmey's positions on social and political issues often are apparent in his paintings, particularly those done in the early 1940s and in the 1960s and the early 1970s. During the Forties, in works such as *Standard Bearer* and *Bread and Circuses,* he protested lynching and the persistence of segregation and social and political dominance by whites. In the Sixties, he again dealt with social and political issues in his paintings. In *Space*, done in 1964, he described the irony of the modern South's enthusiasm for the forward-looking space program at the same time mobs, continuing the region's tradition of violence, attacked those who tried to integrate buses. *Belle* brought together images of bigotry, intolerance, and ignorance, while *Late 20th Century*, done during the Vietnam war years, depicted the chaos of war and waste in modern life.

Despite the strength of his social and political commitments, Gwathmey's most effective work is not art of advocacy but is instead an examination of the nature of community and the relationships between the races and the sexes within his region. For him, Southern heroism has been best exemplified by the strength of common people, particularly blacks, and their families. He painted nameless individuals and places which nonetheless served as universal types which people could recognize and identify with. The power of his art lies not so much in an overt social statement but in his ability to use his craft to focus attention on aspects of everyday life that frequently are overlooked or might otherwise be ignored as not worthy of our concern.

A recurrent image in Gwathmey's work over four decades has been the heroic black woman, exhausted by the many responsibilities that she assumed but nonetheless proud of her labor, her family and her survival within an oppressive social system. It is important to understand the context of the heroism of these black women, for they are an essential part of a black community. Although women appear by themselves in many Gwathmey works, they frequently are portrayed together with men in the field, at home, and in town as full partners in black culture. While oppressed for generations by the dominant elements of white society, that black culture proved both physically and spiritually strong, a characteristic well portrayed by Gwathmey in the generation before historians began to examine it in the 1960s. The paintings discussed here date from the 1940s and early 1950s.

Women in the Fields

The advent of mechanized farming and the out-migration of people to cities changed the rural South dramatically in the twentieth century. But wearisome fieldwork continued to be the predominate experience for many of the region's people, including large numbers of black field hands exemplified in many of Gwathmey's paintings. Knowing that poverty, malnutrition, and disease have been endemic in the rural South, the striking characteristic common to blacks in these artworks is their physical strength. For example, in *Cotton Picker*, the strong back, thickly muscled arms, and large hands give the viewer a sense of the life of a single fieldworker even though we cannot even get a glimpse of his face. The powerful black men who appear in Gwathmey's works helped him express an important message. He was certain that the vitality of the South and its people was not found in the white genteel upper class but rather in the hardworking laborers who typically were disdained by the elite. Gwathmey frequently painted these whites as either grossly rotund (*Standard Bearer* and *Parade*) or wan and emaciated figures (*Ancestor Worship*), in neither case able to do any real work. Physical strength developed through years of hard labor had not demeaned blacks but had brought forth their true heroic character and put the lie to the claims of social superiority of the dominant class of the region.

Women first appeared in Gwathmey's early depictions of fieldwork in a subordinate position in the background of paintings with dominant male figures. The sole woman in his Alabama post office mural is found on the far right-hand side of the painting, the least visible of five figures. The composition of *Hoeing* (Figure 1), done at about the same time, draws attention to a burly male figure in the center of the picture. By contrast, a woman with thin arms and legs appears as almost a second thought, hardly central to either the fieldwork or the artwork.

In the mid-1940s Gwathmey style evolved as he began to break his paintings into carefully segmented planes of flat colors often separated by black lines. It is unclear why at about the same time the women in his paintings began to emerge from their position in the background.

Figure. 1. *Hoeing,* Robert Gwathmey, oil on canvas, 22 1/4" x 18 1/8", Rose Art Museum, Brandeis University, Waltham, Massachusetts; Gift of Edgar Kaufmann, Jr., New York.

While some works, such as *Man with Hoe* (1944) (Figure 2), still featured dominant male figures in relationship to the female, *End of Day* (1943) (Figure 3) is an early example of the emergence of a new kind of woman in Gwathmey's art. Two strapping male figures dominate the center of the work, but they are joined on their left and right by erect black women, both with assertive postures, almost as if they appear ready to assume the lead of the procession of laborers if called upon.

Other paintings reveal the full development of the character of the black woman fieldworker as a heroic type in Gwathmey's art. While the black man in *Hoeing Tobacco* (1946) (Figure 4) still holds the center position in the composition, the two women on either side of him capture attention at least as much as he does. Now a man, his back to the viewer of the painting, faces a heavy-breasted woman, the archetypal black "mammy" figure. Yet here she is in the field working, with sinewy forearms and a determined grasp on her hoe, alongside the man. At the right in the painting is a younger woman, sweatband around her head, perhaps the daughter of the older woman at the left. The presence of the two women together in the painting reminds us that years of this kind of work are the lot of the young as they have been for the old. The strong hands of both women are doubtless already callused from gripping the hoe, and they perform labor at least as difficult as that done by the man, whose back is hunched after years of fieldwork.

In *Sowing* (1949) (Figure 5) Gwathmey focused on a single black woman casting seed from her apron across a field. The sun is low on the horizon meaning she is working either very early or very late in the day. Barefoot on the hard ground like the women in *Hoeing Tobacco*, she is doing work of the kind that few people would seek. Despite these images, the dominant feeling of this work, as with *Sowing*, is not one of pity for these people, particularly not for the women. They certainly are not the stereotyped happy blacks of *Gone with the Wind* but neither are they the wretched of the earth. The countenance of the woman in *Sowing* is serious, almost contemplative, but the sweep of her right arm as she pitches the seed into the breeze is energetic. She displays physical strength in her arms, even though this woman clearly is tall and thin. Such black women may not have been enjoying their work, but they were doing what they needed to do.

Worksong (Figure 6) is a simple evocation of what held members of the black community together as they broke from their labors. Gwathmey does not slight the toll that work has taken on the three people in the painting, for their faces and gestures reveal weariness. But their group singing is symbolic of their mutual effort to which each individual, the woman included, has contributed. In this context, the woman is a vital force in maintaining the spirit of the community.

Figure. 2 *Man with Hoe*, Robert Gwathmey, oil on canvas, 13" x 9", Hirshhorn
Museum and Sculpture Garden, Smithsonian Institution; Gift of Joseph H. Hirshhorn,
1966.

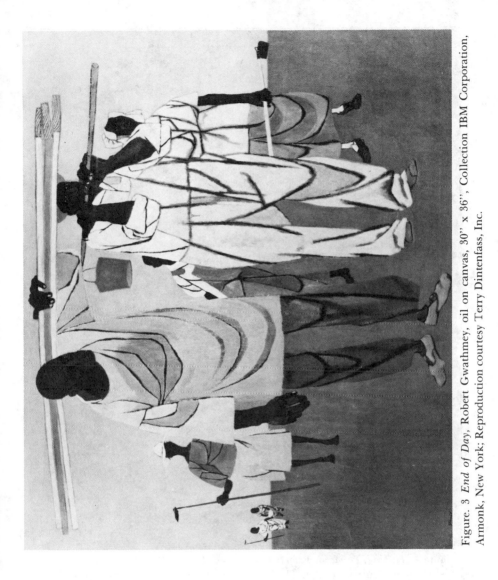

Figure. 3 *End of Day*, Robert Gwathmey, oil on canvas, 30″ x 36″, Collection IBM Corporation, Armonk, New York; Reproduction courtesy Terry Dintenfass, Inc.

Figure 4. *Hoeing Tobacco*, Robert Gwathmey, 1946, oil on canvas, 30 1/8" x 24 1/8", Georgia Museum of Art, The University of Georgia, Eva Underhill Holbrook Memorial Collection of American Art; Gift of Alfred H. Holbrook, GMDA 47.164.

Figure 5. *Sowing*, 1949, Robert Gwathmey, oil on canvas, 36" x 40",
Collection of Whitney Museum of American Art, New York; Purchase,
49.17.

Figure 6. *Worksong*, Robert Gwathmey, oil on canvas, 29 3/4" x 36, Auburn University Collection, photo courtesy of the Montgomery Museum of Fine Arts, Montgomery, AL.

Women at Work in the Home

Women had another life that continued when they were not working in the fields. Instead of depicting women's role in the home as unimportant, Gwathmey featured it as a significant element in the black community and just as heroic as were her activities outside. In fact, the artist used the stereotypical woman's place in the home to emphasize a larger point he wanted to make about the anonymous people the rest of society takes for granted. Within the black home, the woman often labored while men relaxed and several of Gwathmey's paintings juxtapose women working at chores to men at leisure. In *Singing and Mending* (1944-45) (Figure 7) two figures of the kind that frequently appear in the artist's field scenes now sit at home next to a simple table adorned with a single vase. At the left a brawny black man strums his guitar—perhaps playing the blues—as he relaxes after a hard day's labor. To his right, an equally strong and muscular woman pulls a thread taut as she mends an article of clothing. In contrast to the man, who seems particularly serious, the woman has a half-smile on her face as she sings along. Neither meek nor unequal, this woman provides a picture of confidence in the importance of what she is doing for her family and herself.

When he painted *Front Porch* (1947) (Figure 8), Gwathmey was examining the significance of a domestic setting that appears often in Southern literature and art. But he also was creating a complex artistic construction of the contrast between male leisure and female work at home.[7] At the right two men sit on the porch steps, their postures and expressions indicating that they are relaxing after an exhausting day's work. Sitting on a chair behind the porch railing in the left center of the painting is a woman sewing on a piece of cloth draped across her lap. Unlike the men to her left, she sits erect on her chair still actively engaged in labor. Although the woman is partially hidden by plant leaves, the flowers with which Gwathmey surrounds her draw the viewer's attention and remove her from the background of the painting. In this way the artist calls attention to the extraordinary grace with which she pursued her activities even though others have taken her for granted.

Gwathmey also focused on the difficulty and tedium that were part of women's role in the home. *Sewing* (Figure 9) takes the woman figure from *Singing and Mending* and examines her in isolation. The mood here contrasts with that in *Singing and Mending*. The thread here no longer is pulled tight, the smile is gone, and weariness shows on the woman's face. The same sense of drudgery is seen in *Shelling Peas* (1944) (Figure 10), where a simple but monotonous activity seems finally to be wearing down the woman's spirit. Nonetheless, the women of *Shelling*

Figure 7. *Singing and Mending*. Robert Gwathmey, oil on canvas, 30″ x 36 1/4″, Hirshhorn Museum and Sculpture Garden, Smithsonian Institution; Gift of Joseph H. Hirshhorn, 1966.

Figure 8. *Front Porch*, Robert Gwathmey, oil on canvas, 31 7/8" x 39 5/8", Hirshhorn Museum and Sculpture Garden, Smithsonian Institution; Gift of Joseph H. Hirshhorn, 1966.

Figure 9. *Sewing*, Robert Gwathmey, oil on canvas, 12" x 8", Hirshhorn Museum
and Sculpture Garden, Smithsonian Institution; Gift of Joseph H. Hirshhorn, 1966.

Figure 10. *Shelling Peas,* Robert Gwathmey, oil on canvas, 36″ x 20″. Hirshhorn Museum and Sculpture Garden, Smithsonian Institution; Gift of Joseph H. Hirshhorn, 1966.

Peas and *Sewing* remain powerful heroic figures, capable of surviving and overcoming the domestic challenges they face.

Despite Gwathmey's interest in women's domestic work, he also recognized another side of their life. *Children Dancing* (early 1940s) (Figure 11) is a powerful evocation of the woman's significance in black family life. Three children dance in a circle while the father plays the guitar and the mother claps her hands to the beat. Two of the children look admiringly up at their mother. Nothing in the painting gives a hint of the world of work either inside or outside the home. However, Gwathmey presents us with an equally strong woman in this role, where her powerful hands, instead of sowing or sewing, clap to the music. Here the heroic woman delights in her role as mother and model for her children.

In 1946 Gwathmey painted *Field Flowers* (Figure 12), a study of a single black woman seated next to a brightly colored bouquet. The woman seems weighed down with her burdens, but the flowers provide a striking contrast and lend dignity to an otherwise dismal setting. Five years later, he created a similar setting in *Portrait of a Farmer's Wife* (Figure 13), among his most eloquent paintings. An aged woman very much like the woman in *Field Flowers*—perhaps the same woman— is portrayed late in her life. A thinly leaved and flowered potted plant has replaced the bouquet of the earlier work. The elderly woman's strong hands and face have become wrinkled over the years, and shoes now protect her feet. The heart-shaped wicker with wooden cross stick may symbolize her sadness at losing family and friends over the years.

"I know this farmer's wife; I know her husband, her children and her children's children. I know the relatives who have moved to the city," observed Gwathmey. "*Portrait of a Farmer's Wife* is my response to a lady of character who has borne the scars of outrageous circumstance and has refused to be destroyed."[8] Here is the anonymous heroine in her penultimate days, remembering what she and others have done. Through the years she has worked and endured. Just as certainly as the other heroes of history, she has inspired others by example. Not knowing her name, we frequently have neglected her heroism. Because her life was not documented, we often have forgotten her and others like her. By helping us visualize these anonymous women in their many roles, Gwathmey invites us to examines their lives. No less than the work of novelists and historians calling attention to black women, his art requires us finally to give these forgotten heroines their due.

Figure 11. *Children Dancing*, Robert Gwathmey, oil on canvas, 32" x 40", The Butler Institute of American Art, Youngstown, Ohio.

Figure 12. *Field Flowers*, 1946. Robert Gwathmey, oil on canvas, 37 1/2" x 25 3/4" Collection of Whitney Museum of American Art, New York; Gift of Mr. and Mrs. Sidney Elliott Cohn, 56.34.

Figure 13. *Portrait of a Farmer's Wife*, Robert Gwathmey, oil on canvas, 44 1/4" x 34", Hirshhorn Museum and Sculpture Garden, Smithsonian Institution; Gift of Joseph H. Hirshhorn, 1966.

Notes

[1]Alice Walker, *The Color Purple: A Novel* (New York, 1982).

[2]Jacqueline Jones, *Labor of Love, Labor of Sorrow: Black Women, Work, and the Family from Slavery to the Present* (New York, 1985).

[3]Sidney Hook, *The Hero in History: A Study in Limitation and Possibility* (New York, 1943).

[4]*Anonymous Was a Woman*, comp. Mirra Bank (New York, 1979).

[5]Richard Hofstadter, *The Age of Reform: From Bryan to F.D.R.* (New York, 1955), pp. 23-36.

[6]Robert Gwathmey Interview with Paul Cummings, March 5, 1968, Typed Transcript, Archives of American Art, Washington, D.C., p. 8.

[7]See Richard L. Perry, "The Front Porch as Stage and Symbol in the Deep South," *Journal of American Culture*, 8 (Summer 1985), pp. 13-18.

[8]*Contemporary American Painting and Sculpture* (Urbana, Ill., 1953), p. 186; *The Hirshhorn Museum and Sculpture Garden*, ed. Abram Lerner (New York, 1974), p. 699.

Soap Opera Heroines:
Helen Trent's Legacy

Suzanne Frentz

"Time now for *The Romance of Helen Trent*...the real-life drama of Helen Trent, who—when life mocks her, breaks her hopes, dashes her against the rocks of despair—fights back bravely, successfully, to prove what so many women long to prove in their own lives: that because a woman is 35, and more, romance in life need not be over; that the romance of youth can extend into middle life, and even beyond..."

From 1933 to 1960, the voice of Fielden Farrington with a banjo and the humming of "Juanita" in the background intoned the above words as he introduced one of the hundreds of heroines audiences have come to know and love since the birth of soap opera in 1926. As serialized, daytime dramas broadcast first on radio and since 1956 on television Monday through Friday 52 weeks a year, soap operas provide a clear promise to continue for as long as mass mediated entertainment exists. Over the last sixty years, billions have happily suffered along with soap opera's gallant women of the afternoon. And, all this time, audiences, advertisers, executives, researchers, and critics of all sorts have wondered why.

A growing body of scholarly literature exists now to provide insights and suggest answers to the question of why so many continually return to the routine tragedies of daytime drama. An examination of the evolution of soap opera as a broadcast programming genre, in general, and its heroines, in particular, reveals that both have become as complex as the lives they imitate and the medium which delivers them. An exploration of some of the elements in this equation will, I hope, lead to a deeper understanding of drama serial heroines and ourselves.

Roots

A consideration of the contemporary soap opera heroine's gene pool supplies a solid foundation for anchoring archetypcal characteristics. The roots of her family tree untangle in the symbols of relationships

149

and activities etched on prehistoric cave walls. Likewise, Egyptian tomb art and artifacts reveal the importance of the female and the family theme in storytelling. The family continues as a central storyline in Greek mythology and the Greek dramatists' awareness of universal fascination with interpersonal relationships exists in the plays of Aeschylus, Sophocles, and especially Euripides who was renowned for his portrayal of women in the grip of powerful emotion.

While women characters rarely appear in the miracle and morality dramas of the middle ages, the idea that soap operas are modern morality plays deserves attention. Just as "Everyman" serves as an heroic model for later dramatists, the soap opera heroine is similar to an allegorical figure, an "Everywoman."

If Sophocles' Clytemnestra reigns as the first anti-heroine, then Shakespear's Lady MacBeth's confirms the notion that audiences "love to hate" a good villainess. Elizabethan dramatic literature also testifies to the popularity of themes of crime, adventure, romance and power. Charles Dickens, of course, earns the credit of "first" serial writer. It seems important that many of his novels initially appeared in installments in a medium of the masses, the newspaper.

Some studies point out similarities in the area of content between the soap opera and the domestic novel (Stedman, 1977; Weibel, 1977). The English sentimental novel (Keeler, 1980) is also cited as a form containing similar content. Finally, the melodrama gives the soap opera some of its form. The lack of a single, dominate point-of-view in melodrama is found in soap opera's propensity for providing for multiple identification. Soap opera is unique, however, and thus so are its heroines, in that it is the creation of dramatists of a broadcast medium, radio and remains the product of a broadcast medium, television.

Radio

While the history of radio is rich with inventions and events which led to the establishment of this medium of mass communication, the years between the Radio Law of 1912 and the Radio Act of 1927 stand out as most significant. The former act allowed the Department of Commerce to license experimental radio stations and the latter created the Federal Radio Commission. In those twelve years, varying means of support were explored and the commercial basis for radio was firmly established. By 1930, national radio networks organized for profit provided sponsors with a clear signal and large audiences.

Since radio stations and networks supplied only the technical facilities to transmit messages, it was up to the sponsor who bought the air time to fill it. Advertising agencies took over the work of writing the programming as well as the commercial messages for the sponsors.

Even in radio's infancy, advertisers knew they needed to target their persuasion for an audience of women between 18 and 45. At first, sponsors were reluctant to create programming for women during the day but were lured to it by the discounts offered. Manufacturers of products used by women, especially soap and hence the term "soap opera", purchased hour blocks of time and assigned quarters to one particular brand.

Amos and Andy, the first radio serial, aired in 1929 and was broadcast in fifteen minute installments six nights a week. More evening serials followed and soon some were moved to the daytime. Serialized daytime drama was a hit and began multiplying immediately. At their peak in 1940 there were 64 on the air in one day (Cantor and Pingree, 1983:30).

Given radio soap opera's commercial purpose and success, the reasons for it's enormous popularity become even more fascinating. R.W. Stedman (1959:58) delineated three types of radio soap opera stories: (1) the woman alone, (2) problems of marriage, and (3) the family.

Fortunately, for researchers who are just too young to remember anything of radio soap opera except that at a certain time in the day organ music cued a serene expression and far-away look in their mother's eyes, many wonderful volumes exist which capture not only the flavor of the stories but give us hard clues to the heroines' characteristics.

Speculation seems to be non-existent as to why the "woman alone" story dominated radio soaplines. Perhaps, writers at that time felt only an unattached woman was believably free enough to have the sort of adventures these heroines did. One of the most famous and enduring creations of the Hummerts was *The Romance of Helen Trent* which was aired originally during the depths of the Great Depression on CBS on October 30, 1933.

In *Tune in Yesterday*, John Dunning describes the show as "developed as an endless struggle between Good and Evil, an audio simmering pot of primitive emotion, seasoned heavily with unrequited love, murder, tears, and madness, served up daily in 15-minute doses." (1976: 519) Recall the words of the announcer who every weekday for 27 years reminded the audience of what life had done to the heroine-mocked, broken and dashed her! But what did Helen Trent do? Fought back! How? Bravely! Why? To prove that just because a woman is 35, or more, romance in life need not be over! What follows is an example of how the audience was prepared to join Helen's battle:

Glamourous Helen Trent faces a desperate crisis in her deep love for the brilliant, handsome lawyer Gil Whitney. For within 48 hours, a beautiful but evil adventuress Fey Granville is announcing her intention of marrying Gil. As we heard Helen say: "Fay Granville has caught Gil in a trap. She pretended to be a secretary and Gil gave her a job. She pretended to be alone and penniless, and Gil showed her sympathy.

He even took her out! And now Fay is claiming that Gil proposed to her, and she's threatening Gil with a scandal. There's only one way to stop Fay Granville! That is to find some proof of her notorious past—to find someone who knows who Fay Granville really is—if it's not too late." (1976: 519)

Dunning tells us that what Helen really wanted was marriage, children, and a home.

She was absolutely pure, nobly selfless, refusing to stoop to the tactics of her enemies until the last days of her run, when her purity became slightly ridiculous even to her loyal following. She never smoked or drank and seldom allowed herself even a minor show of temper. Only evil women like Helen's arch-rival, the insidious gossip columnist Daisy Parker, did those things. Housewives who went through three packs a day accepted that a woman who smoked or drank on *Helen Trent* was of questionable moral character. (1976: 521)

The Young Widder Brown challenged *The Romance of Helen Trent* and *Stella Dallas* in the area of melodrama and agony. It came to NBC September 26, 1938, the story of "a woman as real as her friends who listen to her—the dramatic story of a very human mother's duty to her children, in conflict with the dictates of her heart." Later the story became one of "attractive Ellen Brown, with two fatherless children to support— the story of the age-old conflict between a mother's duty and a woman's heart."

Ma Perkins brought to listeners from coast-to-coast, Canada, Hawaii, and Europe Oxydol's "mother of the air."

Among the great homespun philosophers of old-time radio, none is remembered with more affection and pathos than Ma Perkins. Flowing into kitchens each afternoon to a slight variation of "My Old Kentucky Home," Ma Perkins was one of radio's most important daytime serials, spanning almost the entire life of network broadcasting, (Dunning, 1976: 383)

The story followed the life of a widow who managed a lumber yard. Ma Perkins' character was drawn as tough but "with a heart of gold." One of radio's great commoners, Ma lived by the Golden Rule and always made time for others' problems. The show's writers became part of the "war effort" as did many other serials' writers. After son John was killed in World War II, and was buried "somewhere in Germany, in an unmarked grave", Ma became an effective spokesperson for the government.

The radio soap opera heroine set the thematic patterns which we see today in televised soaps but stylistically she was not quite the "Everywoman" mentioned earlier. Radio's women of courage were styled melodramatically whereas television, a more intimate medium, encourages more realism and subtly. Indeed, the soap opera heroine has changed as she has moved through time, slowly, patiently, from one medium to another. Ironically, after 40 years the heroine of daytime serials was forced to leave the medium which created her for the same reason she was conceived. By 1962 radio broadcasters could make more money by selling time locally for less expensive programming. Thus, heroines brought their continuous trek of goodness before the eyes of masses as well as their ears.

Television

Indeed, it is definitely the case with soap opera, as Marshall McLuhan said, that the old medium became the content of the new medium. From 1956 to 1962, whole serials moved usually intact from one medium to another. Some were even simulcast. Muriel Cantor and Suzanne Pingree in *The Soap Opera* give us a thorough discussion of the only soap opera to have made the transition from radio to television which is still on the air today, Irna Phillips' creation, *The Guiding Light*.

In keeping with the demands of the new medium and a new era in American society, the soap opera heroine evolved magnificently to accommodate new needs. By 1974, Mildred Downing determined that the soap opera heroine had become more identifiable:

The woman of the daytime television serial drama is strong, warm, and fallible— a more believable human being than her counterpart in many other forms of television entertainment. She is, to begin with, more adequately represented, the proportion of females equaling that of males, compared to the four-to-one ratio in favor of men in prime time drama. (130)

Interestingly, Downing entitled her study "Heroine of the Daytime Serial" and although while not stating it, she seems to mean for the word "heroine" to include all female characters in soap opera or, at least, the 300 episodes of the 15 serials monitored in the summer of 1973.

If one asks soap opera writers, this writer included, if they write for a particular audience, i.e. women, the reply will be a resounding "no" with variations on the theme of "we just try to write good stories." While it is well documented that the largest percentage of the daytime serial drama audience is women of childbearing age, it is also known that men, and elderly and college age people of both sexes represent significant portions of the audience numbers. Nevertheless, when one considers the form and structure of soap opera it appears that they are more feminine than masculine which is significantly different from saying they are written for one sex or the other.

Part of the reason that soap opera's form fascinates audiences is because it defies Aristotle's mandate that drama should have a beginning, a middle, and end in its imitation of life. With soap opera there is no beginning, no end, just infinite middle.

Tania Modlesky in "The Search for Tomorrow in Today's Soap Opera" posits the notion that daytime drama is an uniquely feminine narrative form. She suggests that audiences tune in, not to find out the answers to the questions posed previously, but to see what further complications will defer the resolutions and create new questions.

Thus, the narrative, by placing ever more complex obstacles between desire and its fulfillment, makes anticipation of an end an end in itself. Soap Operas invest exquisite pleasure in the central condition of a woman's life: waiting—whether for her phone to ring, for the baby to take its nap, or for the family to be reunited shortly after the day's final soap opera has left *its* family still struggling against dissolution. (1979: 12)

Just as Modlesky suggests the woman in the audience's central condition is waiting, the same may be said of the heroine on the screen who waits for the good to be rewarded and the wicked to be punished. And, because of the inherent continuous element of this form, the viewer and the heroine are patient. They know that just as in life these things are accomplished over time and in bits and pieces. Why? Because there are many players "strutting and fretting" their hours upon the stage. In other forms of drama, we are given one protagonist, one point-of-view with which to identify. One ego, which Modlesky and others point out is more powerful, more male in orientation than the multiple points-of-view the soap spectator is asked to absorb. This diffusion of power, then fits understandably then into a "female" frame of reference.

Instead of giving us one "powerful ideal ego...who can make things happen and control events better than the subject/spectator can," soaps present us with numerous limited egos, each in conflict with one another and continually thwarted in its attempts to "control events" because of inadequate knowledge of other peoples' plans, motivations, and schemes. (1979: 14)

With multiple identification an important operative in soap opera viewing, the popularity of the anti-heroine becomes even more interesting. Of course on a practical level, it would be difficult for a heroine to represent the forces of "good" if there were no forces of "evil." In the days of melodrama, we had the villain in the form of the landlord demanding the rent, or tieing the heroine to the railroad tracks. And, on radio soaps villains were more sharply drawn. After sixty years though, the men and women of soap opera have evolved into multi-dimensional, well-developed characters.

Granted, there are characters who are consistently depicted as more bad than good or "in trouble" more than they are out of it. But, no central character is always written negatively. This is not to say that at any point in time one would have trouble locating a villainess or two busily manipulating her children, meddling in the lives of others, or destroying another woman's marriage.

Today's soap operas have developed the character of the villianess so deftly that the negative self admires and identifies with her.

...the villainess seizes those aspects of a woman's life which normally render her most helpless and tries to turn them into weapons for manipulating other characters....far from allowing her children to rule her life, she often uses them in order to further her own ambitions. (Modlesky, 1979: 14)

Viewers of *The Young and the Restless* at this writing find themselves faced with an interesting dilemma. Kay Chancellor and Jill Foster Abbott who have been vying for the title of "Queen Villainess" for the last fifteen years are involved in a custody battle over Jill's son Phillip whose father was Kay's dead husband. Phillip, Sr. married Jill on his death bed after a drunken, devastated Kay drove him off a cliff on the way home from the airport because he told her he had just obtained a Mexican divorce. Both Kay and Jill have done so many "bad" things to each other and others that one might wonder with whom the viewers sympathies lie. Of course, the answer is complex. It is neither villianess for the viewer's "good" self and both for the viewer's "negative" or controlling self. Or, on a more conscious level, just the next complication of seeing who will out manipulate whom holds the interest of the audience in the story. Another part of this answer may rest in the propensity of the viewer to look for "good" in a character just as she would in a person in real life. In which case, the audience can consciously identify with Kay, at least for the moment, because she gave Phillip a home and the love his mother did not when she sent him away to boarding school because he might have hampered her desired lifestyle and plans surrounding John Abbot.

Pingree and Cantor tell us that characters on soap operas are easily identifiable as good or bad.

Good characters are family-oriented and hold in check their ambitions and selfish desires. Work, although becoming more important than it has been in the past, is secondary to family ties. Only bad characters are openly seductive and aggressive in their careers. (1983;22)

But they fail to mention that because of the continuous nature of the soap opera and it's ability to dole out rewards and punishment over time that it's possible for a bad character to become easily indentifiable as good, also. The viewer who has been away from a serial for awhile may wonder about the seemingly radical reformation of a bad character when the regular viewer will have seen a gradual change and can usually point to at least one motivating event.

Again, Kay Chancellor, on *The Young and the Restless* functions as an example. At the core of Kay's character is her vulnerability. She is older, a recovering alcoholic, a former smoker, admittedly lonely, a woman with weaknesses. Kay has money but no love, power but no happiness. The audience can easily function as Kay's "ideal" mother. We know her so well and have for so long that even when she does something terribly wrong, we understand. So when Kay bought the pictures of Jill making love with her husbands's son that "one night" they were trapped in a cabin during a blizzard so Kay could ruin Jill's happy marriage, we were glad. Kay was in control and Jill who was flaunting her money and power was going to suffer for her "sins."

As the villianess or "bitch" has gained prominence on soap operas, the truly "good mothers" have all but disappeared. They have not died and they are still on cast lists but we rarely see them. Liz Foster on *The Young and the Restless* has always been written as a "Ma Perkins" type character listening, advising, worrying and never doing anything wrong herself. Jennifer Brooks was Liz's upscale counterpart only she did have a "one-night stand" of which her oldest daughter was the result. Paul's mother, Mary Williams has been seen only rarely for years. The fact that these near-perfect "good mothers" have drifted off marks the end of one-dimensional heroines. It is not a coincidence that at the same time it marks the end of the "housewife heroine" era in soap opera, also. Just as life is more complex so are soap opera heroines.

The writers, the soap opera itself, the ratings, the audience, the network, the sponsors—all these complex factors bonded by the goal of commercial gain form a story telling gestalt that has been entrenched in America culture for the last 60 years. Soap opera heroines have values which are identical to those held by the mass audience. Soap operas entertain American society with stories which reflect American contemporary values. Values come into play as a heroine responds to conflict. Just as in life, a character is not going to behave in a manner which is going to differ from the value system of the audience being entertained by that heroine and her value system. Martin Esslin discusses this mirrored reality in *The Age of Television*.

The feedback process is one of infinite complexity: social, economic, and cultural developments create needs that find expression in the utterances of certain opinion-forming individuals; these expressions find an echo, a confirmation, in the reaction of other individuals who may have been slower to respond to the same set of circumstances. Multiplied on the mass medium of television as well as by other means, these attitudes then reinforce the initial reaction of still other individuals and gradually mold the behavior of the masses. The process is a dynamic one. (1982;45)

Television has changed our lives. It stands to reason that the lives we see reflected on it should also be changed. Our soap opera heroines have left the simpler, purer life of the golden days of radio drama behind. But Helen Trent's courage and stamina live on in television's soap opera heroines who face the same challenges in relationships and families. As we watch electronic images flicker across the screen and wait for "Everywoman" to react to them, for us it seems that Gertrude Stein made a lot of sense when she told those Oxford students, "Everything is the same and everything is different."

Notes

Cantor, M. and Pingree, S. (1983) *The Soap Opera*. Beverly Hills. Sage.

Downing, Mildred (1974) Journal of Communication "Heroine of the Daytime Serial", pp 130-137.

Dunning, John (1976) *Tune in Yesterday*. Englewood Cliffs. Prentice-Hall, Inc.

Esslin, Martin (1982) *The Age of Television.* San Francisco. W.H. Freeman and Company.

Keeler, J. (1980) "Soaps: counterpart to the 19th century's quasi-moral novel." New York Times, March 16, p. 34

Modlesky, Tania (1979) *Film Quarterly* "The Search for Tomorrow in Today's Soap Opera", pp. 12-21.

Stedman, R.W. (1977) *The Serials: Suspense and Drama by Installments.* Norman: University of Oklahoma Press

_____ (1959) "A history of the broadcasting of daytime serial dramas in the United States." Ph.D dissertation, University of Southern California.

Weibel, Kathryn (1977) *Mirror, Mirror: Images of Women Reflected in Popular Culture.* New York. Anchor.

Lady as Tiger:
The Female Hero in Rock

Frank W. Oglesbee

In the work of each performer, there is an attempt to create oneself, to make a new man out of what is inherited and what is imagined.

—Greil Marcus[1]

It seems a basic urge in Western man to change and reshape things, and this is reflected in the history of his music.

—Haam *et al*[2]

Take a look around...there's a woman right next to you.

—Annie Lennox[3]

The Rock Rebellion: "Girls, Stay Back; Boys, Come Ahead"

Rock Music, the contemporary complex arising from both rural (folk and country-western) and urban (rhythm-and-blues, and soul) roots, with its own branches and blossoms, is praised by some and damned by others, often because of different interpretations of the same perceived characteristics. It is a constant musical rebellion (freedom? license?). It is disconcerningly sexual in its lyrics, rhythm, and performers (honest expression? shallow exhibitionism?). It mocks all traditional values (are they all above criticism? is this the way to change things?)

It is the thesis of this essay that to the extent that rock has been a rebellion, that rebellion has been curiously repressive. Whether freedom, license, expression, mockery, or whatever, it has been primarily the province of males; they wrote it, they played it, they sang it, they dressed in strange costume and hairstyle to do so. The open sexuality celebrated in rock has generally been the same old irresponsible sexuality of the roving male. The liberated female in rock lyrics is the one free to say yes. The unliberated female in rock lyrics is the dependent, subordinate character. The "girl groups" of the 50s and early 60s reflect this as surely as the men (even more so in their costuming and delivery), singing songs of dependence on their boyfriends. They expressed desire a bit more openly than in mass-distributed songs of the 30s and 40s, but their longing was still comparatively restrained, and their position inferior.

However, beginning in the mid-1970s, and increasing noticeably in the 1980s, rock has been invaded by its own band of rebels, in the persons of women: women who write most of their music, choose the rest, play "masculine" instruments (drums and electric guitar), work in women groups, or lead a male band, or are equal to male partners. They sing of independence and interdependence. In short, they are popular culture heroes, not heroines, and their appearance is a welcome popular culture icon of progress.

To show how this has developed so far, the remainder of the essay will discuss the concept of the female hero, trace briefly some antecedents of rock, describe the male domination of rock, and show, by examples of a few selected women, how this is changing. That it is not possible, in 1986, to cover every female rock hero in a chapter-length essay, while it would have been in 1976, is one indication of the change.

Heroes and Heroines

Traditionally the hero is a male central character and the heroine a female central character, each representing Good. Classically, Comic heroes succeed in their struggles, Tragic ones fail. Why argue for female heroes, not contemporary heroines, in rock (among all places in popular culture)? Because more than gender separates the ideas. The hero succeeds or fails, taking the heroine with him, or leaving her to a tragic fate. The hero has been the active, assertive male; the heroine has been "the prize to be won, the maiden in distress."[4] If not a maiden in the sexual sense, then one in the helpless sense, as blatantly evidenced by the heroine of most nineteenth-century melodrama, fainting at dramatically opportune moments, when not tied to the railroad tracks or the sawmill. Even if an active character, occasionally given to daring deeds, she does so to restore balance in the established order: she pleads for her falsely-accused lover/husband/father, seeks help to regain her rightful throne— in short is the conscience behind the hero's sword, a moral shield against the villain's devices.

However, the nineteenth-century heroine also adopts some masculine characteristics, such as male costume. Within the dramatic act, this is usually for concealment or protection, and gives the disguised female some male mobility. It also gives the audience some excitement, since a woman is playing the part.[5] However unintentionally, as the Industrial Revolution, the Westward movement in America (i.e., the USA), and emancipation of slaves move from ideas to manifest practice, popular drama shows some possibilities for women.

Ever since Adah Isaacs Menken shocked society by wearing a flesh-colored bodysuit in a production of *Mazeppa* during the Flash Age of post-Civil War New York, women in leotards—or the equivalent (step-ins for flappers; no bras for 1960s hippies)—have typified freedom from convention.[6]

Part of this freedom lies in taking male action, as in *Fidelio* (trouser parts in opera are an interesting class of female performer freedom), as Leonore adopts male guise and the title role to save her (falsely-imprisoned) husband. However, Leonore/Fidelio still acts under the moral imperatives as described by Brownstein, which require the heroine to be "beautiful and virtuous as real people never are, she is the Ideal incarnate."[7]

Something of this is expected of heroes as well, but they have more latitude and a broader charge. Butler defines the hero as a "paradigm who bears the possibilities of life, courage, love—the commonplaces, the indefinables which themselves define our human lives."[8] Marshall Fishwick builds upon this in presenting heroes as one of his *Seven Pillars of Popular Culture*. Finding new heroes, says Fishwick, is an unending task in popular culture. He sees that these heroes may be men or women, and that in our time, "the heroic proposition is linked to the politics of visibility."[9] Lee Edwards' thesis on female heroes agrees with this, calling heroism "a public drama," but looking at the difference between male and female heroes. The woman hero is "an image of antithesis," whose gender is significant, because she threatens masculine authority and the system it supports, not because she is a she and he is a he, but "because of the positions assigned to men and women in every society our culture has devised."[10] She "forbids the presumption that women are innately selfless, weak, or passive."[11]

By doing so, the female hero, although threatening an established order, expands the essence of heroism and suggests a better order, as the heroic essence is to give "individuals a way to incorporate change into private life, to move with confidence into a newly constituted world."[12]

Therefore, revising the first two quotations under the title, some artists seek to make new women of themselves, inheriting the same broader culture as men, and having as good an imagination; they are acting upon a basic urge of Western woman, reflected in her music. As Lennox' line (from the song "Sisters Are Doing It for Themselves") indicates, the other writers are narrow-sighted; new heroes are here to be seen. This is meant here not only heard—the female musician/writer/singer—but literally seen, as the sudden increase of female heroes in rock coincides with the recent mass media genre of music videos. Female rock heroes predate videos, but visual as well as aural presentation of women (costume, movement, facial expression) who insist on their share of the freer culture is important.

Heroines and heroes occur in other types of music, and as with theatrical melodrama, female heroes arise from the base of heroines who take on heroic characteristics, often those assumed to be male-linked by genetics rather than culture. A brief look at rural (folk, country, western) and urban (blues, soul) modes will illustrate this.

Courage and Cowgirls

Percy Sholes distinguished folk music, from which eventually all forms arise, as that of persons without professional training or education, compared to art music, thus the "culture of the countryside," and "the culture of the city."[13] In practice, of course, people with little or no musical training work within urban culture (when they formed the Beatles, John Lennon and Paul McCartney could not read music), and some "countryside" people have had training, including the first female hero of country-western music. Some people have moved into the mass-media area of rock, a primarily urban sound and philosophy, from more elite training, including Pat Benatar (opera) and Annie Lennox (classical flute). Sholes sees rock as arising from blues, although he does not seem to appreciate the rural influences on what is now largely urban.[14] Irwin Stambler sees the process as more complicated: rhythm-and-blues incorporates country blues and big band sounds, and rock and soul are two main branches of rhythm-and-blues.[15]

Turning to the rural side, country-western implies both the culture of the countryside and the mystique of the American Westward Movement. It also incorporates blues, as evidenced by, *inter alia,* Jimmie Rodgers' twelve Blue Yodels. The urban big band sound was incorporated into western swing, pioneered by—again, *inter alia*—Bob Wills. Wills' best-known song, his band's signature tune, "San Antonio Rose," tells of the man's love for that metaphoric rose, much as does "Yellow Rose of Texas." That is, switching from style to lyrical theme, many country-western songs are sung by men about desirable, subordinate, waiting women. Women country singers still often also sing from that viewpoint, as in Tammy Wynette's "Stand By Your Man" (no matter what).

But the Westward Movement gave popular culture the cowgirl as well as the cowboy. This creature might be suspended, like the cross-dressed heroine of melodrama, between gender traditions, and move to the heroic—an early version of the gender-bender rock performer of the 1970s and 80s. The cowboy is also a gender-bender, as shown by male western heroes and western singers (frequently personified by the same performer, as with Roy Rogers and Gene Autry). The cowgirl wears jeans, or split skirts, with boots and hats like the men, so she can ride astirde, dig in her heels, and face the weather. She may carry a gun, toss a lasso, turn a stampede. Contrariwise, the cowboy hero, besides wearing high-heeled boots, may wear a stunning variety of embroidered silk and satin shirts, and trousers, along with rhinestone-bedecked jackets, all in bright or pastel shades, with no indication that his masculinity is in question.

The cowgirl had not achieved full parity, but was in some ways ahead of the typical heroine of urban music, as the cowboy had costume options the urban worker did not. This was not fully in place of a sexual double standard, but congruent with it. For some years, a female hero was likely to be a persona sung about by a male hero. Gene Autry, for example, although he sang of "Pretty Mary," "Sioux City Sue," and "Mexicali Rose," also celebrated the more vigorous charms of some assertive "mamas," including "High-Powered Mama," "Wildcat Mama," "Pistol-Packin' Mama," and "Bear Cat Mama From Horner's Corner." A specific instance of female hero occurs in Woody Guthrie's "Ranger's Command," in which a young woman, eschewing both benefit of clergy and hope of creature comforts, accompanies her lover on a cattle drive. When rustlers attacked in the night, "she rose from her warm bed, a gun in each hand/saying, come all you cowboys/come and fight for your land."

The female hero personified by an actual female performer in country-western music, however, is exemplified with the arrival of Patsy Montana (born Ruby Blevins in Arkansas). Montana, in a life and career which confound Shole's definitions, was raised in the Ozarks, had academic musical training, changed her name to reflect changed musical interests, and achieved her success as the principal member of an otherwise all-male band, performing on the rurally-oriented *National Barn Dance*, a program broadcast from the decidedly urban Chicago. Further, Montana and her band, the Prairie Ramblers, combined country-western with swing, jazz, or blues as seemed warranted by the song.

By the 1930s the mass production of popular culture, begun with mass printing in a time when music and dramatic performance still were distributed by moving performers from place to place, had achieved mass distribution through records and radio—and sound motion pictures. By the time Montana wrote and recorded her cheerful desire for an equitable relationship, "I Want to Be a Cowboy's Sweetheart," diverse musical styles were easily accessible. Paul Whiteman's big band jazz and swing had been significant in winning station affiliations to the fledgling CBS radio network in the late 1920s. Montana claimed, in "Cowboy Rhythm," to prefer the rhythm of the range to jazz, swing, square dance, or rumba, indicating that the audience had some awareness of these styles—the song itself is a blend of country and swing, musically, with a touch of yodeling in her delivery.

Montana's success with this persona is partly due to its place in the larger culture. By the 1930s not only had women won the right to vote, but more women were working outside the home, going to college, and appearing in other areas of popular culture than before. The cowgirl was joined by the aviatrix, the reporter, the detective, and the business executive in books, plays and films.

This does not detract from the work of Montana, and later women such as Patsy Cline, but it's well to keep in mind the conditions and diversity of media in which popular culture heroes occur.

In recent years, female country heroes include Barbara Mandrell and Juice Newton. Mandrell, who often performs in snug-fitted costumes with antecedents in those favored by some male performers (bodysuits, or as called when worn by women, catsuits), can go beyond Montana's rather chaste cowboy's sweetheart lyrics to complain that she's frustrated from "Sleepin' Single in a Double Bed." Newton tends even more toward the hero, controlling the situation and expressing a healthy sexuality as easily as any male singer. she has, e.g., combined long hair and a very feminine pink lace dress and gloves with a short hemline and black lace tights, moving about the stage as freely as the usually more mobile male—and by playing electric, not acoustic, guitar. Her delivery is also that of the hero, not the put-upon heroine awaiting (emotional) rescue. While her lyrics show she knows she's "Heading for a Heartache," her voice almost celebrates the risk, as she presents a persona whose eyes are open, willing to take a chance, strong enough to prevail. If hurt, she is undefeated, and will just take a brief respite—"Love's Been A Little Bit Hard On Me"—before trying for a better relationship.

Expression of the sexual side of romance is also common in blues, and its more optimistic offshoot, soul, which have also given popular culture a few female heroes, and contributed to rock.

I Had the Blues, Then I Got Soul

Sholes identified blues as a form arising from jazz, characterized by bitter-sweet tones in music and lyrics, usually with a slow pace and flowing style, over a twelve-bar bass; both rhythm-and-blues and rock developed from blues.[16] Stambler, as noted earlier, sees a progression from blues to rhythm-and-blues, whence soul and rock.

Whatever the exact chronology—probably not very exact—blues deals with industrial-strength despair, often, although not exclusively, focused on inter-personal relationships. In "St. Louis Blues," the female persona has lost her man to the duplicitous "Saint Louie Woman." In "St. James Infirmary Blues," the (usually male) persona goes to that place to view the dead body of his loved one. In "Empty Bed Blues," the woman, like the one in Mandrells' song, is sleeping single. She expresses her frustration in lyrics which would not have been allowed in mainstream music, or gotten airplay, a generation ago, referring to her lover's abilities: "he is a deep-sea diver, got a stroke that can't go wrong. You know, he can reach the bottom, and his wind holds out so long."

Female blues heroes are difficult to find, because the genre lends itself so well to heroines (and there should be a male version of heroines, as male personas are also often distraught). Bessie Smith and Ella Fitzgerald seem the likeliest candidates, with long careers, which they did much to run themselves. The comparatively lower visibility of blues singers also limits the available heroes. For example, the vocal and lyrical strength of Janis Ian has been expressed for twenty years in a persistent melancholia. Since 1965, when barely sixteen, and her song about racial prejudice, "Society's Child," Ian has sometimes ventured into a blues-rock musicality, but the unrelenting pessimism of her work has limited her heroism. Even Ian's assertive females, those surviving bad love affairs, or openly expressing sexuality, tend to exemplify the currently popular expression, "life's a bitch and then you die," The heroine of "At Seventeen," who "learned the truth at seventeen/that love was meant for beauty queens," later learns that the beauty queens are not so lucky—but that just means that everybody's miserable. The sexually active heroine of "Boy, I Really Tied One On," waking up in a strange double bed, can say, "allow me the pleasure/of taking your measure/though I'm sure you ain't/nobody's treasure," but there's really no pleasure.

Soul, on the other hand, blends blues problems with gospel hope for a better future, and even finds a happier present.

Ray Charles and James Brown are probably the best-known male soul singers; Aretha Franklin and, to some extent Diana Ross, the best-known females. Ross, who started with the Supremes, one of the few 1960s girls groups without a cute or diminutive name, launched her solo career in 1969, and has moved to a more mainstream sound. Franklin, often referred to as Lady Soul, or the Queen of Soul, has also moved into rock occasionally, and been voted into the Rock Hall of Fame. Both women present strong personas, and both exercise control over their careers. In the 1960s, when most girl groups and girl singers were still pretty little things with prom night heartbreaks, Ross recorded "Lovechild," in which the girl refuses her boyfriend, not wanting to risk pregnancy and the birth of a child who will suffer as she has. Franklin has had an enviable string of successful records, but is particularly identified with "Respect," in which the persona celebrates her individual worth, and insists upon "r-e-s-p-e-c-t!"

Oddly enough, despite these examples, when rock became popular, the female heroes of country and soul seemed to be left in those genres. Rock had commercially successful female performers, but almost no heroes, until the mid-1970s. The folk music revival, which began at about the same time as rock's success, produced Joan Baez and Judy Collins, and Joni Mitchell, who moved into folk-rock and rock as a performer and writer, but rock's women were heroines and often tragic ones at that.

Rock: The Limited Rebellion

That rock music rose in the 1950s is not due solely to its inherent merits. The matter is complex, but among the contributing factors is the increase in media outlets, from less than a thousand radio stations and about a dozen television stations in 1945 to several times that number today. As the number of TV stations increased, TV took over the drama forms radio had used, so that radio expanded its music offerings; the need for programming offered more opportunities for rock (and rhythm-and-blues and other forms) than would have been the case without TV. The population also increased as the economy expanded, resulting in huge numbers of that novelty, the "teenager" with leisure time and money to spend. Rock, in a sense, is a result of the communications revolution, not a cause.

Many rock musicians may see themselves as making social statements, which some undoubtedly do; more may see themselves as being social statements: their music is a form of rebellion. But in a capitalist society, where rock began, a continuing rebellion which seeks profits through record sales and concert grosses depends on disposable money, an infrastructure, and an open society, all of which existed before rock. Typically, some backer, often a record company, puts up money for recording, for publicity, for touring expenses. Publicity is affected in a society by the nature of mass communication, which is more free and competitive in societies with some capitalistic or at least socially liberal, philosophy. In a combination of philosophy and economy, any number of rock hopefuls may try for success, while knocking the system which nurtures them. That that system has flaws and excesses is true, but rock music operates more freely in Western democracies and countries like Japan, which have adopted some similar practices, than anywhere else. Whatever changes, good or bad, that rock may start or encourage, are more likely to be successful under such conditions.

In short, rock constitutes a contemporary institutionalized pressure valve for society, as well as a means of musical expression. The popular culture of many societies contain some such means of release and expression, which also are likely to be used to argue for changes, while supporting the perceived virtues of the society. Rock is neither as radical as some of its proponents think, nor as dangerous as some of its detractors hold (in the main; exceptions always exist). it is, in short, part of society. For example, the early sexism of rock (which has not vanished) and the growing resistance to that, expressed in the persons and works of several women.

The outrageous new form of music in the 1950s was balanced by its gender-specificity. This loud, and to many, disturbing, music, was left to the sex that traditionally could strike out in new and disturbing directions, the male sex.

Recent criticism recognizes this. Bruce Elder denotes rock as "so much the work, language, and culture (as well as the metaphor for sex) of straight, aggressive American males that it's difficult for outsiders to imagine its taking on any other meaning."[17] Simon Frith writes that the world of rock is a man's world. "Women—this is independence, a threat to male art."[18] Frith acknowledges female rock singers of the 1970s, but points out that women are still largely excluded as instrumentalists, producers, or arrangers. Iain Chambers echoes this, and further notes the options of peculiar costuming and sexual aberration have been mostly male, "the wider choices and possibilities—from the macho heavy metal guitar hero through the glitter androgynoid to the gay disco star—stubbornly remained with the boys."[19]

A look at some rock histories is also instructive. In the 1970 *Anatomy of Pop* the ratio of men's to women's names in the index is 157/18; illustrations include twenty-nine pictures of men, three of men and women in bands and four of women performers.[20] Busnar's history of 1950s rock has an index male/female ratio of 566/104.[21] Of the twenty-nine articles in Ben Fong-Torres' 1976 book on contemporary music, one is about a woman, Patti Smith.[22] Carl Belz's 1972 history lists 320 males and male groups to 48 females and female groups.[23] None of forty-two articles in Johnathan Eisner's 1970 history is on a woman or female band.[24] His 1969 book is dedicated to several (male) individuals and bands; he also thanks his (female) secretarial help. Of thirty-eight entries in that book, one (eight pages long) is on a female performer, Janis Joplin; another (sixteen pages) is on groupies.[25] For those unfamiliar with it, "groupies" is the generic, usually derogatory, always condescending term, given to young, usually sexually available, females who cluster about male rock stars. Earlier male performers had female admirers willing to do anything, but rock added mass production and open bragging about the string of easy women. This is the sexually-liberated woman too often associated with the world of rock; as she's allegedly making a free choice, the male has more license and less responsibility than before.

All this does not mean the authors are sexist; there were few women in 1950s and 1960s rock, and fewer made major contributions, or exercised significant power. The books are overlooking some women, but the sexism exercised was successful before the books were written.

Girl Groups

The women in rock in those days, so short a time ago, were pop culture heroines, not heroes. Witness the girl group phenomenon of the time (and briefly, how that has changed today). For a few years, groups of girls appeared, made a few popular records, and faded away. Typically, the groups were assembled by producers, recorded what they were told to, and saw little, if any, of the big money. Their songs tended to be immature glosses on teenage longing, if somewhat more sexual than those of Doris Day or Teresa Brewer. The songs, and the names of the groups reinforce their cute, doll-like status. The Chantels lamented "He's Gone." (When they started the Chantels ranged from thirteen to sixteen years old.) The Shirelles asked, "Will You Love Me Tomorrow?," and longed for their "Soldier Boy." The Marvelettes waited for a boyfriend's letter, "Please, Mr. Postman," and warned other girls, "Don't Mess With Bill." These girls and young women were not all without talent, and the songs were often entertaining, but they're quite limiting.[26] Listening to several today is rather like watching re-runs of *Star Trek* three or four nights in a row, and wondering how it is that the alien women throw off their entire acculturation when Captain Kirk plants a big smack on their lips. If rock's rhythms and lyrics constituted the beginnings of a sexual revolution, it was one in which women were either camp-followers (groupies) or members of a submissive auxiliary (girl groups). The term is now used to refer to new groups of women, but the context is quite different. The Shirelles, the Chiffons, and Martha and the Vandellas have been supplanted by the Bangles, Banarama, and Joan Jett and the Blackhearts. Women are still a minority in rock, but they now include instrumentalists, arrangers, and producers. Their singing, too, has undergone changes. It's quite a jump from the Angels exulting in their little-girl voices, "My Boyfriend's Back," to Joan Jett growling in a powerful but unmistakeably female voice, "I love rock and roll— put another dime in the jukebox, baby."

A current example of sameness and difference is the Bangles, who combine an eclectic variety of sixties musical elements and vocal harmonies with today's performance and lyrics. All four women are instrumentalists, as well as singers and songwriters. They are not a vocal quartet, but a woman band, who have been favorably compared to the Beatles (that may seem sexist, but there is no equivalent female group from the 1960s to compare them to). Vicki Peterson (lead guitar), Susanna

Hoffs (guitar), Debbi Peterson (drums), and Michael Steele (bass), work differently from the first girl groups. Rather than conform to an image and sound and song choice imposed by a producer, they write some of their songs and "Banglecize" the rest. The 60s groups often sang in the persona of a teenager looking for the ideal date. The persona of "Manic Monday" is a working woman who has to get up for more pressing reasons, "But I can't be late/'Cause then I guess I just won't/get paid." Another pressure is her lover's circumstances, "I have to feed both of us/Employment's down." Also, their arrangements sound more like male groups of twenty years ago than the girl groups, prompting one critic to compare them to Buffalo Springfield, "four women have managed to recreate a sound that took six men to originate."[27] Steel, interviewed on a European tour, said, "there is a sort of performing flea aspect to it—Let's go and see those weird girls jump up and down...it seems it's not that usual this side of the pond to have women who can play."[20]

To see how conditions changed to favor groups such as the Bangles, a look at the latter 1960s, when two women in particular hung between hero and tragic heroine, the mid 70s, when a cluster of female rock heroes emerged, and the 80s, when the number suddenly increased, is necessary.

Almost Heroes

Janis Joplin and Grace Slick, of the women in late 1960s rock, had the greatest visibility, and illustrated a change from suffering blues singer and the startling new mode of drug-oriented rock. Joplin was a powerful singer, but her generally morose, suffering persona and her early death from drugs and alcohol makes her a tragic heroine. Some may dispute this, but heroes should provide models, and neither Janis Joplin nor Jimmy Hendrix will do.

Grace Slick comes closer, but the drug songs of the 1960s are an embarrassing part of rock. Slick has also admitted she used drugs and alcohol excessively. She did, however, make a radical move, as a female rock singer who sang with the strength, and about the topics, that men did. Unlike Joplin, Slick was not a strong pleader but a strong demander, "when all the joy within you dies—you better find somebody to love." Slick's lyrics and delivery say to take action, not sit and wait.

While the departure of the girl groups removed one obstacle to women as rock heroes, and Slick began showing how they could be developed, the first British Invasion set women back, as the invaders were almost entirely male: The Beatles, The Rolling Stones, The Dave Clark Five, Gerry and the Pacemakers, Freddy and the Dreamers, The Animals, etc. Many of these were, if not unkind to women, condescending in their lyrics. The Beatles did say "I Want to Hold Your Hand," but also bragged, "Everybody Wants to Be My Baby," and complained about the fickle

"Day Tripper" and the greedy "Girl." The Stones were even more critical of one "Stupid Girl," boasted that another was "Under My Thumb," and sang fondly only of a loved one as dead as the one in St. James Infirmary, in "Paint it Black." Not until the mid-1970s is there the first definite cluster of female rock heroes, or rather, two clusters, one of feminine but independent women, the other of women who look, talk and act like the men.

Female Heroes of the 1970s

The feminine rock heroes of the mid-1970s tend to approach their work from folk-rock, using a softer musical sound than Grace Slick, or the typical male band. Given the dominance of the guitar in folk, they also tend to play guitar, and given a folk tradition of solo performance, they also appear solo, or accompanied by musicians, rather than as a girl singer in a band. Joan Baez, Carole King, Carly Simon, and Joni Mitchell are probably the best-known of these women, writing most of the songs they perform, becoming involved in social movements, and singing about that, as well as love. Mitchell may be the first female rock hero to write about the pressures of the rock business, "Free Man in Paris," not only describing some of the daily frustrations, "I deal with dreamers—and telephone screamers," but casually crossing gender in her lyrics, "I was a free man in Paris." Mitchell was the focus of a 1974 *Time* article on women in rock, which pointed out that the women "pay dearly for success."[29] What may appear to be a sexist passage in the article is no more so than Mark Twain's use of the word "nigger" in *Huckleberry Finn* is racist. The pressures of touring, for example, affect men and women: the travel, the continuous interviews with the same questions, the string of hotel rooms, the crowded tour bus, etc. But the guys are more likely to have other guys around than the gals are to have gals, and men are still freer to move about. Moreover, there are always some people in the crowd who confuse the stage persona with the actual person, and for an attractive female singer this is more of a problem than for the male. This is not right, but *Newsweek* was correct to point out its existence. It may have changed in the twelve years since, but probably not much.

The same problems affect the other cluster of female rockers who started in the 70s, the tough chicks in leather. As Grace Lichtenstein puts it, "since the rock business was also downright contemptuous in the treatment of women as song subjects, groupies, or singers, it did not come as a shock that the most exhibitionistic female performers in the entertainment world should be pop singers."[30]

Given the restrictions of women in rock, such exhibitionism doesn't take much; dressing in a snug leather catsuit or appearing in leotard and tights will do it, even if more female skin can be seen on any beach, or at a tennis match. Context has considerable effect, and neither the girl groups nor the folk-rock heroes had dressed that way.

The first such tough chick was Suzi Quatro, who was born in Detroit, but had less success in the USA than in other countries. She formed Suzi Soul and the Pleasure Seekers, in 1965, but her recording success dates from 1974. Most of her forty-five million record sales were outside the USA, where she is more likely to be remembered as "Leather Tuscadero," on the TV series *Happy Days*. Unlike the girl groups or the folk-rockers, Quatro dressed in leather and chains, played raucous guitar, and sang "Your Mama Won't Like Me," "Heartbreak Hotel," and "I Wanna Be Your Man," crossing gender more disturbingly than Mitchell's "Free Man In Paris."

Working in a similar style, but if anything tougher, Patti Smith is the only woman in Fong-Torres' collection of interviews from the 70s. Smith has been called a "female Mick Jagger," which is supposed to be a compliment, but would Jagger be called a "male Patti Smith?" Coarse material (even in titles, e.g., "Piss Factory"), and lesbian imagery kept her off major record labels and many radio stations. Even her less blatant songs are more assertive than Quatro's, as "I Am the Warrior." She is among the heroes of the 70s because of her determination to try things women had been denied before, and she did so consciously, perceptive of her position: "I'm a girl doing what guys usually did, the way that I look, the goals and things I want to help achieve through rock. It's more heroic and heroic stuff has been traditionally male."[31]

In another interview she summed up her approach:

I have my own way of pursuing things, of focusing my anarchistic spirit into form. It's the long way around, I guess, but I do if. Of course, I must say that I don't opt for beauty.[32]

Shortly after Quatro and Smith started recording albums, Joan Jett, a Quatro fan, formed the all-female band, the Runaways, bringing female instrumentalists into rock. It is more accurate to say back into rock, as Fanny, formed in 1970 had been all women, including Suzi Quatro's sister, Patti, but had broken up. The Runaways' name and their album titles show another distinct break for the 60s girl groups: *Queens of Noise, Waitin' for the Night, Flamin' Schoolgirls*.

When the Runaways disbanded, Jett built a new, male band, the Blackhearts. Their albums include *I Love Rock N Roll* and *Glorious Results of a Misspent Youth*. Much of Jett's original motivation came from anger at people who didn't believe a girl (she was fifteen when the Runaways formed) could rock, and she has turned this into a continuing theme, acting on her version of the carthasis theory of drama. "It's *good* hostility. We get it out, and everybody else gets it out." The sources for specific instances of hostility are identified in terms no 60s girl groupers would have used for publication: "There's never an end of assholes. They're all over the place."[33]

The folk-rockers and the leatherclad rockers were ends of a scale which for a while had no center, but popular culture is constantly seeking an expanded middle. Two bands formed in the 70s, combining more feminine-appearing lead singers with the sharper rock style. Blondie centered on Debbie Harry, an attractive blond woman, who at first seemed to be an older version of the group style, an illusion temporarily supported by her clearly enunciated, often soft voice. But what the voice sang left the 60s groups far behind. "X Offender," changed from "Sex Offender," which the record company felt too blatant for the label, tells of a prostitute who develops a romantic attachment for the officer who arrested her, "We sat in the night/with my hands cuffed." "The Attack of the Giant Ants" was also different: "Giant ants from space/snuff the human race/ Then they eat your face/never leave a trace." And the soft delivery of the groups first hit, "Heart of Glass," makes the lyrics more telling, as the philosophical, yet almost girl-like tones describe a failed romance, "Once I fell in love/and it was a gas/I soon found out/it was a pain in the ass." Nice girls didn't use to sing like that.

The other band, Heart, originally all-male, was re-formed around Ann and Nancy Wilson. The Wilson sisters moved to heroism fairly early, by fighting back against their record company's questionable promotional material. The company, at least according to the Wilsons, started the rumor they were dykes to sell records. It certainly distributed an ad referring to their "first time," supposedly a clever way to publicize the first album. The sisters also took the company to court over the matter of non-payment for two and a half million albums.[34] Most of the lyrics, then and now, are written by the Wilsons, and Nancy plays electric guitar. The group has undergone considerable reorganization in recent years, but has survived, continued to record, and given the brief career of most rock bands, especially those few centered on women, has a remarkable longevity. Ann and Nancy Wilson's early assertiveness over money, over the advertising, over creative control has paid off. They were insistent on not being manipulated for their physical attractiveness; not being among the too many women presented as sexy women, who also sing now and then, rather than as good songwriters and singers, who happen to be women. "The sexy image is flattering and all that junk, but it gets dangerous," Nancy said in 1978.[35]

That same year, Paulette Weiss wrote that if "all goes well," the day will come when a study of women in music "will be about as pertinent as one of vegetarians or short people" in music, "when it comes down to making music, will that really matter?"[36] That day is not here, but it may be getting closer. In 1970, few women worked in rock, fewer were successful, and female rock heroes were nearly non-existent. By 1982, Liz Thompson could put together a book of brief biographies of over seventy women in rock—not all heroes, but more than before.[37] In the few years since, some of these women have faded (as have many men) but others among them have become more prominent, and new women have come on the scene. Indeed, there are now so many, compared to the years before, that they cannot all be covered. What can be covered are three representative samples. Pat Benatar combined her petite physicality, her four-octave voice, and her assertive stance into six platinum albums in a row. Annie Lennox moved from classical flute to writing and singing, and is an equal partner, with Dave Stewart, in Eurythmics. Cyndi Lauper, whose first album "She's So Unusual," seems a fair description, is a recent addition to the female heroes.

Rock 80s: Heroisms All Around Us

Newsweek, some eleven years after *Time's* coverage of Joni Mitchell, summed up the rock experience and change thus:

As one of the most influential strongholds of knee-jerk misogyny, the rock scene has long cried out for women with power, ideas, and an independent sense of style. Now, it seems, they're emerging one after another.[38]

The article also says, "never have so many women with such strong images do dominated the music videos shown on MTV."[39] The video presentation of female, as well as male performers has helped revive the pop music industry, and contributed to the success of the new female heroes of rock. While women are still sexual objects in videos by heavy-metal groups, they are also helped by the TV screen's ability to show emotional intensity and different costuming and attitude. Pat Benatar is among the first women to be so presented.

Pat Benatar

Pat Benatar, born in 1953, had a typical middle-class childhood on Long Island. She married her high school sweetheart and worked as a bank teller. Aware the she had a voice, she tried a job as a singing waitress, then moved to New York and spent three years working for a break, divorced, and changed "from the self-conscious, five foot tall girl with the voice that seemed too big for her into a snarling temptress daring to challenge men on her own terms.''[40]

Her first hit song, "Hit Me With Your Best Shot," exemplifies this. The title is a challenge to a Don Juan, "I understand you got a long history/of breakin' little hearts like the one in me." She has no doubt of the outcome, "another notch in my lipstick case." Visually, Benatar worked between the leather-clad and the girlie singer schools, in leotards and leopard or striped tops, moving athletically across the stage. Early videos for "Promises in the Dark," and "You Better Run" show her in performance in variations on such costuming. The latter song is a warning to a lover who has been untrue, "everything I had was yours/ now I'm closing all the doors." As she said in a 1980 interview, the difference between her style and most female singers was that "they seem to be saying, if you love me and then hurt me, I'll die. I say, if you love me and then hurt me, I'll kick your ass."[41] Most of her work is in this vein, with videos favoring her as the heroic character. "Love Is A Battlefield" characterizes love today as a a rough game, "no promises, no demands, love is a battlefield." In the video, she plays a young woman cast out of her family after an argument, who moves to New York, toughens up, and becomes a taxi dancer (a euphemism) in a sleazy ballroom, and leads the other women in a revolt against their even sleazier male boss. Cut-away scenes show that her family misses her. In the end she heads back home, having won on all fronts. "Shadows of the Night," is a lovesong about a couple who will prevail. In the video, she plays a World War II defense plant worker who dreams of herself as an equal member in a team of saboteurs behind enemy lines. She flies one of the planes, climbs over the wall, and places the bomb with her male companions.

In "Lipstick Lies," she is a contemporary factory worker, who dreams of dining in an elegant restaurant and meeting the ideal man—which she then does. It is apparently a four-minute version of the film *Flashdance*, but the central character doesn't have to flaunt her body to get what she wants. More recently, Benatar has also recorded "Sex As A Weapon," which says sex should not be used that way. The lyrics appear to be addressed to one Other, but the video expands the idea to attack the exploitation of female sexuality to sell products, or women as products. A 1986 interview shows a more thoughtful outlook, as her music changes to include songs about equal relationships ("We Belong"). After six platinum albums, and four Grammy awards for best female rock performance, she now schedules albums to avoid the Grammy award deadlines: "making music is one thing, but having to be a rock and roll star is stupid."[42]

Married again (to Neil Geraldo, her guitarist, songwriting partner and record producer) and with a child to raise, Benatar faces problems that are both gender and culture-related. No matter how equal rights become, it is the women who will get pregnant. And while the concept of maternal instinct has often been interpreted in ways favorable to male mobility and female restriction, a woman in rock has an unenviable choice. If she favors child over career, she may compromise her success. For Benatar, the child and family are important, but she has been able to continue her career; not only does recording help, but thanks to music videos, a woman with a young child can appear in elaborate videos, countering the loss of visibility through touring. This advantage applies to other rock performers as well, of course. For those who have Benatar's outlook, it may be an important advantage. And her outlook surely strikes a chord in many women:

To me the point is to be strong but still be a woman, not to be tough.... I'm not gonna be masculine, and I'm not gonna be a frilly girl who gets what she wants because she's frilly. There's a middle ground, and that's where I want to go.[43]

Another female rock hero has expressed sentiments is Annie Lennox, of Eurythmics, who took a more different approach early in her career, but now is developing the fertile middle ground, visually, and lyrically.

Annie Lennox

First off, Annie Lennox does not like the topic "women in rock." In a 1986 TV interview, she said, "when people ask me to do interviews, and the caption is woman in rock, I have to say, no, I'm not interested in doing interviews like that."[44]

She's also said, "I don't want to be the head of a movement. I don't represent any movements. I'm singing that purely out of my own feeling of satisfaction, my good feeling about women."[45] "That" is the song "Sisters Are Doing It For Themselves," identified in its lyrics as about "the conscious liberation of the female state." Lennox classifies it not as a feminist call to arms, but as "a song for people in a situation like mine, people who now do things through their own assertion, through their own power, that they would never have been able to do before."[46] The song notes formerly male occupations women now hold, but also reminds the audience, "a man still loves a woman, and a woman still loves a man."

The song, among others she has written, and Lennox' own perception of current possibilities, makes it appropriate to put the discussion on her between Benatar, with the erotic spandex catsuits and the kick-your-ass attitudes, and Cyndi Lauper, with the feminine but bizarre costumes and rapid-paced songs arguing for women's right to enjoy themselves and for the right to be different. Also, Lennox works in the most visible equal partnership in rock. While Benatar and Geraldo certainly seem to have an equal partnership, he has not been as visible as Dave Stewart, the other half of Eurythmics, who produces records and videos for other performers. If he had any problems with the spotlight falling on Lennox in 1983-84 when their work became successful, he didn't let them affect the work.

Lennox was born in 1954. The exact year is not too important, but women born between say, 1950-56, were little children when rock became prominent. They were old enough to understand newspaper and TV news as the women's and civil rights movements exploded in the 1960s, along with the British rock invasion. In Lennox's case, this means she was also aware of music coming into Britain which fueled British pop music and resulted in the invasion. Lennox, although fond of popular music, planned a career in classical flute. At seventeen, she was one of two finalists for one performing position at the Royal College of Music; the other finalist was male. She was asked, "wouldn't you rather become a teacher, we think it's more realistic, your being a girl?" She said, "No, I don't want to be a teacher, I want to play the flute."[47] The boy got the place and she went to the Royal Academy of Music in London, but after three years, decided to be a singer and songwriter.

After she and Stewart met they worked in a band called the Tourists, which broke up in 1981; they stayed together and formed Eurythmics, which became successful in 1983 with "Sweet Dreams." In stage appearances, and more importantly in the 1980s, in the music videos, Lennox attracted much attention for her orange crew-cut and for wearing men's clothes. Sometimes she looked disturbingly (to some people) androgynous, other times, as in the video for "Who's That Girl," and in her live appearance at the 1984 Grammy awards show, as a male character. This was partly to make a complete break with the frilly girl blond singer of the Tourists—"I had to get rid of the blond poppy Annie Lennox. The strain was unbearable so I killed her."[48] Another reason was to avoid the sexual comments female singers get all too often (especially in a struggling band, playing less desirable venues) "This is a more androgynous visual portrayal, but it isn't meant to be butch. It is very useful in transcending the bum-and-tits thing, though."[49] At the 1984 Grammy Awards show she responded to press coverage of her masculine appearance, and her own interest in experimenting with costume, by appearing in full male drag as a 1950s rocker. Although this has been covered frequently in print and TV stories about Eurythmics no one has bothered to point out that her appearance complemented the rest of the band, all dressed in styles associated with aspects of American popular music: Stewart in a glitter jacket, a guitarist as a cowboy with sheepskin chaps, backing singers in Motown wigs and dresses. The restrictions associated with the limited radicalism of rock are clearly demonstrated in this response: an opera audience and the opera press would not have made so much of a woman in a trouser part, but commented on how effectively she performed.

The relation between male dress and female strength, between male and female strength, between male and female options has been noted by Lennox, by critics, and for that matter, by Blondie's Debbie Harry. Harry remarked,

basically, I've always felt that I was a woman with a man's brain, a man trapped inside a woman's body. I always had the initiative of a man, but was always treated like some idiotic creature, some buzzy little beauty.[50]

Lennox has commented, "I am very feminine. I'm not gay. But I feel, as a woman, sometimes, very masculine, powerful."[51] Hollander, writing of andrygonous appearance for both male and female performers, says the meaning is still "the male is the primary sex, straightforward, simple and active."[52] Marsh, citing Lennox as a prime example of the independent female singer of the 1980s, categorized her male drag as "a way of highlighting the independence available to Lennox, as a star regardless of gender, and of emphasizing that the basic rock roles remain male-oriented."[53]

In her lyrics, one of Lennox' strongest statements about equal options occurs in "Regrets." The persona ends a relationship with a declaration of mobility formerly associated only with males, usually in folk or country-western songs, "Where I go to, no one knows/Find me where the cold wind blows." This is followed by a statement combining a mystic phrase (also often found in folk song) with an insistence on personal freedom and integrity, "Black is red, and red is white/In this country, I do *what I like*!" The performance features a long passage of variations in pace and inflection of those lines, and concluding with an almost staccato, "That's right, that's right, that's right, that's right!"

Since about August, 1984, Lennox has demonstrated strength without the masculine guise. In the video for "Would I Lie To You? she appears as a club singer who has broken up with her chauvinistic boyfriend. Unlike blues singers of the girls of the 1960s, her delivery is exuberant, celebrating her decision. Her costume is a short, scoop-necked blue dress. The title contrasts the persona's ethos with that of the boyfriend, who is told, "You're the biggest fake/that much is true/Had all I can take/Now I'm leaving you." When he climbs on stage, she pushes him off.

Lennox, in an interview, said "I don't relate to this male macho shit anymore, and that's what the song is really about."[54]

Neither Lennox nor Benatar sing exclusively of women who reject or defeat deceitful men. Both have written and recorded songs dealing with affectionate, but interdependent, equitable relationships. however, to establish female persona independence in rock music, and to gain control over their own careers was important, both for themselves, and for the arrival of the full-fledged female hero in rock.

The third example, Cyndi Lauper, also owes some of her success to the publicity surrounding her unusual visual presentation. Of the three, she is the only one who has characterized herself as a feminist, although her definition of the term is close to their statements about the middle ground, and about people now doing things through their own power.

Cyndi Lauper

I've learned a lot from men. I work in a male field. I've worked with men half my life. I have a power position and I run my life. I have people working with me and for me on it and I have creative control over my career and my work. It's great to have that now. You know why? I had to fight so hard for it.[55]

Lauper's parents divorced when she was five; her mother raised three children alone. By twelve, she was dying her hair and wearing unusual clothes. Later, she tried art school, and started working as a professional, if not successful, singer at twenty. From 1977 until 1983 she worked in numerous local bands, and was part of a group that did manage to record an album. In 1983 she got a recording contract with CBS, resulting in the album *She's So Unusual*, with the hit song and video, "Girls Just Want to Have Fun." Lauper, more consciously feminist than Benatar or Lennox, exercised control over her first video, which she calls "an artist's video, not a video with an artist in it."[56] The song has been misconstrued by some as saying that all girls want is to have fun, but it says that girls, i.e., working women, just want the right to have fun after work, as men do. As a young girl in New York City during the counter-culture of the 1960s, she noticed that "people were supposed to be breaking free. The only people who were not breaking free were women."[57] In the same interview she compared the socialization of men and women, applying management theory to her own work, and to women in general. "Men learn to take the ball and run with it"; a woman may drop it because "she doesn't know that she is being thrown the ball... If any man gets thrown the ball, *he* will run with it. Women have to learn to do the same." And, lastly, "if something was good enough for a man to do, then it was good enough for me to do."[58]

In her case, work, luck and her perception paid off handsomely; her first album sold some five million copies in the USA alone, won five Grammy nominations, and produced four Top 10 singles, a record for one album. The video for "Girls Just Want to Have Fun" clearly shows a difference in visual style from Pat Benatar and Annie Lennox. Benatar favored snug-fitting costumes for her athletic compact body, or overalls or dresses appropriate to the roles played in concept videos. Lennox went from androgyny to a variety of stylish outfits, over her five foot-seven frame (tall for a pop singer). Lauper, a middle-sized woman with a soft round face, featured multi-colored hair (or long on one side, short and shaved into a checkerboard pattern on the other), and clothes that might be called eclectic thrifty-shop chic. In her first video, she wears a forties skirt and a mannish hat, as she dances down the street under the vocal. While setting up a party with other working-class women, she reminds her parents (played by her mother, who is in all her videos, and Captain Lou, a professional wrestler), of their circumstances, "we're not the fortunate ones/and girls just want to have fun." The video culminates in a crowded, exuberant party with people brought in from all over the neighborhood, enjoying themselves with great good nature. As a feminist tract, it is unusually upbeat, while insistent.

The song and video for "She-Bop" celebrate female sexuality in unusual ways. "Bop" is used not only in the sense of having fun, or referring to a form of music, but as a synonym for masturbation, hardly the usual topic of choice for male and female singers aiming at a large audience. Indeed, a diverse sexuality is expressed, beginning with scenes at a drive-in restaurant. People move mechanically in a line, as their processed burgers do; the stagnating industrialization (Chaplin worked it out in more detail in *Modern Times*, but videos have only about four minutes) is countered by a strapping waitress, moving to her own rhythm. Lauper is seen in a 1950s Chevrolet, with the windows steamed, as she sings of her interest in men, although some referred to would not be interested in her: "you can see them every night in their tight blue jeans/ in the pages of a *Blueboy* magazine." Dressed in gold trousers, leather cap, and other colorful attire separating her from the plainly-clad burger eaters she announces she's "lookn' for a new sensation/pickin' up good vibrations," and rides off in a biker's sidecar, pursued by a morals S.W.A.T. team, which takes her to court. There she admits she "can't stop messin' with the danger zone." Visual clues abound: she plays a game of Masterbingo, turns down full service for self-service at a gas station, wears dark glasses. She escapes from the courtroom, and in the closing scene sings and dances in an imitation of Hollywood production numbers. After all, as she notes in the chorus: "I bop, you bop, and he bops/we bop, you bop, and they bop."

In her second album, released in 1986, Lauper showed a more tender aspect (included in the first album with "Time After Time") on "Your True Colors," as a woman telling her lover he doesn't need to hid behind male posturing. "Show your true colors/your true colors are beautiful, like a rainbow. . . . Your true colors are why I love you."

The difference between the persona who points out the near universality of masturbation and the one who asks for true colors is less then might at first appear. The essential appeal is to honesty and equality in sexuality and relationships, which fits into Lauper's concept of feminism, which, like Benatar's middle ground and Lennox' sense of satisfaction, is not simply for women and against men, but for both.

She decries the idea that "a feminist is a wild woman from Borneo with a spear in her hand and a ring through her nose who hates men." A woman "is a sex object when someone else makes her into that object. If a woman feels sexual, she has as much right to being sexual as a man does. . . . You don't have to sell yourself like they do cars. *You don't have to do that.*"[59]

These three women have, in ways similar and different at the same time, shown that women can succeed on their own terms in one of the most blatantly male-oriented fields of pop culture, rock music, which is also the favorite music of most of the young men and women (and boys and girls) today. They, along with others mentioned, and some omitted for space (but including Tina Turner, Sheila E., and Sheena Easton—who changed from a 60s-clone packaged image into a woman running her career), have had to usurp some characteristics associated with males. Their work has also shown the cultural, rather than the genetic nature of such traits as assertiveness, management skills, and sexuality.

Role Models

Would you want your daughter to grow up like that? Not unless you wanted her to use her brains and talent as well as she could. That goes far beyond rock music, but the female rock heroes need not be that specific a role model. Returning to the title, women's roles need not be confined to lady (in the sense of the sweet, deferential heroine) or tiger (in the sense of the tough, but often unpleasant villainess or bitch), but can be both feminine and strong, as men can be masculine and strong without being arrogant, overbearing chauvinists (gentlemen and tigers, perhaps). The search for pop culture heroes is a continuing one, and both men and women should have both men and women to observe in those roles. None of the women, and for that matter, none of the male pop culture heroes of today, is likely to enter the pantheon occupied by Hercules and Ulysses, but most people will not have to break open the western end of the Mediterranean, or lay siege to Troy. Heroes for the commonplace, found in the current commonplace (as, rock and videos) are essential. Benatar, Lennox, and Lauper are three quite suitable examples: they look differently, sing differently, differ in some views. At this writing, Lennox is divorced, Benatar re-married, Lauper engaged—significant in that, again, female heroes need be identical no more than males. (Joan Jett is unmarried; Ann Wilson calls Heart "the most married band in the business"). Female heroes, rather than heroines, are still too rare. Fortunately, this is changing somewhat. In television, strong women are still likely to be the super-bitches of *Dynasty* and *Falcon Crest*, but we have also had Ann Romano of *One Day At A Time* and Clair Huxtable of *The Cosby Show* (the former, a divorcee who works her way to partnership with another woman in their own public relations firm; the latter, a lawyer and mother of five married to her childhood sweetheart).

Much of popular culture is mercurial and uncertain; careers rise and fade quickly sometimes. But one can certainly hope that the female rock hero will survive individual career changes, as it has so far, and be a continuing part of rock music. The folk song, "Jimmy Taylor," describing the aftermath of an incident, runs, "When we reach the spot where the blood was shed/Girls, stay back; boys, come ahead." Whether the girls stay back now is up to them.

Notes

[1]Griel Marcus, *Mystery Train: Images of America in Rock 'n' Roll* (New York: E. P. Dutton, Inc., 1982), p. 7.

[2]Charles Haam, Bruno Nettl, Ronald Byrnside, *Contemporary Music and Music Cultures* (Englewood Cliffs, New Jersey: Prentice-Hall, Inc., 1975), p. 161.

[3]Annie Lennox, "Sisters Are Doin' It for Themselves," *Be Yourself Tonight*, RCA ALJ1-5429, 1985.

[4]Bill Butler, *The Myth of the Hero* (London: Rider and Co., 1979), p. 25.

[5]For a concise discussion of the development of the melodrama heroine, see Gabrielle Hyslop, "Deviant and Dangerous Behavior: Women in Melodrama," *Journal of Popular Culture*, 19, No. 3 (1985), pp. 65-78.

[6]David Black, "Reflections in a Glass Eye," *Harper's* Aug., 1986, p. 73.

[7]Rachel M. Brownstein, *Becoming A Heroine: Reading About Women in Novels* (New York: Viking Press, 1982), p. xxi.

[8]Butler, p. 6.

[9]Marshall W. Fishwick, *Seven Pillars of Popular Culture* (Westport, Connecticut and London: Greenwood Press, 1985), pp. 60-79.

[10]Lee R. Edwards, *Psyche As Hero: Female Heroism and Fictional Form*

(Middletown, Connecticut: Wesleyan University Press, 1984), p. 4.

[11]Edwards, p. 5.

[12]Edwards, p. 4.

[13]Percy A. Sholes, *The Oxford Companion to Music*, 10 ed. (London: Oxford University Press, 1970), p. 368.

[14]Sholes, p. 368.

[15]Irwin Stambler, *Encyclopedia of Pop, Rock, and Soul* (New York: St. Martin's Press, 1974), pp. 1-5.

[16]Sholes, p. 368.

[17]Bruce Elder, "Born to Rock," *Village Voice*, 26 Feb., 1985, p. 74.

[18]Simon Frith, *Sound Effects: Youth, Leisure, and the Politics of Rock'n' Roll* (New York: Pantheon Books, 1981), p. 87.

[19]Iain Chambers, *Urban Rhythms: Pop Music and Popular Culture* (New York: St. Martin's Press, 1985), p. 128.

[20]Peter Cole, Meirion Bowen, Ray Connolly, Richard Mabey, Richard Gilbert, Jeff Nuttal, *Anatomy of Pop* (London, BBC, 1970).

[21]Gene Busnar, *Let's Rock'n' Roll: A Musical History of the Fabulous Fifties* (New York: Julian Messner, 1979).

[22]Ben Fong-Torres, ed., *What's That Sound?: Readings in Contemporary Music* (New York: Doubleday Anchor Press, 1976).

[23]Carl Belz, *The Story of Rock*, 2nd ed (New York: Oxford University Press, 1972).

[24]Johnathan Eisner, ed., *The Age of Rock 2* (New York: Random House, 1970).

[25]Eisner, ed., *The Age of Rock: Sounds of the American Culture Revolution* (New York: Random House, 1969).

[26]See Alan Betrock's *Girl Groups: The Story of a Sound* (New York: Delilah Books, 1982), and Robert Santelli, "The Girl Groups," *Sixties Rock: A Listener's Guide* (Chicago: Contemporary Books, 1985), pp. 49-63.

[27]Bruce Kaplan, "Reviews—The Bangles," *Music Connection*, Aug. 16-29, 1984, p. 32.

[28]Adam Sweeting, "Americans in Paris," *Melody Maker*, 2 Mar., 1985, pp. 20-21.

[29]"Rock'n' Roll's Leading Lady," *Time*, 16 Dec., 1974, p. 66.

[30]Grace Lichenstein, *Women and Daring* (New York: Doubleday and Co., 1981), p. 263.

[31]Dave Marsh, "Patti Smith: Her Horses Got Wings, They Can Fly," in Fong-Torres, p. 246.

[32]Steve Simels, "Patti Smith," *Stereo Review*, August 1978, p. 80.

[33]Karen Schlosberg, "Good Hostility," *Rock*, Oct., 1985, n. p.

[34]Patrick MacDonald, "Heart: The Hassles Paid Off," *High Fidelity*, Feb., 1978, p. 108, and Air-Wreck Genheimer, "What Makes Heart Beat," *Creem: Heavy Metal*, Summer, 1981, p. 38.

[35]MacDonald, p. 107.

[36]Paulette Weiss, "The Pop Beat: Women in Music," *Stereo Review*, Oct., 1978, p. 72.

[37]Liz Thompson, *New Women in Rock* (London: Omnibus Press, 1982).

[38]Jim Miller, "Rock's New Women," *Newsweek*, 4 Mar., 1985, p. 48.

[39]Miller, p. 48.

[40]Drew Moseley, "Acts of the Year: Pat Benatar," *The Rock Yearbook 1982*, Al

Clark, ed. (New York: St. Martin's Press, 1981), p. 115.

[41]Pamela Brandt, "The New Woman Sound Hits the Charts," *Ms.*, Sept., 1980, p. 88.

[42]Paul Grein, "Benatar's Music, Image in Transition," *Billboard*, 11 Jan., 1986, p. 50.

[43]Steve Pond, "Pat Benatar," *Rolling Stone*, 16 Oct., 1980, p. 15.

[44]*Today*, National Broadcasting Company, 1 Aug., 1986.

[45]"The Ministry of Truth," Melody Maker, 4 May, 1985, p. 29.

[46]Simon Garfield, "Who's That Girl?" *Spin*, Aug., 1985, p. 46.

[47]"The Face Interview: Annie Lennox," *The Face*, Jan., 1985, p. 27.

[48]*Melody Maker*, 11 Feb., 1984, n. p.

[49]Kurt Loder, "Eurythmics: Sweet Dreams Come True," *Rolling Stone*, 29 Sept., 1983, p. 22.

[50]"Quotes of the Year," *Rock Yearbook 1982*, p. 192.

[51]Barry Sherman, "Eurythmics," *Boston Rock,* Aug., 1983, p. 14.

[52]Anne Hollander, "Dressed to Thrill," *New Republic*, 25 Jan., 1985, p. 32.

[53]Dave Marsh, *The First Rock and Roll Confidential Report* (New York: Pantheon Books, 1985), p. 160.

[54]"Ministry of Truth," p. 29.

[55]Gael Love and Glenn O'Brien, "Cyndi Lauper," *Interview*, April, 1986, p. 100.

[56]David Frankel, "Funny Girl," *New York*, 26 Dec., 1983-2 Jan., 1984, p. 113.

[57]Margy Rochlin, "Cyndi Lauper," *Ms.*, Oct., 1984, p. 73.

[58]Rochlin, p. 75.

[59]Love and O'Brien, pp. 98-99.

Contributors

Elizabeth Bell teaches at the University of South Carolina at Aiken. She has published articles on composition as well as literature and is the editor of a collection of essays by Kay Boyle.

Valerie Broege teaches Humanities at Vanier College in Montreal, where she is Coordinator of the Department. She has published articles and book reviews in the areas of Classical Studies, Canadian Studies, Women's Studies, science fiction, and Jungian literary criticism. Currently she is a member of the Planning Committee of the C.G. Jung Society in Montreal and is in training to be a psychosynthesis practitioner.

Pat Browne, editor and business manager of the Bowling Green State University Popular Press, is the editor of *Clues, A Journal of Detection.* She is also co-editor of *Dimensions of Detective Fiction.* She has been involved with the Popular Culture Association since its inception and presently serves as the annual conference coordinator. She is co-editor of a forthcoming volume on women's domestic culture.

Diane M. Calhoun-French is Associate Director of Jefferson Community College in Louisville, Kentucky. Her research interests in the area of popular culture include contemporary romance fiction, inspirational Christian romances, daytime serials, and the application of popular culture studies to serious literature.

Mara E. Donaldson is Assistant Professor of religion at Lafayette College in Easton, PA. The present essay is part of a larger project, "Theology Beyond Narcissism and Altruism: Women's Fiction and the Problem of Self-Affirmation."

Ann E. Egenriether is completing her Masters degree in English at St. Louis University in anticipation of beginning studies on a Ph.D. to prepare for a teaching career. "Scarlett O'Hara: A Paradox in Pantalettes" is Ann's first published piece and represents a years' long fascination with Scarlett and *Gone With The Wind.*

Suzanne Frentz is an Assistant Professor of Speech Communication and the director of the center for the study of Serial Drama at Wichita State University in Wichita, Kansas.

Anne K. Kaler is a professor of English, specializing in Mythology, Women Writers, Shakespeare and Speech, at Gwynedd Mercy College. She has published academic articles and poetry and has delivered many papers at professional conventions. As a fiction writer, she is concentrating on why romance, fantasy, drama, and mystery have the same basic appeal and is currently writing a novel and a juvenile novel.

JoAnna Stephens Mink is an Assistant Professor and Director of Writing Programs at Atlantic Christian College. She has presented papers and published articles on nineteenth-century fiction and authors, as well as on the composing process. She is interested in the changing role of women in the nineteenth century, and her current projects include books on the significance of birth order and of widowhood in literature and a writing center tutor training manual.

Gwendolyn Morgan currently teaches English at the University of South Florida. She is primarily involved in the study of Medieval literature and drama. She is also active in the criticism of film and modern literature.

Frank Oglesbee is Associate Professor of Speech Communication, Eastern Illinois University, Charleston. Professionally, he works in academia as a teacher of TV production, writing, and criticism, and writes on TV and music as part of popular culture (he is the Popular Culture Reviewer for *Communication Booknotes*).

Charles K. Piehl is Associate Dean of the College of Arts and Humanities at Mankato State University. His primary research interest is the cultural history of the South, particularly the visual arts. He has published articles in the *Missouri Historical Review, Georgia Review, Reviews in American History, Southern Quarterly* and other scholarly journals. He is at work on a study of the social and historical context of the life and art of Robert Gwathmey.

T.J. Ross is Professor of English at Fairleigh Dickinson University, where he teaches courses in modern British literature and American film genres. He edited the anthologies *Film and the Liberal Arts* and *Focus on the Horror Film*. He has contributed film essays to numerous journals ranging from *College English* to *Take One*.

Carol A. Senf is an Assistant Professor at the Georgia Institute of Technology. She has always been interested in ghosts, goblins, vampires, and other "things that go bump in the night." She has written short pieces on both Victorian fiction and popular literature, and her book, *The Vampire in Nineteenth-Century English Fiction*, will be published this year by Popular Press.

Gail B. Walker is Associate Professor of English at Kennesaw College. Her area of specialization is Victorian literature, with particular emphasis on Women's studies.

29 417HOU
FM
12\95 6333-109 SWLE
756

INDEXED IN _MCA, EWE IV_

DATE DUE

R0123545825   HUMCA   809
                        .9355
                        2
                        H559

HEROINES OF POPULAR
CULTURE   PAPER

R0123545825   HUMCA   809
                        .9355
                        2
                        H559

HOUSTON PUBLIC LIBRARY
CENTRAL LIBRARY

1/96

BIND COVER IN